THE COMPLETE
GUN OWNER
YOUR GUIDE TO SELECTION, USE, SAFETY AND SELF-DEFENSE

James Morgan Ayres

©2008 James Morgan Ayres

Published by

kp **krause publications**
An Imprint of F+W Media, Inc.

700 East State Street • Iola, WI 54990-0001
715-445-2214 • 888-457-2873
www.krausebooks.com

Our toll-free number to place an order or obtain
a free catalog is (800) 258-0929.

All photos are by M.L. Ayres, except where otherwise indicated.

Library of Congress Control Number: 2008928404
ISBN-13: 978-0-89689-715-1
ISBN-10: 0-89689-715-X

Designed by Heidi Bittner-Zastrow

Printed in the United States of America

Dedication

For my sons: Shawn, Ashley and Justin—all good men.

When I was considering whether to take on this project one of my sons said, "Dad, do the book. You taught us all we know, but not all you know." I still haven't accomplished that. Does any man? I didn't even get everything about guns into this book. But I have tried to pass on something of value—to them and to you.

Contents

Acknowledgements

I've never before known a publisher to come down into the trenches and do the meticulous work of a dedicated editor. Dianne Wheeler, Krause publisher, did exactly that, and with great patience and determination to overcome all obstacles. Thank you, Dianne.

The initial concept for this book was Derrek Sigler's. Derrek gave me the freedom to develop and expand his concept into this book. Derrek, thanks for all your work and your confidence in me.

A special thanks to Joe Kertzman for bringing this project to me and for years ago helping a beat up old trigger puller find his way back to the world of words.

Mary Lou Ayres shot most of the photos and was the Fixer-of-All-Things on this project, as she has been on so many other projects over the last thirty years. Thanks love. Nothing would be the same without you.

Additional credit and thanks for photography goes to Justin Ayres, a talented young man who has been shooting (photographing) professionally since he was fifteen and whose work has appeared in many national publications.

Thanks to Cris Lauren and Jim Marlar for their patience during a long morning of photography, and for the use of the range at The Desert Marksman Rifle and Pistol Club in Palmdale.

Our entire crew thanks The Oak Tree Gun Club, its owner James Mitchell, Morgan Cina for helping to organize our visit, and all the folks at Oak Tree for their hospitality: Brian P. Dillon, gunnie extraordinaire; Shawn Eubanks a fountain of firearms knowledge; Doug Bamforth helpful range guide and Gene Gulseth range master.

To Jacobi Wynne, a young man who allowed us to tell his story and photograph his first experience with firearms, sincere thanks and best wishes.

Thanks also to two students of Combatives who agreed to demonstrate shooting positions and techniques in the How to Shoot and the Self-Defense chapters.

I also drew on the resources of Nomadic Productions International. Thanks guys.

www.nomadicprods.com

Introduction

Welcome to the fraternity of shooters. We are a diverse group: men, women, and children, doctors, lawyers and some Indian Chiefs, car mechanics, home builders and bakers of bread, millions of folks from all walks of life. The fraternity sprawls worldwide and is open to all of good intent. People in dozens of countries collect firearms, shoot competitively, and hunt. You'll find something in common with many of them.

Some of us are gun nerds, like computer nerds into the intricacies of guns and having no real application for them. Some are professional soldiers or law enforcement officers, some are military or former military, but the greater majority is regular folks who enjoy the shooting sports, or who collect guns much like others collect art, stamps or French wine.

This book goes a fair distance beyond the basics and introduces the first-time gun owner or the gun owner with limited experience, to many uses of the gun, such as hunting, sporting competition, and self-defense. Given the critical nature of self-defense, this book contains considerable detail on effective self-defense with firearms. Also included are resources for additional information on the legal aspects of gun ownership, manufacturers of guns and related products, and other helpful hints and directions for new gun owners.

I have been a gun user for a half-century. I have either carried a firearm or kept one close at hand, more or less daily, for over thirty years. I have never yet had an accidental discharge. I generally hit what I aim at and have never shot anything I didn't mean to shoot, although I've regretted some of the shots I have taken. I've successfully hunted large and small game and have been obliged to defend myself and others in armed conflicts in various countries around the world.

My intent in giving you a little of my history is not to impress you with my background and knowledge, which is undistinguished and meager as compared to many others. It is rather to let you know that the information in this book comes from someone at least minimally qualified to write on the subject. There are experts on various aspects of the gun and its usage whose opinions differ from mine. I cannot say they are wrong because their experience has led them to their own conclusions. But based on my own experiences I can, and do on occasion, respectfully disagree with them.

Stories are often remembered long after facts and figures have drifted away. So I have included a few stories meant to illustrate certain points and possibly to entertain and stimulate reflection, with all of them taken from true life events. I hope you find the information in this book to be helpful if you decide to take to the field in pursuit of game or to the range in pursuit of that perfect score, and that you never have occasion to use any of these skills in defense of your life or that of your loved ones.

James Morgan Ayres

2008

Firearms Terminology

ACP

An acronym for Automatic Cartridge Pistol refers to cartridges designed to be fired in automatic pistols, such as: .45ACP, .380ACP. (It's an Army thing to reverse the natural order of words.)

ACTION

The portion of a firearm that places rounds into the chamber.

ARTILLERY PIECE

A combat arm used by armed forces to discharge large projectiles of various kinds, including explosive and illuminating rounds; also known as a cannon or big guns.

AUTOMATIC

Generally refers to both fully-automatic firearms and semi-automatic firearms.

1. Fully-automatic firearms will continue to fire as long the trigger is held back, until the magazine is empty.

2. Semi-automatic firearms fire one shot each time the trigger is pulled.

BARREL

The tube through which projectiles pass.

BEATERS

In certain kinds of hunting, English wing-shooting or tiger hunting in India, people are sent ahead of the shooters to beat the bushes and drive out the animals so they can be shot.

BOLT

A sliding rod that chambers and ejects rounds in a bolt action firearm.

BOLT ACTION

A firearm that uses a manually operated bolt to chamber a round, also called a bolt gun.

BORE

The inside of a barrel of a gun.

BOX MAGAZINE

A magazine that resembles a box and can be removed from the firearm.

BULLET

The projectile portion of a cartridge fired from a rifle or handgun.

BUTT

The bottom of the stock of a shoulder firearm; the part that touches the shoulder.

BUTT PLATE

A plate covering the butt, in military firearms, it is usually steel; in civilian firearms, usually rubber.

BARREL

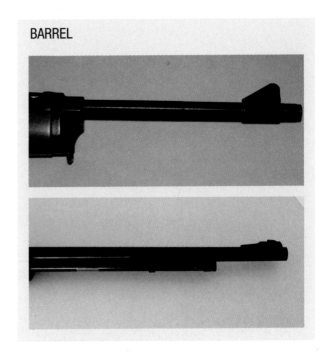

BOLT ACTION

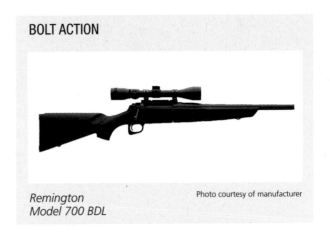

Remington
Model 700 BDL

Photo courtesy of manufacturer

BOX MAGAZINE

BULLET

BUTT PLATE

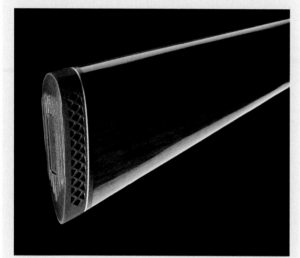

Photo courtesy of manufacturer

CHAMBER

CALIBER

A measurement, either in inches or millimeters, of the inside diameter of a rifled barrel.

CARBINE

A lightweight shoulder firearm similar to a rifle.

CENTERFIRE

Type of ammunition that has a primer in the center of the base of the cartridge.

CHAMBER

A tightly fitted area just behind the barrel where the bullet is placed (chambered) in preparation for being struck by the firing pin.

CHAMBERING

1. To put a round into the chamber

2. Another term for caliber, as: chambered for a forty-five or forty-five is a good chambering.

COCKED

DOUBLE BARREL

COCKED

When the hammer of the firing pin is ready to drop.

DOUBLE BARREL

A rifle or shotgun having two barrels, which can be arranged either side by side or with one over the other. Usually referred to as side-by-side or over and under.

DOUBLE ACTION

A mechanism in which the hammer is cocked by the movement of the trigger.

FIRING PIN

A pin or protrusion of steel that strikes the primer of the cartridge, thereby initiating ignition (firing) of the cartridge. A firing pin may be contained in a bolt or be situated on a hammer.

FMJ

Full Metal Jacket; any bullet that is covered with a kind of metal instead of lead.

FOREARM

A support under the barrel commonly made of wood or synthetic material where the hand is placed.

GARAND

The M1 Garand, the standard battle rife of the U.S. Army in World War II and Korea, named for its designer John Garand.

GAUGE

A measurement of the inside diameter of a shotgun.

GRIP

1. The handle of a handgun.

2. The method of grasping a handgun.

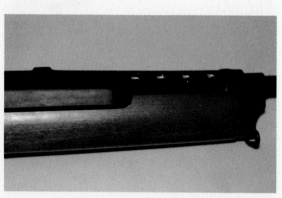

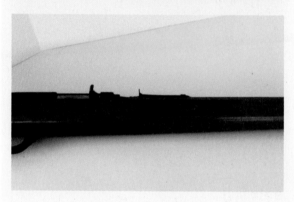

GROUP

A number of bullet holes in close proximity to each other, commonly measured by the distance between the two holes that are farthest apart as in: two-inch group, three-inch group.

GUNS

Everybody has seen the movie where the Marine Drill Instructor makes the recruit run around like an idiot screaming, "This is my rifle, this is my gun…"etc. Properly speaking, a "gun" is a smoothbore, which lacks rifling or an artillery piece. But common usage is to call all firearms

GROUP

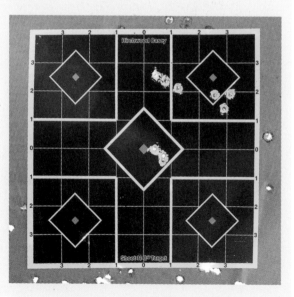

guns. So we'll call them guns too. (Just don't join the Marines and tell your Drill Instructor I told you it was OK to call a rifle a gun; it won't help you avoid the consequences.)

GUNNIES

A non-gender specific term referring to gun enthusiasts, usually also a term of respect, as the Marine gunnery sergeants are the highest ranking enlisted men and the best Marines. (Not to be confused with Gun Nerds.)

GUN NERDS

Gun Nerds are so far into the objects of their devotion, that like computer nerds, they have lost contact with the real-world usage of the object. Gun Nerds, like computer nerds, often have no real-world application for the device and are simply fascinated by the workings of it. (Not to be confused with gunnies.)

HAMMER

Photo by Tom Nelson

The mechanism that strikes the primer of a cartridge thereby firing it.

HANDGUN

Handguns are firearms designed to be fired with one hand and have no shoulder stock. Handguns are also commonly referred to as pistols; however, properly speaking, a pistol is a semi-automatic, not a revolver. They are also commonly fired with the use of two hands, but they are not called handguns.

HARDBALL

An old gunnies term for .45 ACP FMJ.

HOLLOWPOINT

A bullet with a cavity at the point, designed to expand.

HOPPES #9

A cleaning solvent that removes cartridge residue from the bore and other parts of a gun. It has been in use since the Napoleonic Wars, possibly longer, and possesses a distinctive scent that gun nerds, and even some gunnies, consider comparable to Chanel #5.

IRON SIGHTS

Standard metal sights, not optical.

JHP

Jacketed Hollow point, a hollow point bullet with a metal jacket.

LEVER ACTION

A type of action in which the cartridges are chambered by manipulating a lever.

IRON SIGHTS

LEVER ACTION

MAGAZINE

1. A device that contains cartridges in the firearm before they are chambered; magazines may be detachable or integral.

2. A building in which munitions are stored.

MAGAZINE RELEASE

A button or lever that releases a detachable magazine from the firearm.

MANUAL OF ARMS

The correct procedures for handling any given weapon.

MALFUNCTION

A failure of a cartridge to feed into the chamber or otherwise operate properly.

MISFIRE

An event that occurs when the firing pin or hammer strikes the primer, but fails to ignite it.

MAGAZINE RELEASE

MUZZLE

MUZZLE

The front of the barrel; the place where the projectile (s) emerges.

PERFORMANCE ENVELOPE

Refers to the expected limits of performance of any kind of system or mechanism. For example, the performance envelope of a service handgun could include specifications such as the ability to deliver accurate fire to a distance of 25 yards and to be operable with one hand.

PUSH-PULL METHOD

A two-handed method of gripping a handgun whereby one hand pushes against the force exerted by the other hand.

RACE GUNS

High performance, custom guns designed for competition.

RECEIVER

The part of the gun that houses the chamber and related parts.

RECOIL

The backward movement of a firearm when it is fired.

RED DOT SCOPE

An optical sight on a firearm that superimposes a red dot on the target.

REVOLVER

Revolvers are distinguished by cylinders containing a number of chambers. Each chamber houses a round and is revolved into firing position by the pull of the trigger. In the case of a double-action revolver or by manually cocking (usually with the thumb), the hammer of a

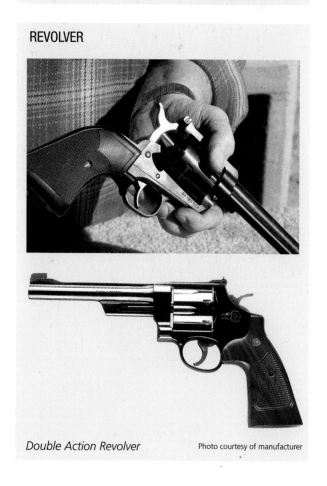

RECEIVER

Photo courtesy of manufacturer

REVOLVER

Double Action Revolver   Photo courtesy of manufacturer

RIFLE

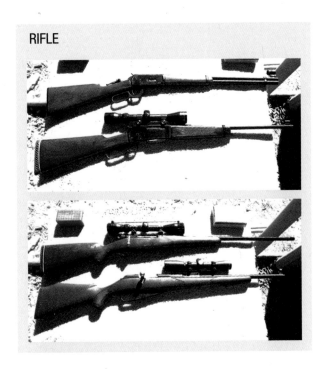

single-action revolver. Double-action revolvers can also be revolved and cocked manually.

RIFLE

A rifle is a firearm designed to be fired from the shoulder and having spiral grooves commonly referred to as rifling, cut into the interior of the barrel. This rifling imparts spin to the bullet, stabilizing it and enabling accuracy. Rifles are made in many different actions types.

RIMFIRE

Ammunition that has the primer contained in the rim of the base of the cartridge.

ROUND

SCOPE

Photo courtesy of manufacturer

ROUND

One cartridge or one shot; derived from the term used to describe one round of fire from the days of muskets and single shot rifles.

SCOPE

An accessory that is used on a rifle or a pistol to optically increase the apparent size of anything viewed through the sight.

SHOTGUN

A shotgun is a firearm designed to be fired from the shoulder (there are shot pistols, but they're not in common usage) and distinguished by having no lands or grooves. Shotguns are also know as smoothbores and are designed to shoot a number of round pellets commonly know as "shot," therefore: shotgun. The pellets are contained in one cartridge and discharged with one pull of the trigger. Shotguns can also shoot "slugs" solid projectiles similar to rifle bullets but much larger and slower. Lacking rifling, no spin is imparted to the slug and they are less accurate than rifle bullets.

SEMI-AUTOMATIC

Almost everyone calls a semi-automatic handgun an automatic, so we will also. A true automatic can fire many rounds with one press of the trigger. A semi-automatic requires the trigger to be pressed each time a round is to be fired. Very few pistols have selector switches which allow the shooter to fire in full-automatic mode. The automatic uses the energy of a fired round to chamber the next round, and after the first round is chambered manually all other rounds are chambered automatically.

Single-action automatics must be manually cocked before firing. This is usually done by retracting the slide and releasing it, which also chambers the first round. They are commonly carried "cocked and locked," that is with the hammer cocked and a safety engaged.

Double-action automatics are commonly carried with the hammer down. The hammer is

SHOTGUN

SEMI-AUTOMATIC

Walther PPK and FN FiveSeveN

APERTURE OR PEEP SIGHT

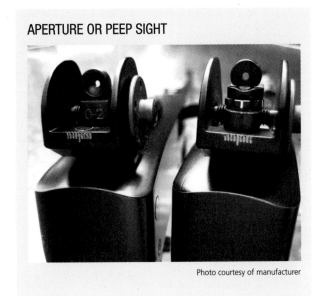

Photo courtesy of manufacturer

FRONT SIGHT

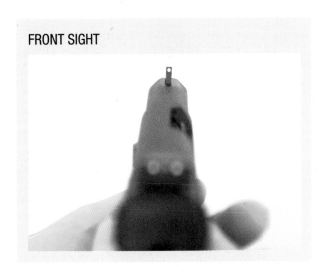

OPEN SIGHTS

cocked for the first shot by trigger action. In general, most consider the double-action automatic to be safer than the single-action. This may be debatable in some circles, but the statistics from the military and law enforcement agencies are clear: there are fewer, accidental discharges with double-action autos than with single-actions.

SAFE ACTION

This is a term coined by Glock, an Austrian firearms manufacturer to describe their proprietary trigger, which is a hybrid, but functions as a double action.

SIGHTS

Sighting devices that enable the accurate sighting of a gun. There are many different kinds. Most common are:

Aperture or peep sight

A hole through which the shooter looks to center the front sight.

Front Sight

Commonly a post or bead that the shooter aligns with the rear sight.

Open Sights

Various kinds of open notches the shooters align with the front sight.

Telescopic Sights

Gun accessories that optically increase the apparent size of anything viewed through the sight.

SAFETY

There are various types of safeties, many specific to a particular firearm. All are designed to block the trigger or firing pin in order to prevent accidental discharge of the gun.

S.E.R.E.

An acronym for Survival Escape Resistance and Evasion, a body of survival knowledge and skills taught in military schools and specialty civilian schools.

SERVICE HANDGUN

Handguns suitable for use by military or law enforcement, usually large caliber automatics.

SLIDE

The part of an automatic that moves back and fourth when the gun is fired.

SMOOTHBORE

Another term for a shotgun.

SOLID

A solid bullet, not a hollowpoint.

TELESCOPIC SIGHTS

Photo courtesy of manufacturer

SAFETY

Safety-On

Safety-Off

SLIDE

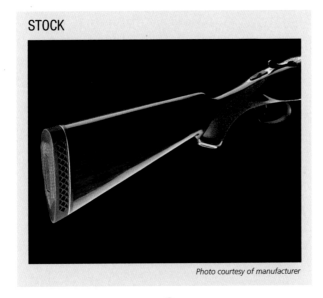
STOCK

Photo courtesy of manufacturer

STOCK WELD

TARGET

STOCK

The part of a shoulder weapon that is placed to the shoulder or the part of the gun to which the barrel is attached.

STOCK WELD

The contact point between the shooters cheek and the stock of a firearm.

STOVEPIPE

A malfunction wherein the ejected case is caught by the slide and sticks up like—well—a stovepipe.

STRIKER

The portion of the firing pin or hammer that strikes the primer.

TARGET

An object at which you aim and which you desire your bullet or shot to strike.

TARGET OF OPPORTUNITY

A target discovered serendipitously. A bulls-eye at a shooting range is a formal target. A pine cone on the ground under a pine tree could be a target of opportunity.

TRAJECTORY

The arc all projectiles describe after being fired. Gravity, being a force that acts upon all objects, pulls the projectile to the earth.

TRIGGER

A lever which when pulled releases the hammer or bolt containing the firing pin.

TRIGGER GUARD

A device that surrounds the trigger and is designed to protect the trigger from being accidentally tripped.

WINDAGE

1. The amount of deflection the wind will produce in a projectile.

2. The amount needed to adjust the aim of a projectile to counter wind deflection.

3. The adjustment of sights from side to side.

WINGSHOOTING

The practice (or attempt) of shooting birds while they are in flight.

TRIGGER

TRIGGER GUARD

SECTION 1

GUN SELECTION

CHAPTER 1

A Case For the Twenty-Two

Your first gun should be a target grade rifle or handgun chambered for the twenty-two long rifle cartridge. This principle used to be gospel. All new shooters were advised to start with the little rimfire. Then something changed; I'm not sure what. This now appears to be a minority opinion, one that many experts today disagree with. I have read that some think it's best to go right to the gun and caliber the new shooter intends to use for big game or self-defense, especially if the object is self-defense.

BUILDING A FOUNDATION FOR MARKSMANSHIP

I believe a foundation of marksmanship laid down with a twenty-two will better serve a shooter than any other introduction to shooting. About the only exception I can think of would be the shooter who plans to shoot only trap or skeet and never intends to do any other kind of shooting. Even then, starting with a twenty-two is not a bad thing.

A strong and solid foundation for marksmanship is best built on a few thousand rounds of .22 ammunition, expended in both fun and in serious practice. There's a good deal more to shooting than hunting and self-defense, but if either of these endeavors is your goal, you won't go wrong starting with a twenty-two. Target shooting, from plinking to Olympic level, bench rest, trap and skeet are only a few of the shooting sports that have occupied and entertained millions. Virtually all of these activities can be built on a foundation laid down with the lowly .22 rimfire.

Further, the twenty-two is more than a training round. It is a useful and versatile cartridge. I know more than one person who relies on a twenty-two for subsistence hunting, and others who, for various reasons, have used it for self defense. (You can find more detailed information about the twenty-two as it specifically relates to hunting and self-defense in those specific chapters.)

FUN TO SHOOT

Twenty-twos are just plain fun to shoot. They have none of the muzzle blast and recoil that intimidate so many new shooters. I have seen more than one first-time shooter try his hand with a large caliber rifle or pistol only to be driven away from the sport forever with ringing ears and a sore shoulder from a Monster Magnum rifle, or a stinging palm from that Dirty Harry special. There's no excuse to not use good ear and eye protection when shooting. However, even with the proper protection, the kick of a full power .44 Magnum revolver can be a bit much for a new shooter, or even some experienced shooters to deal with.

ACCURACY

Accuracy always matters. But it can be especially important when you're learning to shoot. A new shooter should expect to make many mistakes as part of the learning process. He or she will not benefit from a firearm that cannot be relied upon to produce consistent, excellent accuracy. With an inaccurate firearm a new shooter cannot be sure if a miss is his fault or that of the gun. Select one of the twenty-two handguns or rifles recommended in this chapter, buy good ammo, zero your gun (as explained in How To Shoot) and you can be sure a miss is yours, not the guns. With a "no excuses" gun, you can focus on improving your marksmanship and not worry about the gun.

COST

Twenty-twos have the virtue of being inexpensive to buy and to shoot. A thousand rounds of twenty-two long rifle ammo costs less than dinner in a cheap restaurant, less than a car wash in Los Angeles, less than…well, you get the idea. Twenty-twos are cheap to shoot, even if you're buying top quality ammo. The guns are also inexpensive to purchase. Unless you go for a top match-quality pistol or rifle, or a highly decorated one, you can get a twenty-two that will shoot the ears off a rattlesnake at fifty yards.

EFFECTIVENESS OF THE TWENTY-TWO

Make no mistake; the twenty-two is far more than a training round. It is effective beyond what its limits would appear to be. In part this is due to good sectional density, which enables it to penetrate well. There are subsistence hunters the world over who use the twenty-two to take whatever game is available, including large game.

Mike, one of my friends who happens to be an Inuit from Alaska, uses a .22 rifle to hunt caribou and moose to feed his family and to kill marauding walrus when they destroy his nets and eat his fish. Caribou and moose are very large animals. The technique Mike uses for caribou and moose is to get very close and shoot a burst of at least five rounds into the heart and lungs. He shoots walrus, which can weigh four hundred pounds and have sharp tusks a foot long, from about ten feet using head shots. The point is that the .22 is much more effective than most people think it is.

The military and various other government agencies also use the .22 to good effect. I was taught to always keep a Bug Out Bag close at hand to be used in the event I had to E&E (Escape & Evade) and found myself in a survival situation.

I was to always keep in my BOB, a target-grade twenty-two pistol and two hundred rounds of ammunition. The reasoning for this specific handgun was that it would take any reasonable game; it was effective as a self defense weapon; its report was relatively quiet; and, the entire package, pistol and ammunition, weighed very little.

Today this kind of training is called SERE, Survival Escape Rescue Evasion and is taught to elite units, covert operators, and pilots. In one military school, I am aware of the trainers and students take everything from frogs to deer with twenty-two handguns as part of their SERE training. They do so legally on a military reservation.

Make no mistake, the twenty-two is an effective all-around cartridge. It's good to know that in a survival situation, you can take large game with a twenty-two. However, do not go out in search of your autumn whitetail with your new twenty-two pistol or rifle. Doing so would be in violation of virtually all game laws in the U.S. and the Fish & Game officers will confiscate your firearm and put you in jail. Be sure to check regulations with your local Fish & Game authorities to learn which firearms are legal for the game you pursue. In general, small game is fair game for a twenty-two, but check and make sure.

Twenty-twos are also commonly used as self-defense weapons by various individuals and members of certain organizations. (I'll give more information on this in the Self Defense section.)

When you select your twenty-two, be aware that performance will vary with various brands of ammo. You should try as many different variations as you can find in order to determine which one groups best and which is most reliable in your gun.

Without exception, everyone in my Basic Training and Advanced Infantry Training classes who qualified as Expert, which none of us considered a major accomplishment, had owned and shot a .22 since they were kids. There is simply no substitute for expending thousands of rounds for fun without the recoil and muzzle blast of large caliber weapons.

SUGGESTED FIRST GUNS

So, start with a .22. Learn it well before going on to more powerful guns. You'll be glad you did. And, who knows, you may one day be in a situation where that .22 will be just what you need to bring in game or defend yourself.

TWENTY-TWO AUTOMATIC HANDGUNS

BERETTA

This five-century-old company makes a space age looking .22 called, appropriately, the U22 Neos. I have not yet had the chance to try one, but from all reports, the Neos lives up to Beretta's reputation.

BROWNING

Browning's best known .22 automatic pistol is the Buckmark, which comes in about fifteen variations. All of them that I have used are accurate and reliable and do not seem to be unduly ammunition sensitive. Personally, I like the feel of this one in my hand.

RUGER

The Mark III Standard is the current generation of a series that had become an American icon. This series has been in production for over thirty years. It is a solid, well made, reliable and accurate handgun that will last for generations if well cared for. It has an enclosed bolt and a grip angle that many find points well for them. Available in at least a half dozen versions, all

Browning Buckmark 22

Beretta U22 Neos

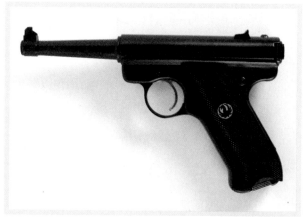

Ruger Standard   Photo by Kris Kandler

that I have fired shoot well and seem to accept almost any ammo.

Ruger 22/45 Mark III is similar to the Standard except that its grip angle and magazine release matches that of the Model 1911 .45ACP. In addition, it has a polymer frame and is lighter weight than the Standard. We've had one of these in our family for over ten years and during that time it has had uncounted thousands of round fired through it with no problems. I have found no difference in accuracy or reliability between the Standard and the 22/45. Both the Standard and the 22/45 are in current use at SERE schools.

SIG-SAUER

The Mosquito certainly looks like a Sig. It's lighter weight than others in this category and given Sig-Sauer's reputation for excellence, it should be a good choice. I have not yet had the opportunity to fire one. Truth is, there are only a very few .22 target autos being made today. The Sig and the Beretta are new and unproven. The best thing I can say about them is that they come from companies with excellent reputations.

Sig-Sauer Mosquito   Photo courtesy of manufacturer

SMITH & WESSON

Currently, Smith & Wesson produces a half-dozen variations of its 22A series. All seem to be well made and the few I shot had good accuracy and handling. I particularly like this model because it fits my hand very well and is lighter weight than the Rugers, while having accuracy that is at least equal to the Ruger and Browning Buckmark. This is one of the handguns in use with some of today's SERE trainers.

All of these twenty-two automatics should be able to produce one-inch groups at twenty-five yards from a rest with iron sights if the shooter does his part. They also lend themselves to mounting a scope, which many do, including the guys at the SERE school mentioned above. A scope on a handgun makes long distance shots at small game, easier than with iron sights. There are other pistols that will fill the bill, but these are available at most gun shops and are reasonably priced.

S&W M22A   Photo courtesy of manufacturer

TWENTY-TWO REVOLVERS

Twenty-two revolvers, such as the Smith & Wesson Kit Gun served generations of outdoorsmen as trail guns. Colt, Smith, Ruger, Taurus and others continue to make high-grade, twenty-two revolvers; including a .22 Magnum—a somewhat more powerful rimfire cartridge. However, for our purposes, I believe you'll do better to select an automatic for your first handgun.

Competent revolver work requires mastery of the double action trigger. In addition, the revolver is slower to fire should you need rapid fire. The automatic holds more rounds and reloads much faster by an order of magnitude.

Having the facility to fire ten rounds rapid fire, reload, and fire another ten rounds in a few seconds is a very valuable attribute; one that the revolver lacks. This could be especially important in a firearm of low power. Who knows? Maybe your first gun will be your only gun. In that case, you won't regret buying the automatic.

Automatics are subject to fewer mechanical problems under field conditions. This is one of the reasons many of the world's military forces use them. If you were to slip while crossing a stream and give your handgun a thorough dunking, it would be much easier to field strip, dry, clean an auto than a revolver.

TWENTY-TWO RIFLES

For the same reasons mentioned earlier, I think the semi-automatic rifle is the best choice for your twenty-two. The only reason to buy a lever action twenty-two is if you have been swept away with the romance of the old west or if it's to be an understudy for a large caliber lever gun. If you're aiming for Olympic competition, start with a good bolt action twenty-two. You might do the same if your goal is big game hunting, as most is done with a bolt action rifle guns. Otherwise a good, reliable, semi-automatic will serve you better.

Browning SA22 Rifle

Photo courtesy of manufacturer

BROWNING SEMI-AUTO

This is a beautiful example of the gun maker's craft. Introduced in 1987 and popular with those who like the look and feel of well-made traditional firearms, the Browning comes in six levels of finish Grade I has an attractive walnut stock, traditional bluing, fine checkering and retails for about 500. Grade II adds some engraving and retails for about 700. Higher grades have more engraving, finer burled walnut stacks and retail for over 1,000. Of course this rifle is accurate and reliable as you would expect of any gun bearing the Browning name.

CZ 511

CZ makes their guns in the Czech Republic with old world craftsmanship and tight tolerances. They are attractive, well made and accurate. The 511 .22 rifle shoots as well as the rest of the CZ line up and is stocked with nice walnut.

MARLIN

Marlin enjoys a well-deserved reputation for accuracy, reliability, and quality. They are also a terrific value. Every 60 and 795 series Marlin I have fired has had outstanding accuracy. This may be due to their well-known "Micro-Groove" rifling, which is used in all Marlins and which the company claims is more precise than standard rifling.

The Marlin Papoose is a take-down rifle that comes with a padded case. The small package can be stored just about anyplace. I have only shot one Papoose, and it, too, possessed the well-known Marlin accuracy.

REMINGTON

The Remington 552 BDL Deluxe Speedmaster is a nicely finished, well-made, accurate, rimfire at about twice the price of The Marlin Model 60. It feels heavy and sturdy in the hand which many feel aids a steady hold.

Marlin 795 Rifle

Photo courtesy of manufacturer

REMINGTON'S 597

The 597 has a plain finish, but retains Remington's manufacturing quality and is priced comparably to the Marlins. This is basically the BDL without the fancy checkering.

RUGER 10/22 CARBINE

Ruger seems to have a knack for designing guns that become classics. The 10/22 is such a classic having been in production since 1964. Ruger makes a number of variations on the basic theme, but they're all from the same family and have the Ruger virtues: reliability, durability, and, reasonable accuracy.

Remington 552 Rifle   Photo courtesy of manufacturer

Remington 597 .22 LR rifle   Photo courtesy of manufacturer

Ruger 10/22 Rifle

Photo courtesy of manufacturer

77RCM Bolt Action

Photo courtesy of manufacturer

Savage Model 64

Photo courtesy of manufacturer

SAVAGE

The Savage Model 64 is a decent rimfire rifle for under a couple of hundred bucks. From all reports, it's a good shooter. The one I have had experience with shot to point of aim out of the box and looked like it would keep on doing so for years. Please give some specifics that make it a "good shooter."

Of the rifles mentioned above, the Marlins seem to have the best and most consistent accuracy, at least in the models I have shot. Any of these should serve the needs of the new shooter.

Don't think you'll have to put your twenty-two aside when you learn to shoot. You'll still have many uses for it. There are many true stories of lives being saved with the little rimfire. I can't think of a better tool to store in case of emergencies other than a high quality, twenty-two and a thousand rounds of ammunition.

CHAPTER 2

Where to Buy Them and Where to Shoot Them

When you buy your first gun, and all the others, do so at a local gun shop. The independent gun shop owner will give you more service, more information and more support than you'll ever get at the counter of the mass merchants where the clerk you talk to was selling shoes last week and cabbages the week before. You might pay a couple of bucks more at, say, Fred & Martha's Shooting Emporium, but you'll get it back and more in knowledge and help. The people who run independent gun shops, like those who operate independent bookstores, they do so out of love of the product. None of them are getting rich. You need them in your corner, especially if you're a new shooter.

THE OAK TREE GUN CLUB STORE

Recently I took a photo crew with me to a local range that had an attached gun shop. The Oak Tree Gun Club is located just north of Los Angeles and is open to the public, has ranges for skeet, trap, sporting clays, rifle, and pistol. They offer onsite instruction and the gun shop has a wide selection of handguns, rifles and shotguns, as well as a number of antiques. All in all, I thought it would be a good place to shoot and show the new shooter what a nice facility was like.

There are hundreds of good gun shops across the country; some of them have similar facilities,

Oaktree Gun Club Store interior

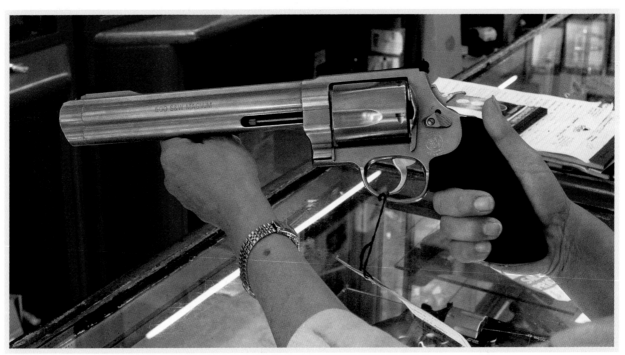

Guns For Sale — S&W 500 Magnum

Walther P38

Photo by Justin Ayres

Selection of revolvers at Oaktree Gun Club Store

Photo by Justin Ayres

some not. I can't visit them all, but Oak Tree is close by and the folks there agreed to let my guys come in and trample over everything with our cameras and questions.

While we were there, a small drama played out that couldn't have made my point any better if I had it scripted it myself. All this happened as it is presented. We asked for and received permission from everyone involved to take photos and use their names. You can follow the story in the accompanying photos.

We were bugging the fellow behind the counter with questions and taking pictures of all the cool guns when a young man came in. He said hello to the guy behind the counter who introduced himself as Shawn Eubanks. He shook hands with Jacobi Wynne, the customer.

Jacobi was a clean-cut, young fellow with a story of tragedy all too common today. He and

Employee of Oaktree Gun Club Store, Shawn Eubanks

Photo by Justin Ayres

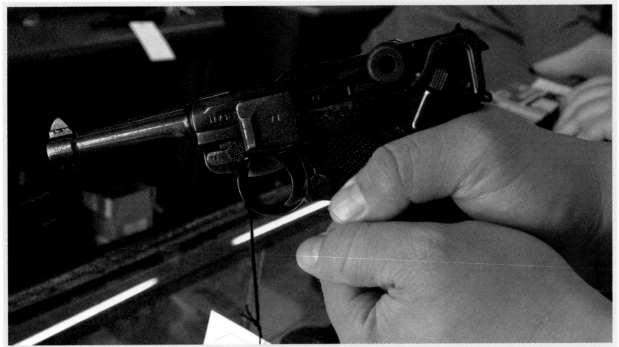

Luger

Photo by Justin Ayres

his family had suffered a home invasion by a criminal gang that resulted in one family member being hospitalized with severe wounds. Jacobi told Shawn he never had any interest in guns and still didn't. He didn't like guns and doubted he would ever shoot one for fun. But he had decided it was incumbent upon him to protect his family and that the only way he could do so was with a firearm.

Shawn has worked at Oak Tree since he was fourteen years old. He knows more about guns than the average Marine Drill Instructor. He could have buried Jacobi in information, but he did not. He patiently drew Jacobi out about his needs, abilities, and tolerances. As they talked, Shawn displayed various pistols and revolvers and gave them to his customer to handle. (It was immediately apparent that Oak Tree customers were not treated like somebody who dropped in to buy a cabbage on the way home.)

Shawn Eubanks showing Jacobi Wynn a handgun
Photo by Justin Ayres

Jacobi Wynn holding a handgun
Photo by Justin Ayres

Three important points emerged from their conversation. One was Jacobi was not going to become a gun enthusiast at any time in the foreseeable future. Two was that he was totally committed to his goal of providing protection to his family and that he was willing to train as hard as was required to get the expertise he would need. He fully accepted and understood that he needed training and practice in order to be able to actually use a gun to defend his family. Third was that he has no intention of carrying the gun outside his home. Based on Jacobi's commitment and his needs, Shawn guided him to the service pistols.

Shawn told Jacobi that the .45 autos they had been looking at were not for him. "All of us shooters like them, because we can customize them and they're fun to shoot in matches. But they're not right for someone who is not into guns." He then handed Jacobi a Glock. "This is a good gun for people who don't care about guns." He went on to explain the workings of the Glock. He also showed Jacobi the workings of revolvers and explained that they also were good guns for people who don't care about guns. Based on the fact that the home invasion had been carried out by a gang of people, Jacobi decided he wanted more rounds available than a revolver provided.

Shawn then showed his customer pistols made by Springfield, Smith and Wesson, and other makers that shared similar characteristics with the Glock: high capacity, simple manual of arms, and so forth. He emphasized that it was very important that Jacobi should select one that best fit his hand. Shawn explained that he needed to be comfortable with his choice so that he would follow through and do the needed practice.

Shawn spent almost two hours with his customer helping him to decide which gun he needed and counseling him on how to proceed. Between them they narrowed the choices down to two models. Shawn then called the range master and asked for an instructor to show Jacobi the basics of shooting a handgun so he could try the pistols at the range before he made his final choice.

Within a few minutes Jacobi was on the firing line with Brian Dillon, a courteous and professional gunny of the first rank, an NRA Certified Master and Instructor. On the way Gene and Doug, the range managers helped Jacobi get fixed up with a rental gun and eye and ear protection. Brian showed Jacobi the ropes: safety, range etiquette, how to handle, load, and fire a pistol.

Keep in mind that so far Jacobi had not yet purchased anything other than a bag of ammo and had only spent a couple of bucks to rent a pistol. If he did decide to buy a gun at Oak Tree, the total purchase would be about the price of a week's groceries. I don't know where else you can get that kind of service and professional attention than in a good gun shop.

When Jacobi squeezed off his first round of 9mm, he jumped like a hand grenade had exploded. It was to be expected: first gun, first shot, loud noise, and recoil. But Brian had shown him how to correctly hold the pistol and control recoil. So, Jacobi realized that it was just a loud

Entering Oak Tree Gun Club pistol range   Photo by Justin Ayres

Oak Tree Gun Club firing line   Photo by Justin Ayres

Brian Dillan, range master illustrating gun handling to Jacobi Wynn   Photo by Justin Ayres

noise and the bump in his hands didn't really amount to much at all.

He stayed with it. Brian continued to coach him. Jacobi was hitting the target before he expended his first magazine. By the time he had fired ten rounds he had settled into the workings of the gun. His determination was palpable. He had no intention of being deflected from his goal by a little noise.

Jacobi tried two or three different 9mms. He fired about fifty rounds with Brian always at his side, talking quietly, encouraging, coaching, and teaching. By the time he had fired his second magazine, he was hitting the center of his target. Before Jacobi left the Oak Tree facility,

Shooting instructor Brian P. Dillon showing the S&W Model   Photo by Justin Ayres

Brian Dillan, range master, demonstrating correct two-hand hold Photo by Justin Ayres

Jacobi Wynn with S&W automatic Photo by Justin Ayres

Jacobi Wynn firing S&W 9mm automatic Photo by Justin Ayres

he made a decision and bought his first gun. California has a ten-day waiting period. During those ten days, Jacobi could come and practice with his gun on Oak Tree's range. If he wanted more professional instruction, it was there for the asking.

Can you imagine any big box store providing this kind of service for any kind of product? We're talking about a sale that's going to net the company, maybe, forty bucks. As an aside, Brian Dillon is also an archeologist with a U.C. Berkeley PHD, a world traveler, witty, friendly, and knowledgeable about a wide range of subjects. Brian made Jacobi feel at home and taught him some important foundational skills.

Everybody made this new shooter feel comfortable and helped guide him through a difficult and stressful situation. Keep in mind that Jacobi wasn't out for a good time or shopping for a new pair of sneakers. He was making a decision that could affect the future safety of his entire family and it was clear from his demeanor that the recent home invasion weighed heavily on him. Where are you going to find people like this to guide you in your first steps as a new shooter if not at your local gun shop or range?

GET SHOOTING INSTRUCTIONS

Don't be reluctant to ask for instruction. Even if you have a little experience, you can probably benefit. I had a friend once who had some kind of cognitive disconnect. Roger thought he could outshoot Wyatt Earp. But in fact, he couldn't hit a barn with a shotgun if he was inside of it. He wouldn't let me show him anything; he already

knew everything there was to know. Eventually, after he shot out the windows in his truck while trying to hit a tin can, he agreed that, maybe, he could benefit from some high level combat style shooting lessons from a retired Marine.

My Marine buddy had some time on his hands and agreed to give Roger some basic marksmanship instruction under the guise of jungle combat training, or hunter killer sniper training, something like that. After a little bit of dedicated practice, Roger got good enough that I could take him afield without worrying about friendly fire.

Most of us can benefit from professional instruction. If you're lucky enough to buy your first firearm from a place that offers instruction, jump at it. If not, do contact the NRA and get hooked up with a local instructor. Failing that, almost any good range will have some people hanging around who can show you how to get your rounds on target.

If you're not going to do any of that, then do yourself and the rest of the world a favor and follow the instructions in this book and practice until you acquire a reasonable level of competence.

S&W Model 19   Photo by Justin Ayres

Small bore range

Brian P. Dillon with FN FiveSeveN Photo by Justin Ayres

S&W Model 19 & FN FiveSeveN Photo by Justin Ayres

Shooter on firing line with a Walther PPK .380

Three generations of handguns Photo by Justin Ayres

LOCATING AN INFORMAL SHOOTING PLACE

Almost every locale has an informal "shooting place." Ask the folks at the gun store, gun club, or shooting range where you can go to do a little informal target practice. At present I'm based in Los Angeles, one of the largest and most sprawling metroplexes on the planet. Yet, there are dozens of safe shooting areas within an hour's drive.

L.A. County recently passed an ordinance that no discharging of firearms was allowed anywhere in the county except at ranges. Sixty minutes and I'm out to where the coyotes howl. I know of legal, safe places to shoot within an hour of Washington D.C., Manhattan, and a dozen other cities across the country. The key is to get plugged into the local shooting fraternity.

An Internet search or a quick look in the Yellow Pages will turn up gun shops, clubs, and ranges almost anywhere in the country. Don't be shy about dropping in, even if you are not planning to buy anything at the moment. As I said in the introduction, the shooting fraternity is widespread and welcoming to newcomers.

SECTION 2

GUN USE

CHAPTER 3

How to Shoot a Rifle

FOUNDATIONS OF MARKSMANSHIP

Marksmanship, the ability to hit what you intend to hit is the heart of the matter. The fundamentals of marksmanship are simple in description and at an entry level, relatively easy to attain. Identify your target; align your sights on the target; and, press the trigger without disturbing the sights. That's about it. Not hard to understand at all, hardly magic or rocket science. Actually, achieving this goal under any and all field conditions is another matter. Reasonable competence at hitting non-moving targets at modest ranges can be achieved by anyone in a relatively short period of time, say a few hours, maybe a day or two, as long as he or she really puts their mind to it. True mastery takes somewhat longer and can be the practice of a lifetime.

NATIONAL RIFLE ASSOCIATION BASIC INSTRUCTION

The best possible way to learn any physical skill is with hands-on instruction. Most areas have local NRA instructors who will show you the basics. You can locate them by going to the NRA website, www.nra.org. Some ranges also offer basic instruction or will refer you to an NRA certified instructor.

ONE GUN

In the following paragraphs, we'll explore the fundamentals of shooting rifles, shotguns and handguns: body alignment and grip for a steady hold, trigger control, breathing, sight picture, tracking on moving targets and more. You'll learn the basics of shooting with sights and without sights. I'll touch on the internal stillness that lasts only a fraction of a second, but allows the kind of marksmanship that enables you to shoot quickly, as well as accurately and can save your life in a lethal encounter.

Start with one gun and learn that one gun before trying another gun. It's fine to fire a few rounds from a variety of different guns just to get the feel of them. But once you select your first firearm—stick with it. If you're a beginning shooter, you will find that switching back and forth between firearms before you have mastered the first one will make the goal of becoming a marksman much more difficult to achieve. At a time when you should be focused entirely on skill development, you will be distracted by variations between the firearms. If you just want to make noise on a Saturday afternoon, then by all means go to your local range and bang away with whatever gun strikes your fancy. But, if you're committed to the goal of becoming a good marksman and a safe and responsible shooter, stay with one gun until you have mastered it.

Many people go their whole lives with one gun or maybe two—one rifle and one pistol, perhaps one shotgun. There's a good reason for

gaining such a level of familiarity with a particular gun. Operating it becomes as familiar as driving your family car. There's an old saying among shooters, "Beware the one gun man." All of us who have been around shooting long enough have seen the old guy that shows up at a local range and shoots the socks off the resident big guns with his worn, but well-oiled Springfield 30-06 or his .38 Smith & Wesson revolver with the blue worn away.

HOW TO SHOOT

Fundamentals of marksmanship are the same for any rifle; rifles shoot a single projectile at high speed. The shotgun shoots multiple projectiles at slower speeds and those projectiles slow down much faster. Therefore, somewhat different methods are required for the shotgun. The handgun, lacking a shoulder stock requires its own methods.

DRY FIRE

Before shooting live rounds you should "dry fire" your gun. First make sure the gun is unloaded. Put your ammo away. Then, even though you know it's unloaded do not point your gun at anyone. Remember, treat all guns as loaded. Follow the instructions on how to shoot as if you were firing a loaded gun. Do not take your ammo out until you have finished practice. **If you reload your firearm, do not continue to practice.**

The advantage of dry fire include the opportunity to gain familiarity in handling your gun without expending any ammunition. Another is that it provides a means to check your hold and trigger squeeze. For example, it is easy to miss the fact that you are jerking the trigger when you are firing live rounds.

A good practice is to balance a coin on your front sight or barrel, and squeeze the trigger as if you were firing a live round. If the coin does not move, you've got a steady hold and a smooth squeeze. It the coin falls when you squeeze the trigger, you do not. Continue to focus and practice until the coin does not fall when you squeeze the trigger. Snap at least a hundred dry rounds with full concentration to begin to get your muscle memory grooved in. You will come back to this practice time and time again. (Most good shooters fire ten dry rounds for every live round.)

ZEROING YOUR GUN

Before commencing shooting practice, you must insure that your gun is shooting to point of aim. To do so you must zero your gun. First, set a target in a safe location with a backstop. A good range is really best for this, but you can accomplish the same thing if no range is available. Bulls-eye targets are best for zeroing.

Secondly, take a steady rested position. If no shooting bench is available, use one of the positions explained below, prone being the most steady. If you cannot get steady enough in prone, use an informal rest, such as a tree limb at least until you can improve your prone position. For the zero to be valid you must shoot from a steady position.

Prone position

Get a good sight picture on the center of your bulls-eye. Fire three rounds, pausing to get a sight picture for each shot. Take your time. Fire the tightest group you can. Chances are the group will not be centered in the bull. However, if it is centered, fire three more rounds to confirm. If all six rounds are centered in your bull, the gun you are shooting is zeroed for you, with that load, at that distance.

If your three round group is not centered you must adjust your sights. Following the directions for your particular gun and sight, first adjust your windage left or right to the point where you think your round will now be in line with the bull. Fire three rounds and check the group. If you are now directly above or below the bull you are ready to adjust elevation. If not, repeat until you have a centered group.

Now adjust your sights' elevation up or down, again following the directions for your particular gun and sight, so that your group, to the best of your judgment will be centered. Fire three rounds. If your group is centered, fire another three rounds to confirm. If all six rounds are centered you are zeroed with this gun and load.

PRACTICING WITH BULLS-EYE TARGETS

You should practice shooting the bulls-eye at various ranges and utilizing all the shooting positions you wish to master. Bulls-eyes don't lie; they are tough taskmasters. Shooting bulls is your basic training. You should invest at least

500 rounds in this kind of shooting. Practice until you can shoot three tight shot groups from all positions you wish to master at all reasonable distances.

CALLING YOUR SHOTS

By the time you have fired about a hundred rounds, you should be able to call your shot. This means you should know where your shot is going at the moment the hammer or striker hits the primer, and before the bullet hits the target. You should be able to look at your target after your shot for confirmation of what you already know.

INFORMAL PRACTICE

Wandering through woods and shooting at pine cones and other targets of opportunity create a familiarity with a gun and a level of shooting proficiency that little else can equal. As soon as you have attained a level of expertise on bulls-eyes, but not before, begin to shoot informal targets and targets of opportunity.

Find a secure location where you can shoot without endangering anyone. This kind of practice is much easier to engage in if you're shooting a twenty-two rather than, say, a 30-06 (which would require a considerably larger safe zone). The warning on the side of the twenty-two ammo box indicating that the bullet will carry for a mile—is correct. You should walk the circumference and study of any area where you are considering to do this kind of informal practice.

Even though you might be shooting at pine cones or twigs on the ground, or leaves floating in a stream, you must take care with every shot that there is no possibility of the shot going astray. In all cases, you must insure that no person or living creature is in your line of fire, no matter how distant. Fire each shot as if it was your only shot and be aware of its path. There is never any excuse for endangering others, certainly not for the sake of shooting practice.

In addition to targets of opportunity, such as pine cones, you can improve your marksmanship considerably by using such informal targets as half-inflated balloons, tennis balls, and soft drink cans tied to low lying branches or placed on tree stumps or on the ground. (Full soft drinks cans are more fun to shoot than empty ones in that they blow up with a satisfying spray.)

I often have young or first time shooters start by shooting a full soft drink can with a twenty-two. Doing so engenders respect for the diminutive cartridge. Having the contents of a soft drink can blow up and spray everything and then examining a blown-out soft drink can is a clear visual demonstration of the power of even this, the smallest caliber.

Since you are the kind of responsible person who would buy this book, you will like all responsible shooters, pick up and pack out any debris, blown out cans, perforated balls, popped balloons, and so on. You don't want other shooters to mistake you for a careless, inconsiderate gun owner who uglifies the world and leaves his empty ammo boxes and other debris lying around for others to clean up. Right?

Low Speed .22 solid impacting soft drink can

Hi-Speed .22 hollow point meets soft drink can

Hi-Speed .22 hollowpoint meets soft drink can

Low speed .22 solid meets orange

RAPID FIRE

Once you can call your shots on informal targets, you are ready for rapid fire. Start the same way. Fire your first shot as if it was your only shot. Then, without a moment's pause, trigger your second shot. If you've done everything right you will find two holes in your target so close together they might be touching.

The next method of rapid fire is to regain your sight picture and then immediately fire another round. This is moot with a twenty-two due to the lack of recoil. Odds are you won't lose your sight picture at the shot with a twenty-two. Repeat the process to put more than two shots on target.

Hi-speed .22 hollowpoint meets orange

MOVING TARGETS

Half-filled balloons left to blow along the ground or to float downstream, make good moving targets. Unless you're in a hurricane or you've tossed those balloons into a raging river, they won't be moving too fast. Paper plates tied to branches and left to blow in the wind also work well.

Look at your target and bring your gun to bear so that your sights come to the target. Then track the target as it moves and squeeze your round off as you continue to move with the target.

Paper plates hanging from a tree

Paper plates as informal targets

PPK .22 and student's target

Tracking paper plate target

Glock 19 and student's target

59

THE FLINCH

I will deal with flinching at some length because of the reluctance of many people to actually discuss the issue. The most common cause for misses that I have observed is the anticipation of recoil and muzzle blast leading to jerking the trigger, or pushing, pulling or "heeling," the handgun or "shouldering" the rifle or the shotgun. All of these actions move the weapon out of alignment. (It is also the most common cause for new shooters to get discouraged and quit the sport.)

Few shooters, especially male shooters will admit to a flinch. Flinching is the absolute bane of the shooter and is one of the most common causes for misses and the limiting factor in shooting powerful weapons. Female shooters seem to have no problem admitting to a flinch and therefore experience less trouble overcoming one. It's difficult to cure something you deny exists. This is one of the key reasons, but far from the only one that I advocate starting with the twenty-two. Flinches are caused by recoil and muzzle blast; the twenty-two has virtually none of either.

Among certain groups of shooters, the issue of the flinch is sort of a dirty little secret—something many have but no one wants to admit to. This seems to be a uniquely American phenomenon. I have shot with men in other countries, experienced shooters, some of them professionals who openly complained about the kick of a big gun and talked about how they were working to overcome their flinch.

Indeed, this is an important point of discussion among African Professional Hunters—men who hunt the largest and most dangerous game on earth. These men deal with guns, such as the .500 Express to insure dropping large dangerous game in its tracks at close range during a charge.

Over drinks one night in a transit lounge in the Dubai airport, I talked with a Professional Hunter who had been at the game for over twenty years. He told me that he took pains to make sure his clients were armed with a rifle they could shoot accurately. He was quite clear that he would rather have a client with 30-06 shooting 220 grain solids, who could place his shots every time on a moving target the size of a playing card, than a client who insisted on shooting a big double rifle he couldn't handle.

In his view, it was part of the Professional Hunter's job to back up the client with a big gun. Few non-professionals could afford the investment of time and money to maintain proficiency with the big guns. (As we talked further, I found that he was afflicted with severe arthritis and a fair amount of hearing loss; part of the price the big guns extract for mastery.) Even an ordinary 30-06 takes some work to get accustomed to for most people.

When I was young, in military training and still dumb enough to volunteer, I became the designated shooter to use up the extra ammo after the day's training was over. The other troops would load up on the back of the duce and a half's (2 ½ ton trucks) and head for the barracks while I stayed at the range with one or two of the training sergeants until the ammo was all fired—or the sergeants got tired of hanging around.

The range had pop-ups and a "jungle walk" and other entertaining attractions. I often burned up an extra two to three hundred rounds of .308 and would continue to shoot for an hour or so after dark when the sergeants didn't drag me away earlier. In truth, I welcomed the opportunity to improve skills I expected would be instrumental in my future survival. Sometimes, I arrived back at the barracks after the mess hall had closed, which will give you some idea how serious I was about my shooting. (Missing chow for an eighteen-year-old paratrooper was a BIG deal.)

A couple of decades later, after not having occasion to fire a high-powered rifle for three or four years, I dusted off my old M1 Garand (chambered for the 30-06 the M1 was the predecessor to the M14 and the rifle I learned in basic training) and went to the range. Have you ever seen an angry horse kick out with his hind leg? That was roughly comparable to the severity of my flinch. I was stunned. What, me? I had a flinch? Yes! Sure did; it took me a couple of days to relax into that Garand again. I let that flinch go like the bad habit it was. But it can happen to anyone and with much less of a gun.

DIAGNOSING A FLINCH

The basic technique for diagnosing a flinch is to have a coach load a dummy round in your magazine without telling you which is the dummy round. When you squeeze the trigger on a dummy round it will become immediately appar-

ent if you have a flinch. The diagnosis is also part of the cure. Return to dry fire for, about fifty rounds. Then, when you resume live fire, you will retain the memory of the dry fire. Do not anticipate the shot. Squeeze the trigger and just let it happen; relax into the shot. Have your coach again load a dummy round after you resume live fire. You should find that the flinch has been corrected. Most people flinch more from the muzzle blast, the noise, than from the actual recoil, However, if you're still having a problem, upgrade your ear protection. Nine out of ten times that will do the trick.

Some people cannot get over a flinch induced by a powerful gun. In that event, simply choose a gun with less recoil. I am no great believer in power as the defining characteristic of any firearm. If the shooter cannot fire the gun accurately, the gun is basically useless except as a noisemaker. In other sections, I distinguish between carbines and rifles, but practically speaking the basic shooting methods are the same.

BASIC RIFLE MARKSMANSHIP

The fundamentals of shooting a rifle accurately are:

- steady position,

- target observation,

- aligning the sighting system with the target, and,

- firing without disturbing the alignment of the sights.

STEADY POSITION

1. Foregrip: The foregrip rests in the non-firing hand, that is the left hand if you're right handed. The forearm should be held firmly but lightly. The elbow should be under the forearm; this will enable a relaxed but steady position and allow the rifle to move freely to engage moving or multiple targets.

2. Butt: The rifle butt is placed firmly into the hollow of the firing shoulder. This will aid in acquiring a steady position and minimize the effects of recoil. The trigger finger is placed so that the rifle will not be disturbed when the trigger is squeezed. A slight rearward pressure on the stock with the remaining three fingers will aid in stabilizing the firing position and reducing recoil.

3. Cheek-to-Stock Weld: Your neck should be relaxed, allowing your cheek to be placed naturally on the stock. The stock weld must provide a natural line of sight through the center of the rear sight aperture, or notch to the front sight post and on to the target. This alignment is critical. You may find that some rifles do not allow you to achieve a proper cheek-to-stock weld, but you should be able to acquire a general sense. If not, ask an experienced shooter to help you get fitted. (Often a cheek pad will do the trick.)

Foregrip Illustrated

Rifle butt firmly in pocket of shoulder

Showing cheek-to-stock weld

4. Support: Correct body alignment will, as much as possible, use your bones to support the rifle. In field firing, if any fixed support such as a tree is available it should be used. But the shooter must learn to support the rifle without a rest.

5. Muscle Relaxation: When your correct position is attained you should be able to relax into the position and hold it for some time without muscle fatigue.

Bench rest

In order to become a marksman, a steady, consistent position with a solid cheek weld must be acquired and mastered, to the point where it is reflexive when the rifle is brought to the shoulder. If these basics are in place, you can build on them and eventually be able to shoot quickly and accurately even under difficult conditions. The key is to develop a natural point of aim, one that will allow you to align your rifle and sights exactly in line with your target every time you shoulder your rifle.

TARGET OBSERVATION

Observing and identifying your target is a simple matter when you're shooting bulls-eyes at a shooting range, but is somewhat more difficult in the hunting field. However, you must always insure that you are aiming at what you think you are shooting. Do not mistake Farmer Brown's cow for a deer. When you are sure of your target, start the aiming process.

Correct body alignment

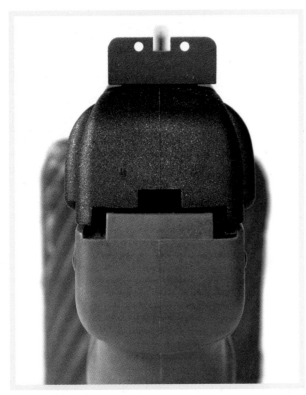

Correct sight alignment

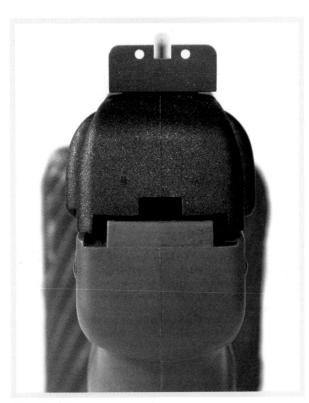

Correct sight picture

ALIGNING THE SIGHT SYSTEM

1. Sight alignment: To align your sights correctly place the tip of the front sight in the center of the rear aperture of a closed sight (or notch if using open sights).

2. Focus: Focus your eye on the front sight. Doing so will naturally center the front sight in the rear sight, thus aligning them. This causes the target to look slightly blurred, although the front sight will be in sharp focus. Every shooter must learn this fundamental technique. If your focus in on the front sight, only minor aiming errors should happen.

3. Sight Picture: A correct sight picture consists of the aiming point on the target, the front sight post, and the rear sight—all in alignment. If you have practiced the points above a good sight picture should naturally form.

BREATH CONTROL

Controlling the breath aids in maintaining stability and alignment while squeezing the trigger. There are two breath control techniques commonly used.

1. When there is sufficient time to allow natural respiration, you should squeeze the trigger after exhaling and during the natural pause before inhaling.

2. If there is not enough time to allow for this technique simply hold your breath at the moment you squeeze the trigger.

FIRING WITHOUT DISTURBING THE SIGHTS

TRIGGER SQUEEZE

A proper trigger squeeze will fire the rifle without disturbing the alignment. A sudden movement (jerking) of the trigger will move the rifle out of alignment causing a miss. A flinch will also move the rifle with the same result.

The index finger should be placed on the trigger so that it touches between the first joint and the tip of the finger. Some prefer to place the pad of the first joint on the trigger; some prefer to use the area just behind the pad. Either will do, so do what works for you.

The trigger must be squeezed directly to the rear with a steady movement. In the beginning, care must be taken so that the squeeze is not off center. Pressing the trigger to one side or the other will result in pulling the shot out of alignment. When forming this skill, visualize pressing the trigger directly to the rear of the butt as if a rod connected the butt and the trigger. In time, this pull will come naturally.

WOBBLE

Unless you are shooting from a solid rest, your sights will wobble somewhat, moving your sights away from your target and back to it. If you have a strongly supported position, there

Correct finger position; ready to fire

will be very little wobble. This wobble is normal. Do not try and anticipate the wobble by jerking the trigger. If your sights move off target during your squeeze, wait until they return to the target and resume your controlled squeeze.

Getting a good position, acquiring a proper sight picture, and, executing a trigger squeeze may well take an extended period of time for the beginning shooter. If you're totally new to shooting you may take five or ten seconds just on the trigger squeeze, with the entire process consuming two or three minutes. With diligent practice, you will learn to perform this sequence in a split second. But first go slow and don't concern yourself with speed.

SHOOTING POSITIONS

The above fundamentals apply regardless of the shooting position. However, a good, solid shooting position will improve your ability to hit. After mastering the fundamentals, you should be able to shoot from almost any position.

Off hand field 1

Off hand field 2

Off hand field 3

Note that in each body position pictured, the alignment of the rifle and the sights are unchanged. The cheek-to-stock weld remains the same. The arms and hands are in the same positions. (I have arranged the positions from top to bottom in the order in which I find them useful in field use, as opposed to range or competition.)

OFFHAND FIELD

The offhand field position is dynamic and relaxed. It is a position from which the shooter can see, shoot, and move with secure footing for field movement. If you have any experience with the martial arts, you will see that below the waist the position amounts to a half horse.

Off hand field 4

SQUATTING

The squatting position is one of my favorites. Lightning fast to drop into and to step up from; both arms are supported; good accuracy is enabled; and it lowers your silhouette, which can be important in certain situations. Good, lower back flexibility, indeed good general flexibility, will aid in assuming this position and in making it comfortable. Dropping into this position and then returning to a standing position is similar to a deep knee bend. If this position is a problem for you, try doing a couple of dozen slow deep knee bends a day for a week or so. Also, sitting in this position for short periods at first, will aid in flexibility. (The position will also keep your bottom dry when the ground is wet.)

Squatting 1

SUPPORTED

If you are alert to your surroundings, you will often find something on which to rest your rifle. Whether shooting from a bench at a range or taking a rest on a tree limb, supported positions provide maximum stability, thus the best accuracy. Often you can find a position that offers both—good support and good concealment. This is definitely the optimum when hunting as it will help to hide you from the ever alert vision of your quarry.

Shooting from a bench rest 1

KNEELING

Kneeling is a quickly-assumed position that is more stable than offhand, although less mobile. The key in this position is to place the upper arm so that the fore elbow is forward of the knee. (Some find this easier to assume that squatting.)

Shooting from a bench rest 2

Kneeling position 1

Kneeling position 2

Offhand target 1

OFFHAND TARGET

I distinguish between the two offhand positions because they are quite different in form and in function. The designations, offhand target and offhand field are my own. The offhand target position is a relaxed, erect standing position providing good stability with a good range of vision, but with much less mobility then the field position.

SITTING

Slow to get into and out off, sitting is comfortable for long periods and gives both arms good support. In kneeling, one arm is supported. In sitting, you place the upper arms so that your elbows are in front of and supported by your knees, thus both arms are supported.

PRONE

The prone position is the most stable, but unsupported position. In fact, the position is very well supported by the alignment of the body and its firm connection with the ground. Done correctly, the direct bone-to-earth connection forms a shooting platform that is as stable as a rest. As a field and hunting position, it excels where there is an open view and a long shot such as you might encounter with plains game.

Standing (offhand target), sitting, kneeling, and, prone are positions used in competition. The formal versions of these positions can be learned from an NRA instructor.

Offhand target 2

Offhand target 4

Offhand target 3

Offhand target 5

Sitting

Prone 1

Prone 3

Prone 2

Prone 4

POINT SHOOTING OR SNAP SHOOTING

Point shooting or snap shooting (as it was called when I was a kid), has been pretty well understood since the invention of firearms. For some reason, though unknown to me, there is currently considerable controversy involving this shooting technique with various experts arguing that this basic skill does not, in fact, work at all. Recently, I heard convoluted arguments against the use of this technique, both for riflemen and hand gunners. Some younger, but experienced shooters even tell me that such techniques belong in the realm of fantasy.

I'm not entirely sure how this controversy got started, or what the point of it is. Perhaps it helps to sell hobby magazines by the time-honored practice of setting up a straw man to knock down. Or, possibly something has been lost during the development of something called, "The New Technique," which as far as I can see amounts to shooting fast with sights and both hands.

When our country was engaged in the Vietnam conflict, feedback from the combat zone was clear and unequivocal. The traditional marksmanship that was being taught to our troops wasn't doing the job for them in fast breaking firefights, especially at close range, in poor lighting, and in brush. Something else was needed. The Army introduced a program called Quick Kill that used a Daisy BB gun without sights, and various training aids and targets to teach Quick Kill, which amounted to snap shooting, or instinct shooting, or point shooting. BB guns were used because they made it safer to engage aerial targets and because there was no recoil or muzzle blast to deal with, thereby freeing the trainee to focus on learning the skill.

The program worked. Trainees quickly learning to hit static and moving targets without the aid of sights, such as candy wafers and coins tossed into the air. Some experts argue that in this type of shooting the shooter is unconsciously using the sights. Obviously these soldiers were not unconsciously using the sights, as there were no sights to be used. These skills served thousands of soldiers and saved many American lives.

Forty years later, the military is still teaching Quick Kill, only now they call it Quick Fire.

Before I was twelve, I learned to "snap shoot" fairly well with my twenty-two. Heck I had been doing it with a bow since I was five. From my personal experience, I thought the Army did a good job of teaching men who had never fired a gun how to shoot, both with and without sights. Point shooting, snap shooting, whatever you want to call it has worked well for me within its limits. Those limits, for me, are about fifty yards. Others successfully snap shoot at much longer distances. On more than one occasion I have been obliged to shoot at moving targets at night. No sight picture was possible, yet I hit my targets. Thousands of others have done the same.

Later I was trained in the use of the handgun using what our instructor called "instinct shooting" or "shooting to live," which amounted to the same thing, but using pistols instead of rifles. I'll deal with the use of this technique for handguns in the self-defense section. Here I'll explain how it works for rifles. It is a valuable part of any shooter's skill set and well worth spending some time to learn.

No matter what you call it, the following is the method for point or snap shooting. Here is how to do it:

1. Bring the rifle up to your shoulder and look down the barrel. Focus on your target, preferably a small part of your target such as a letter on the logo of a soft drink can, or a red spot on a bullseye. Squeeze the trigger.

2. The key is to look at your target, not your sights. The better your focus on the target; the better your hits will be.

If you've done your foundational work and have your body alignment grooved in, cheek-to-stock weld and so forth, you'll find your sights are roughly lined up and that you can consistently score hits on small paper plates out to about twenty-five yards without taking time to acquire a sight picture. With a little more practice, you can extend that range to about fifty yards. There are quite a number of people who can effectively snap shoot at much greater distances. Maybe you can as well with good, tightly focused, concentrated practice. But just about anyone can accomplish the basic level in a couple of days, assuming they have already learned basic gun handling.

If you would like to improve your skills in this area, practice with informal moving targets such as I mentioned earlier. If you find yourself looking for a sight picture while practicing snap shooting, try putting tape over your sights—that's what our sergeants had us do.

If bow hunters can hit a small paper plate at twenty-five yards, and most of them can, you can certainly do the same with a rifle without sights. I've known more than one bow hunter who could, and did, hit birds on the wing, no sights used or needed. Give it a serious try before accepting anyone's word that it can't be done.

CHAPTER 4

How to Shoot a Handgun

The basics of handgun shooting are very similar to that of rifle shooting. In order to shoot well, you need to identify your target; align your sights on the target; and press the trigger without disturbing the sights. A solid grip and foot stance become even more important than in rifle shooting, as there is no stock to stabilize your handgun. Handguns also lack the long sight radius of the rifle, which magnifies mistakes in alignment. However, with good technique and practice, most people can become proficient with the handgun.

HANDGUN FUNDAMENTALS

Handguns are firearms designed to be fired with one hand and have no shoulder stock. Handguns are also commonly referred to as pistols, however, properly speaking a pistol is a semi-automatic—not a revolver. (Yes, they are also commonly fired with the use of two hands, but they are still not called *handsguns*.)

There are three kinds of handguns in common use today: semi-automatics, revolvers, and single shots. Handguns are also referred to as pistols. Properly speaking, a pistol is a semi-automatic, not a revolver. But everyone uses pistol to refer to all handguns, so we will too. Semi-automatics are generally referred to as automatics. Handguns are also fired with the use of two hands, but they are still not called handsguns.

It's important to realize that practical ranges with the handgun are much shorter than for the rifle. In the movies, it's common to see the hero snap shooting or point shooting and hitting the bad guy while he's running at distances of fifty yards and more, uphill and downhill, on rooftops, or while driving at 100 miles an hour. In real life, not so much. As with the rifle, aimed shooting with sights is foundational and the preferred technique for hitting targets at longer ranges. Formal bulls-eye target competition is done at distances out to 25 yards and other kinds of competition utilize targets as far away as 100 yards. Long range for handgun point shooting is anything over approximately seven yards, although this distance varies for each person. There are some who can reliably hit their target with a handgun using point shooting over longer distances.

If you choose to hunt with your handgun, you should limit the distance of your shot at any game animal, to that which you are certain you can hit reliably. For, a squirrel or rabbit, your effective target is no larger than a teacup; for a deer, the size of a small paper plate.

As stated earlier, in handgun shooting you will apply most of the fundamentals of rifle shooting, albeit somewhat modified:

- steady position,

- target observation,

- aligning the sighting system with the target, and,

- firing without disturbing the alignment of the sight.

STEADY POSITION

GRIP

The handgun shooting grip is as important to accuracy as the shoulder position and cheek weld is to rifle shooting. Ideally the handgun becomes an extension of the hand and arm with a firm, uniform, consistent grip utilizing the muscles of the arm and shoulder as well as those of the hand.

One-Handed Grip: Grasp the handgun with the V formed by the thumb and index finger. This V should be placed as high as possible on the back of the grip and in alignment with the barrel and sights. Wrap your lower three fingers around the grip and grasp firmly, placing strong pressure primarily toward the rear of the grip. Too much sideways pressure from the fingers can torque the gun out of alignment and lead to missing your target. (A firm grip is critical in all handgun shooting, with the exception of formal bulls-eye target shooting where a more relaxed grip is commonly used.) The index finger is placed above the trigger on the frame, unless you are drawing to fire at once.

Two-Handed Grip: The two-handed grip, correctly applied provides more support and stability for the firing hand. Close the fingers of the non-firing hand over the firing hand with the fingers placed in the grooves between the fingers of the firing hand. Apply firm pressure to obtain maximum stability. Some favor the "push pull" method to aid in recoil control, applying forward pressure with the firing hand and backward pressure with the non-firing hand. Others prefer an all around firm grip. You will need to do a bit of experimentation to determine which works for you. In no event allow the non-firing hand to pull the firing hand out of alignment. Be sure to maintain full grip pressure with the firing hand.

Correct grip

Gripping pistol so that it is in line with the arm

Two-handed field 1

Two-handed field 2

Two-handed field 3

Two-handed field 4

TARGET OBSERVATION

As in shooting a rifle, observing and identifying your target is a simple matter when you're shooting bulls-eyes at a shooting range but somewhat more difficult in the hunting field. However, you must always insure that you are aiming at what you think you are shooting. Do not mistake Farmer Brown's cow for a deer. When you are sure of your target, start the aiming process.

Two-handed field 5

Correct sight alignment

Aligning the sight

ALIGNING THE SIGHT SYSTEM

1. Sight alignment: Few handguns use an aperture sight, although some are fitted with a "Ghost Ring," a large aperture. Most common is the square notch sight. To align this sight, place the front blade into the rear notch. The top of the front sight should be level with the top of the rear sight and centered in the rear notch.

2. Focus: Focus your eye on the front sight. Doing so will naturally center the front sight in the rear sight, thus aligning them. This causes the target to look slightly blurred, although the front sight will be in sharp focus. Every shooter must learn this fundamental technique. If your focus is on the front sight, only minor aiming errors should happen.

3. Sight Picture: A correct sight picture consists of the aiming point on the target, the front sight post and the rear sight —all in alignment. If you have practiced the points above a good sight picture should naturally form. Sight alignment is more important to accuracy than sight placement. The eye cannot focus on the front sight, the rear sight, and the target. Focusing on the front sight is most important to accuracy. The best way to do this is to look through the rear sight and focus on the front sight when it is placed on your target.

FIRING WITHOUT DISTURBING ALIGNMENT

There are two breath control techniques commonly used.

1. When there is sufficient time to allow natural respiration, you should squeeze the trigger after exhaling and during the natural pause before inhaling.

2. If there is not enough time to allow for this technique simply hold your breath at the moment you squeeze the trigger.

TRIGGER SQUEEZE

A proper trigger squeeze is even more critical in handgun shooting than in rifle work. A sudden movement (jerking) of the trigger will move the handgun out of alignment to the extent that a shooter can miss a life size silhouette target from five feet. In my experience the most common cause for jerking the trigger is a flinch.

The index finger should be placed on the trigger so that it touches between the first joint and the tip of the finger. Some prefer to place the pad of the first joint on the trigger; some prefer to use the area just behind the pad. Either will do.

The trigger must be squeezed directly to the rear with a steady movement. In the beginning care must be taken so that the squeeze is not off center. Pressing the trigger to one side or the other can torque the handgun out of alignment. When forming this skill, visualize pressing the trigger directly to the rear of the butt, as if a rod

Front sight on target; rear sights blurred

Another view of front sights on target

Index finger placed on trigger

connected the trigger, the back of the grip and your forearm. In time this will come naturally. Dry firing is probably the single most important practice to insure you are squeezing the trigger properly.

If you are using a double action automatic the trigger pull will be greater and require more pressure than subsequent single action shots, perhaps twice as much. Extra attention should be used to master double action fire. In double action revolvers, all shots are double action unless the revolver is manually cocked.

WOBBLE

The wobble effect that the rifleman experiences will be more pronounced with the handgun. You should do your best to control wobble with proper breathing, grip, and trigger control.

SHOOTING POSITIONS

Handgun shooting positions are similar in form and function to the rifle positions. All provide greater stability than the offhand positions. Utilized properly and with the right pistol, you can get amazing accuracy.

Some years ago, I knew some shooters who were enamored of the 9mm Sig 210, and understandably so. The Sig 210 was once the Swiss Army's issue sidearm and easily the most accurate service pistol made. These fellows considered it great fun to haze a coffee can back and forth at a hundred yards. Like them, I found a coffee can to be an easy target at a hundred yards using this pistol. By shooting from one of the positions described below, we could toss a

Author's Advice

As in rifle work, breath control is critical. The same techniques applies with handguns.

coffee can around at well over a hundred yards. I won't strain your credulity with the actual distances. Learn a solid field stance first. Then try the positions below. You might be surprised.

FIELD STANCE

In the rifle section, I called this position the offhand field position. For the pistol, I'll call it the field stance. It is basically the same as the rifle position from the waist down and equally important in order to have a solid base from which to fire. Lacking the rifle's shoulder stock a stable hold is dependant on correct alignment of the shoulders and arm, or arms. This is an especially important position in that you will likely do most of your shooting from. It is a dynamic and powerful position from which the shooter can see, shoot, and move with secure footing over broken ground.

As the accompanying photos show, a one or two-handed grip can be used in the field stance. A two-handed grip is usually used in other positions such as kneeling, squatting, and prone.

SUPPORTED

"Taking a rest" is a good practice with rifle or handgun. A tree limb or any solid object will enable you to have an almost unwavering sight picture and resultant accuracy.

PRONE

As with the rifle, the prone is the most stable position other than shooting from a rest.

Prone 1

Prone 2

Prone 3

Prone 4

SQUATTING

The squatting position works well in the field as it is quick to assume and offers good stability.

KNEELING

The kneeling position offers less stability than squatting for some shooters, but more stability for others. The comparative utility of the two positions is determined by the individual's physical make up.

Squatting 1

POINT SHOOTING OR SNAP SHOOTING FOR THE HANDGUN

I cover point shooting in some detail in the *How to Shoot A Rifle* chapter. For the handgun, the primary difference is that you do not have the stability provided by a rifle. However, within

Squatting 2

Squatting 3

Kneeling

the limits of the handgun, this method works equally well.

Here is how to do it:

1. Start with your gun hand at your side. Bring your gun hand up with your arm fully-extended towards your target. You may use only one hand or you can bring your other hand up and grasp your gun hand to better stabilize your gun. Look down the barrel. Focus on your target—preferably a small part of your target. Squeeze the trigger.

Focus on target, not sights

2. The key is to look at your target, not your sights. The better your focus on the target, the better your hits will be.

Please review *An Approach to Self-Defense* chapter for more detailed information regarding handguns and the Quick Fire method.

DRY FIRING FOR THE HANDGUN

Dedicated and concentrated dry fire practice is vitally important to learning the handgun and maintaining skill. This is true for both aiming with the sights and point shooting. An intensively concentrated half hour of practice in the evening is something you can do anywhere you have your firearm—no range or ammo required. Once skills are acquired, much less practice is needed to maintain them.

If your dry fire practice is to be of maximum benefit, it is critical to practice as if you were shooting a loaded gun. First, make absolutely sure your gun is unloaded. Second, put the ammunition away, say, in a drawer, or if traveling, perhaps in your case. Third, put yourself in the frame of mind you would be in if you were shooting under actual field conditions. Shoot fifty imaginary rounds with full concentration. Balancing a coin on the barrel of your gun for the first five rounds and the last five rounds is an excellent way to see if you are jerking the trigger or in any way not squeezing off your imaginary rounds correctly.

I have experienced extended periods, usually while traveling internationally, when I had no access to any shooting facilities. I have found that during those periods I was able to maintain my skills by two simple exercises. One was a few minutes of dry fire in the privacy of my hotel room, perhaps once a week, preferably just before retiring for the night. (Any skill practiced immediately before sleep will take on a sort of momentum effect as if you had continued to practice while sleeping.) The second was to visualize a perfect shot after getting in bed just before sleep. Visualization is a key technique to improving your skills. (I will discuss this in more detail in the *Tao of Shooting* chapter.)

CHAPTER 5

How to Shoot a Shotgun

Since a shotgun possesses no rear sight, only a front sight (unless set up for slugs, in which case it is fired as a rifle), there is no point to separating shooting techniques into aimed with sights and aimed without sights, or point shooting, instinct shooting, or any of the other designations. All shotgun shooting amounts to point shooting.

The basic method of mounting the shotgun to the shoulder is the same as for the rifle. The most effective shooting position is what I refer to as the "Offhand Field" position. The Offhand Target position lacks the needed stability. Since shotguns are most commonly used for wingshooting, there is no need to consider the other shooting positions.

OFFHAND FIELD

The offhand field position is dynamic and relaxed. It is a position from which the shooter can see, shoot, and move with secure footing for field movement. If you have any experience with the martial arts, you will see that below the waist the position amounts to a half horse. The position is illustrated in accompanying photos. Although they show the shooter with a rifle, there is no difference in application.

Let's assume you're shooting at a moving target—clay, pheasant, quail, or other flying bird. As with the rifle or handgun, look first at your target and bring the gun to the target. Look down the barrel and swing your shotgun to follow the target. Lead your target to allow for the load you are using and squeeze the trigger.

You must know your load and where it shoots to be successful. You will learn this with practice. Since the projectiles of a shotgun travel much more slowly than those of a rifle, or even a handgun, you cannot aim directly at a fast-moving target. Instead, you must aim in front of your target, and continue to move as you squeeze the trigger, thus "stringing" or placing your shot pattern where your target will be. You must also know the pattern your shotgun shoots with the load you are using. Each load will pattern somewhat differently.

Off Hand Field position

FUNDAMENTALS OF SHOTGUN SHOOTING

In shotgun shooting, you must apply most of the fundamentals of rifle shooting, albeit somewhat modified.

- steady position,

- target observation,

- aligning the sighting system with the target, and,

- firing without disturbing the alignment of the sight.

Off Hand Field position

Foregrip Illustrated

Rifle butt firmly in pocket of shoulder

STEADY POSITION

1. *Foregrip:* The foregrip rests in the non-firing hand, that is, the left hand if you're right handed. The forearm should be held firmly but lightly. The elbow should be under the forearm. This will enable a relaxed but steady position and allow the shotgun to move freely to engage moving or multiple targets.

2. *Butt:* The shotgun butt is placed firmly into the hollow of the firing shoulder. This placement will aid in acquiring a steady position and minimize the effects of recoil. The trigger finger is placed so that the shotgun will not be disturbed when the trigger is squeezed. A slight rearward pressure against the stock with the remaining three fingers will aid in stabilizing the firing position and reducing recoil.

Correct body alignment

3. *Cheek-to-Stock Weld:* Your neck should be relaxed, allowing your cheek to be placed naturally on the stock. The stock weld must provide a natural line of sight along the barrel to the front sight and on to the target.

4. *Support:* Correct body alignment will, as much as possible, use your bones to support the shotgun.

5. *Muscle Relaxation:* When the correct position is attained, you should be able to relax into the offhand field position and hold it for some time without muscle fatigue.

Showing cheek-to-stock weld

Bench Rest

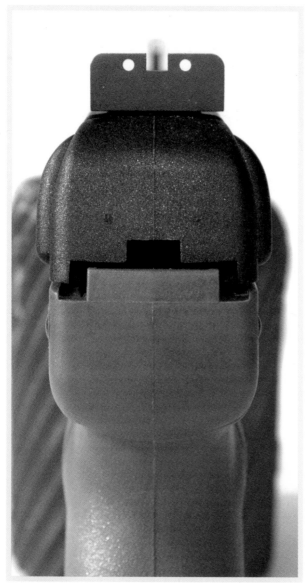

Correct sight

A steady, consistent position with a solid cheek weld must be practiced, acquired, and mastered to the point where it is reflexive when the shotgun is brought to the shoulder. If these basics are acquired, you can build on them and eventually be able to shoot quickly and accurately even under difficult conditions. The key is to develop a natural point of aim, one that will allow you to align your shotgun in line with your target every time you shoulder your shotgun.

TARGET OBSERVATION

Observing and identifying your target is a simple matter when you're shooting clays at a shooting range. These basics can be more challenging in the hunting field; however, you must insure that you are aiming at what you think you are shooting. (Do not mistake Farmer Brown's prize turkeys for pheasants.)

ALIGNING THE SIGHT SYSTEM

For the shotgun, aligning the sighting system amounts to looking down the barrel to the front sight. Although this is simpler than aligning the rear sight and front sight of a rifle, it is no less critical.

FIRING WITHOUT DISTURBING SIGHT ALIGNMENT

Breath control aids in maintaining stability and alignment while squeezing the trigger. There are two breath control techniques commonly used.

Correct finger position; ready to fire

1. When there is sufficient time to allow natural respiration you should squeeze the trigger after exhaling and during the natural pause before inhaling.

2. If there is not enough time to allow for this technique simply hold your breath at the moment you squeeze the trigger.

Trigger Squeeze

A proper trigger squeeze will fire the shotgun without disturbing the alignment. A sudden movement (jerking) of the trigger will move the shotgun out of alignment causing a miss. A flinch will also move the shotgun with the same result.

1. The index finger should be placed on the trigger so that it touches between the first joint and the tip of the finger. Some prefer to place the pad of the first joint on the trigger; some prefer to use the area just behind the pad. Either will do and should works for you.

2. The trigger must be squeezed directly to the rear with a steady movement. In the beginning, care must be taken so that the squeeze is not off center. Pressing the trigger to one side or the other will result in pulling the shot out of alignment. When developing this skill, visualize pressing the trigger directly to the rear of the butt, as if a rod connected the butt and the trigger. In time this will come naturally.

Perhaps even more so than with rifles and handguns, many people have a tendency to try to shoot more gun than they can handle when using a shotgun. This is always a mistake. I have seen fine wingshooting by men and women with light 28 gauge shotguns. Their take of birds fully equaled that of their more heavily-armed companions who were shooting the standard 12 gauge.

FIELDS OF FIRE

Understanding fields of fire is of maximum importance when upland shooting with companions. When shooters form to cross a field or to make a firing line, they will set out individual fields of fire in accordance with the shooters on each side of them. Generally, each shooter's field of fire will extend from his position in an imaginary cone down range, perhaps slightly overlapping his companion's range to either side of the fields of fire. Once established, fields of fire should be maintained, and not transgressed in the excitement of shooting.

GENERAL SHOOTING COMMENTS

Try to find a coach you can work with. It's not hard to meet folks at ranges and gun shops, and many are well informed and willing to lend a hand. Better yet, contact your local National Rifle Association. They offer basic classes in marksmanship and in most of the shooting sports. The cost is very low and the quality usually very high.

If you can find a moment of stillness within yourself at the moment you squeeze your trigger, and learn to focus all your attention for just one fraction of a second, you will have taken a giant step towards shooting mastery. The skills outlined in The Tao of Shooting apply to the shotgun, as well as to the rifle and handgun.

One day last year at a sporting clay range, I saw a man trying to teach his young wife to shoot a 12-gauge slide action shotgun. The poor woman was a good sport, but she weighed maybe 100 pounds and had obviously been given no instruction on how to hold a shotgun to absorb recoil. Each time she fired, the stock slapped her cheek and the butt slammed her shoulder, moving her back a couple of steps. It was painful to watch, but certainly not as painful as what this young woman was enduring.

I noticed that the report of their guns was much louder than that of my gun, or those of my companions. When they moved ahead a station I examined one of her expended shells. She was shooting high base three inch magnums. This is a round suitable for ducks and geese, and grossly inappropriate for clays. In addition to throwing a pattern that makes it harder to score a hit on clays, the round kicks like a mule. The woman certainly had gumption, but I doubt her husband will ever get her to the range again. Maybe that was his purpose. Maybe he wanted some time alone or with the guys. But if he wanted a shooting companion, he lost her that day.

CHAPTER 6

The Tao of Shooting

Tao means "way"—nothing more—nothing less. Taoist meditation, which I am going to tell you a little about, has nothing to do with religion. It is a method or "way" of focused attention; a discipline practiced by Asian warriors, hunters, and, sages for centuries. The methods are similar to those used by Native American hunters, shamans and warriors, and First Peoples from the Arctic to the Amazon. Today certain elite military units and covert action groups practice these techniques.

I have seen bowmen and users of various primitive projectile weapons like blowguns, use exactly these methods. I have also seen champion competitive shooters use these methods, and recommended them. Perhaps most importantly, I have seen these methods used in actual firefights by combat survivors. I use them myself and have done so for years.

I suspect all cultures that lived close to the earth once, knew these methods, but that our European ancestors forgot about them long ago. We gained a great deal with the age of reason, but some things were also lost. We are fortunate that Asian cultures codified and passed those methods down to us.

These skills are enjoying a renaissance and are practiced by many world-class athletes, not only martial artists and competitive shooters, but golfers, tennis players, track stars, and ball players of

When I first qualified for a military pistol team, I was exhausted each day by the concentration required to meet and maintain the team standard. I worked so hard and concentrated so intensely that I dreamed of the bulls-eye with ten shots centered in it. Although I did not know it at the time, this is actually a formal technique called *visualization.*

After about a week of daily shooting, I discovered that I did better when I focused tightly just at the moment of firing and to relax when I was off the trigger. After some more time, I learned to get the same results when I was relaxed. This is the Tao in its essence.

all kinds. Such well-know teams as the Oakland Raiders employ these methods. (There is nothing frou frou, silly, or mystical about the Tao.)

The idea behind the Tao of Shooting is that after learning basic methods and disciplines, you can, by using focused attention, integrate those skills into your reflexes so that you do the correct thing without consciously thinking about it. I first came to formal study of the Tao through martial arts. It was only after I had practiced for some time that I realized that I had been using certain Taoist techniques for years without being aware of it. I am sure this is true for many others.

First, learn your foundation skills. Nothing can replace them. Learn them well. Take your time and go step-by-step. Skip nothing.

FIRST EXERCISE

Find a quiet and comfortable spot. Sit in whatever position is comfortable for you. You do not have to sit on the floor or cross your legs. An easy chair will do just fine.

Let all thoughts of your day slip away. Don't fight with yourself or try and tell yourself to think of nothing or try to force your thoughts to go away. It's OK if you find yourself reliving that moment when that truck cut you off on the freeway. Just don't dwell on the moment. Let that thought, and all other thoughts, slip away like bubbles in a steam.

Now recreate the feelings in your body when everything was correctly aligned and you made the perfect shot. Really feel in your body the muscle memory of your rifle or handgun. Feel the stock against your shoulder, the grips in your hand, and the trigger under your finger. Remember and relive and feel that moment when you made that perfect shot—the best shot of the day—the best shot of the week—the best shot ever. The more attention you put into this inner vision, the better your results will be.

SECOND EXERCISE

Once you have felt your body position in fine detail, visualize your sight picture over your target. Really see the target. Remember the best shot you've made on that target. Once you can see the target, see your bullet flying straight to your target, as if it's on a cord being pulled to the target.

You will be distracted. Don't be discouraged. Like any skill, this takes time to acquire. When you lose your concentration, just relax and let it go for a moment; gently move your attention back and recreate the first or second exercise.

These two exercises can be done separately or sequentially. Doing them at night before sleep will help focus your unconscious and get it to work for you.

THIRD EXERCISE

Go to your safe shooting spot; the familiar one where you have been shooting. The one where there is NO possibility of anyone being down-range. Set up one target. Go to your shooting position; look at your target. Fire without thinking about each individual step in the process.

Focus with intensity on your target. Do not think about the drive to your shooting spot, the weather, the fly buzzing around your nose. Don't think. Just do. Shoot three shots and check your group.

If you've done all the steps, or even most of them, you'll have a good group. Repeat the exercise.

Just as when you begin martial arts, ride a bicycle, or to drive a car, you have to consciously learn the basics. In martial arts you stand and move consciously and thoughtfully in a classic horse for hours and days, maybe weeks. But once you have it grooved in, you don't have to think about it. When you snap out a punch you don't think, horse position, hip rotation, snap

etc. But it's there because of the hours you invested in training; so too, with the fundamentals of shooting. These steps in Taoist focus are in some ways a shortcut to shooting mastery.

There is more. But this is foundational, and all we can go into in this book. These exercises will help to get skill foundations into your unconscious and muscle memory, both of which are much faster and surer than your conscious reasoning mind.

CHAPTER 7

Hunting with Your Gun

Many books about guns for hunting go into deep, detailed discussion and analysis regarding caliber, load, gun models, scopes and so forth. This is not that type of book. In this chapter, I will discuss some hunting methods and some particular guns, then help you to select a gun that's right for you and for the kind of game you pursue. Guns do matter. But the shooter matters more.

If you know what you're doing almost any decent gun will do. It's vitally important to keep this in mind. Do not fall into the trap of buying a rack of firearms in an attempt to compensate for a lack of hunting success. If you enjoy firearm collecting, by all means build your collection, but be aware that collecting has little or nothing

to do with hunting. As you go further into the sport, you may wish to expand your knowledge of various calibers and their performance, but to be a successful hunter, make sure you've got the basics down first.

Also, as a hunter you have an ethical obligation to acquire competency in shooting under field conditions. Ethical hunters reduce their game to possession by inflicting as little pain and suffering on their quarry as possible. The ideal is the clean shot; the unwary animal that drops without knowing what hit him. This ideal is not always achieved, but it should be attempted. We are, after all, sporting hunters. We hunt for the most part, by choice, not by necessity. (I have hunted with subsistence hunters in various places, including Asia and Latin America. I have found they have their own methods that are useful to know if faced with survival conditions, but not part of sport hunting.)

I have witnessed so-called "hunters" driving fire roads in 4x4 trucks with racks of lights, the shooters standing in the truck bed ready to shoot the first deer they see. Don't do this. Don't be any part of it. It's illegal. It isn't sporting. It's just plain wrong. If you're caught you'll be arrested. If not, you'll know you have earned the contempt of all true hunters.

HUNTING BIG GAME

Current conventional wisdom has it that only extremely powerful large caliber rifles are suitable for large game. Yet, each year thousands of deer, elk, moose, and bear are taken with bows. Yes, I'm familiar with the argument that arrows kill by cutting vital organs and bleeding, and that guns kill by shock and tissue destruction, or neural interruption. In this example, the razor sharp arrow is superior to the bullet in causing blood wounds, but I don't think it's so simple. I've hunted successfully with both bow and gun and seen the results of many other hunters. I've witnessed deer run hundreds of yards before finally bleeding out and dropping after taking a lung shot from a high-powered rifle. I've seen virtually the same thing occur with an arrow-shot buck.

My observations and experience indicate that it is the accurate placement of the arrow or the bullet in a vital spot that gets the job done, rather than an excessively powerful rifle. Generally speaking, the best placement on large game is in the heart or lungs. Head and spine shots, being smaller targets, are much more difficult to make and should only be taken if you know you can make the shot.

Many gun hunters would do well to emulate the bow hunter and get closer to their quarry in order to make sure they hit a vital spot. All too many hunters try to substitute power for marksmanship and shot placement. I hate to see a gut shot deer, as does any hunter with respect for the animal he hunts. (A new hunter might do well to try bow hunting. Experience with primitive weapons sharpens hunting skills. It also leads to a better appreciation of modern firearms.)

I recently observed an instructor, who was teaching a state-approved safety class for first time hunters, advise his students to choose nothing less than a .308 to take their first deer. By a show of hands, most of them had never even hunted rabbits. This occurred in a state where the average buck wasn't much larger than my neighbor's German Shepard. He went on to say that a .338 Winchester Magnum or something more powerful was the only chance the students would have to anchor a Colorado elk, given the enormous size and legendary hardiness of the elk. This is nonsense.

This kind of advice has a good chance of driving a new hunter away from the sport. By all means use enough gun, but no more than you can handle or that is appropriate for the game.

As my sons frequently remind me, I'm an old-school guy. I don't think a new hunter has much business going after large game until he's built a foundation of experience on small game. I also believe a new hunter needs a solid foundation of marksmanship and needs to develop a close familiarity with his weapon of choice. In addition, I do not think one has any business taking to the field unless he has at least a rudimentary understanding of the habits and habitat of his intended quarry. (Careful reading can help the new gun owner identify customary and successful methods for hunting.)

Many years ago, I was hunting with two friends and a local contact, George, for deer and elk on a combination tag in Colorado. One of my friends, Dexter, was outfitted with a beautiful new rifle. As I recall, it was a Remington 700 BDL, chambered for the .300 Winchester Magnum and mounted with a good quality variable scope.

Bob and I were somewhat envious of his rifle and the rest of his gear. We were both still in college; funds were limited and our guns and gear were considerably more modest.

Bob carried an ancient Springfield Model 1903 with a "sporterized" stock his father had installed on it when it had been his rifle forty years previously. The old Springfield sported its original aperture (peep) sight and its original chambering: 30-06. The stock displayed the nicks and dings of four decades of use. However, the bore was bright and shiny, there was no rust anywhere on it and it was well oiled. Of major importance, Bob shot his rifle regularly, was very familiar with it from years of use, and had spent a few days at the range zeroing it with the ammunition he had selected for this hunt. He knew where his rifle would shoot with this particular load.

Remington Model 700 BDL Rifle

I wanted to try handgun hunting and had brought my duty revolver, a Smith &Wesson, Model 19 .357 Magnum with a four-inch barrel. I had fired thousands of rounds with a half dozen different loads with this revolver. The Smith was superbly accurate. I could shoot two-inch groups at fifty yards, hit the skittering balloons floating along the ground, and so on. Further, I planned to shoot within my limits. I had no intention of trying, say, a 150-yard shot.

Smith & Wesson Model 19 .357 Magnum

Dexter and George didn't think much of Bob's chances at an elk. They were of the opinion that the 30-06 was severely underpowered, and incapable of dropping a "monster elk." They also thought that without a scope he didn't have a chance, because he couldn't get close enough to bag an elk in the high country, maybe a deer down in the trees, if he was lucky. As for me—I was beneath consideration.

On our first day, just after dawn, about twenty miles down a logging road we saw a herd of elk in the middle of a meadow, or park as meadows are called in Colorado.

All of us were out of the Land Cruiser in a flash and moved a hundred yards or so from the car, which as I recall, was about the minimum legal distance. (It is not legal or sporting, to shoot from or near a car.)

BLAM! Dexter's muzzle was to my immediate left, about fifteen feet away. He had fired without warning. I moved back a few yards, as did Bob. Dexter fired again. BLAM! This time I was watching Dexter and saw him stagger backwards from the recoil and poor footing. I watched with amazement as the elk totally ignored us. None of them went down. None of them even bothered to run. I had never before seen an elk herd, but I was amazed they had not scrambled for cover at the first sight of us. Dexter fired another magazine from his sitting position without hitting anything other than trees. No one else fired a shot. I think we were all stunned by the display of firepower and the lack of result.

We talked around the campfire that night and Dexter admitted he had only fired one magazine from his new rifle before leaving California. Later he admitted that the rifle kicked him so bad when he tried to zero it from a bench, that he had given up, and hoped to get a hit on his first shot or two.

(Dexter made a number of errors, one of which was to fire before alerting us of his intention to do so. My ears were still ringing.)

However, his first error, made long before reaching our hunting grounds, had been to select a rifle that was beyond his ability to handle. His next mistake was failing to get enough practice with the big magnum to master it. He would have done better to select a more modest caliber, but Dexter had been seduced by the myth of the invincible elk. (Thousands of hunters annually make the same mistakes.)

We fanned out after that first day, and hunted separate meadows and ridges over the next week. Bob took his first elk cleanly with a nice ninety-yard (we paced it off) shot. He filled his deer tag, so there was plenty of meat for all. George filled his deer tag by gut shooting a doe at about three hundred yards and then finishing her off with another three or four rounds. Dexter went the whole week without getting a hit on anything that moved.

And me? I bagged a six-point elk at about twenty yards. I put one round behind his ear and he dropped like, well, like a few hundred pounds of meat. Anyone could have made that shot. Anyone with rudimentary shooting skills and certainly anyone who had spent as much time working with that revolver as I had. The .357 isn't as powerful as even the .223 rifle. But it was powerful enough to do what I asked of it.

Author's Advice

- *Use enough gun, but no more than you can handle.*
- *Shoot within the limits of your gun and your skill.*
- *Do your homework and know the habits of your quarry.*

CHOOSING A HUNTING GUN

Generally speaking, whatever arms your state allows to legally hunt with will do the job—if the hunter does his. This is not to say you can't take pleasure in a fine firearm. When you select your hunting gun, pick one that calls to you. You'll practice more and shoot better with it, if you have a gun that you really like.

Another suggestion is to arrange to test a friend's guns or go to a rental range where you can try various guns before making your decision. You'll quickly determine if you're recoil sensitive. (Almost everyone is. Those who say they are not, have, for the most part, trained themselves to ignore recoil. If you're at all recoil sensitive, choose the lightest legal caliber and practice extensively with it before taking to the field.) If you're one of the few who are unaffected by recoil, choose whatever caliber you like, but make sure you get a good deal of practice with it before going after game.

MY BIAS FOR BOLT ACTION RIFLES

There is little mystery left in bolt action rifles. Mauser got the rotating bolt sorted out over a hundred years ago. And the bolt gun in general, is well understood by all its makers. There are only two bolt guns that I have any personal bias for. One is the Springfield 1903 in its original chambering, 30-06. After I shot a friend's 1903 extensively, I bought one, though my funds were extremely limited. I disliked the stock and so re-stocked it with one having less drop and providing a straighter line of sight, given my particular cheek -to -stock weld. It did everything I asked of it.

The 30-06 has fallen from favor due to the advent of the .308. This is understandable, given that the .308 is our service cartridge, has a shorter case length, and thus is chambered in shorter actions. You can do most things with a .308 that you can do with a 30-06, but there are still more loadings available for the 06. As has been proven time and again, with the proper loading you can take anything from squirrel (maybe a little overkill there) to brown bear. (I won't tell you it is better; I just like it.)

My second bias was a Mannlicher Schoenauer with the graceful and slender full stock, the short carbine length barrel, and the "butter knife" bolt handle. Chambering was in the classic 6.5X54 cartridge. The rifle balanced like no other; quick to the shoulder and easy in the hand. The action was silken and smooth as a lover's skin (and that's not just a metaphor). The smoothness of the action was due to fine machining and polishing. To my eye, it was simply a sweetheart; a beautiful little rifle that would take anything from elephant to mountain goat, as long as the shooter did his part.

I bought it in the old Abercrombie & Fitch. (No, not the store that sells pre-wornout jeans and t-shirts at absurd prices to suburban teenagers.) The old Abercrombie & Fitch stocked virtually every worthwhile firearm on the planet, plus clothing, luggage, and gun cases like you can't imagine unless you've been to a hunting store in Paris. Teddy Roosevelt shopped there, as did every outdoorsman of note, and quite a few of us who were not at all notable but happened to have a couple of extra bucks. I don't remember what I paid for the Mannlicher. All that mattered was that I had enough cash for the little rifle, 500 rounds of 6.4x54 and a saddle leather case that made my Louis Vuitton carryall look like a reject from a garage sale.

Part of my infatuation with the Mannlicher was the sheer romance of the rifle and caliber. WDM "Karamojo" Bell used it. Hemmingway used it. (It had to be right if Pappa shot with it.) Aside from all the romance, the rifle and caliber combination really did work. The little 6.5x54 chambering in the hands of Bell and others took thousands of African Elephant and Cape Buffalo, two of the most dangerous and hard to kill animals on our planet. This was due to the high sectional density of the projectiles. They were long and heavy in relation to their diameter and were capable of deep penetration through muscle and bone. This combined with low recoil made for easy accurate shot placement into vital organs such as the heart, and better yet the brain—Bell's preferred target. In his books, Bell writes of taking over a thousand elephants, mostly with brain shots; some of them while they were charging.

How did one of the world's greatest hunters achieve his success? He did so by having intimate knowledge of the game and the habitat, and by choosing a weapon that was accurate, comfortable to shoot, and up-to-the-job. Shot placement, not power was the key to his shooting.

You can pick a gun with your head. You can analyze power, trajectory; so much of this and so much of that, and you'll probably get a good gun. But if you ever find a rifle that calls out to you like that Mannlicher did to me, grab it and hold on to it like a drowning sailor clutching a lifesaver, because you'll have found your gun.

MODERN HUNTING RIFLES AND SHOTGUNS

Remington, Winchester, Marlin, Savage—all American rifle and shotgun manufacturers—make terrific rifles and shotguns. So do the European makers. I've never seen a bad Browning, Beretta, CZ, Sako, or Styer. You can't go wrong with any of them. The standard of manufacturing quality in terms of fit and finish vary, but in terms of function, any of these will do. (I doubt there's a bad rifle or shotgun made in America or Europe.)

BOLT ACTION RIFLES

- *Browning* has a great line-up of centerfire rifles; all of them very nicely finished.

- *CZ* rifles are uniformly of high quality. They make a handy, little, full-stock carbine that balances well. In addition they manufacture a full range of large calibers.

- *Dakota* rifles are considered state of the art today. Most of offerings cost about the same as a good used car.

- *Kimber* makes a few models. All are priced in the low four figures and all with the same quality as their pistols.

- The *Remington* 700 Series is probably the most popular centerfire rifle being made in America today. It does pretty much everything right and is available at a price that is affordable for the middle range of hunters.

Remington Model 700 BDL Rifle

Photo courtesy of manufacturer

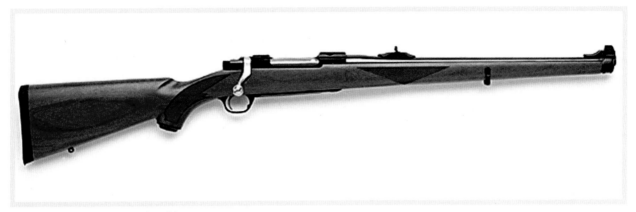

Ruger M77RSI International Carbine

Ruger M77 Mark II Rifle

Photo courtesy of manufacturer

- *Ruger* rifles, like their handguns are famous for durability and good performance. They are available in dozens of variations and all popular calibers, and all at reasonable prices. (One of their models, the International Carbine is close in concept if not in actual design to the old Mannlicher.)

- *Sakos* are made in Sweden. The Swedes know a good bit about making quality rifles, as their manufacturing meets a very high standard.

- *Savage* is an old and well-regarded name in American arms. They make a wide range of very good, very affordable centerfire rifles.

- *Steyr* is still making excellent rifles in a variety of models, and at good prices considering their quality. The Steyr Classic Mannlicher SBS bears a resemblance to their old carbine and is available in a 20" barrel, as well as longer (23" and 26") barrels. (My old Mannlicher had an 18" barrel. Well, still has I guess; wherever she might be.)

• *Weatherby* continues as a premium American made rifle with a model that will suit anyone who can afford them.

LEVER ACTION RIFLES

I was never bitten by the cowboy bug and so never developed and affection for lever rifles. But many love their lever guns and do excellent work with them. The lever action 30-30 made by Marlin and Winchester has probably been used to take more deer in America than any other rifle. Fast on follow up shots and handy in its carbine lengths, it is an American icon. The Winchester is now discontinued, but Marlin keeps the lever action flag flying and makes an excellent, accurate rifle in a wide range of models.

Feeding a round into the magazine of a Winchester 30-30

Marlin Model 336C Lever Action 30-30

Winchester 30-30 rifle with tubular magazine

Browning also has a lever action in the game. Browning lever gun has a detachable box magazine with the Browning traditional, exceptional fit and finish.

SLIDE ACTION (PUMP) RIFLES

Remington makes a slide action rifle and a carbine in calibers from .243 to .308. This is a good choice for the shotgunner who wants to maintain a similar action in both rifle and shotgun. (I had one once in 30-06 and liked it.)

Browning BLR Lightweight/Pistol Grip

Remington Model 870 12 gauge –Loading a shell

Remington Model 870 –Shell loaded; Ready to fire

SEMI-AUTOMATIC RIFLES

Most centerfire rifles have a military appearance, with notable exceptions being offered by Benelli, Browning, Winchester, Remington, and Ruger's handy little Mini14 series. There's nothing particularly wrong with going afield with a military rifle as long as the magazine is blocked so that the numbers of rounds on tap conform to your local Fish and Game regulations. You may get some odd looks from fellow hunters, but most military rifles are accurate enough for hunting and far more durable than a sporting rifle.

For those who prefer an autoloader, you will find the Benelli R1, the Browning BAR, the Remington Woodsmaster, and the Winchester Super X to be perfectly suitable for large game. Ruger's Mini-14 series is chambered for .223 (which many states confine to small game). The Ruger is also chambered in 7.62x39, which is legal for deer in most states.

Ruger Mini 14   Photo courtesy of manufacturer

Browning Bar Safari Semi-Auto Rifle   Photo courtesy of manufacturer

Winchester Super X Semi-Automatic Shotgun   Photo courtesy of manufacturer

MILITARY SURPLUS RIFLES

Military surplus rifles are generally either bolt guns or semi-auto. Many are quite reasonably priced and serviceable. The Mosin Nagant I mention is typical in some ways of other surplus rifles currently available.

MOSIN NAGANT

I have recently seen this rifle at ranges around the country. Many hunters use it with good results.

Lyudmila Pavlichenco, a famous Russian female sniper scored over 300 kills against Nazi armies with this model rifle. Even more impressive was Simo Hayha, and his use of the Mosin Nagant. He was a Finnish sniper in the "Winter War" in 1940 when Russia invaded Finland with over 160,000 men. Against incredible odds, a few thousand Finns held off the Russian Army and extracted a terrible toll. Simo Hayha became known as "The White Death" due to killing over 500 Russian soldiers, many of them at over 400 meters, and with iron sights.

The rifle was designed in the late 19th Century and used by various armies well into the 20th Century. It is still highly functional today. Not as finely finished as a commercial grade sporting rifle, it is very inexpensive and has the robust build of a military firearm. It obviously has good accuracy.

Top—Surplus Mauser Bolt Action Rifle
Bottom—Mosin Nagant Bolt Action with Scout Scope

SCOPES FOR YOUR HUNTING GUNS

Most hunters today, whether after elk or bunny, scope their rifles. There are distinct advantages. You can see your target better from a longer range. It can be easier to get and hold a good sight picture, as you don't have to line up a front and rear sight. Your sighting is all on one visual plane. Today's riflescopes are generally quite sturdy and not subject to the fragility that so many scopes suffered from in years past, (although not so sturdy as iron sights). Scopes can be divided into two general divisions: variable and fixed.

VARIABLE SCOPES

The 2x4 power scope is a popular selection for all-around deer hunting in woods or forested mountains. Two x four means that the image is magnified from two to four times. For open prairie, many shooters go to a 4x12, which obviously make the image much larger. Some might think that bigger is better, but not in this case. Bigger is just bigger. When magnification is increased, the field of view is narrowed. If for example you tried to use a 12 power in the woods, you wouldn't be able to see the forest for the trees, or the game for the leaves. Varmint and target shooters will go up to 18x32. This works for them since magnification is more important to them than field of view.

Top—Thompson Contender single shot rifle with variable scope
Bottom—Ruger single shot rifle with a variable scope

Thompson Contender with a variable scope

FIXED POWER SCOPES

About the only shooters who use scopes and don't use variables are handgun hunters and riflemen who adhere to the "Scout Rifle" idea. Most handgun hunters seem to go with a fixed 2 power scope, as do the Scout rifle shooters. The Scout Rifle concept includes a low power scope with long eye relief mounted well forward. There are various reticules, which are what you might think of as the crosshairs. Except that there are many more options in aiming points than crosshairs.

Leopold and Bushnell are two well-known makers of good quality and reasonably priced riflescopes and other optics. Zeiss produces optics of the highest quality. There are at least a dozen makers of good scopes, but a review of them is beyond the limits of this publication.

In spite of the advantages, I rarely hunt with a scoped rifle. It may be true that today's game is more wary than in the past and that it's harder to get close enough to shoot without a scope. Maybe so. But for me, it's as much a matter of style as anything else.

I'm not starving. I can choose my method. I don't mind using my lungs and legs, getting down on my belly and crawling, or spending two days slowly working my way close enough to a mulie's bed to take a shot from close range. I like the feel of the earth, the sound the leaves make in the wind, the scent of a deer at ten yards. I

Top—Surplus Mauser with variable scope,
Bottom—Mosin Nagant with Scout Fixed scope

Bushnell Elite 2.5-10X50

Photo courtesy of manufacturer

started hunting this way when I was a kid and a riflescope was so far beyond my reach I never considered owning one; and I have kept to it.

> I remember a long ago fall day about a week before school resumed. I was eleven. I spent the better part of a crisp autumn afternoon crawling slowly and silently through dry, crunchy leaves, then sliding through foot-high river back grass to get to a spot where I could get a good shot on a wary old ground hog. I wasted none of him. I kept his skin and cooked him over my own campfire.

COMMONLY USED RIFLE CALIBERS FOR HUNTING

There are hundreds of rifle calibers, most of them suitable for hunting. However, I have focused on those that are readily available in the United States. Ammunition in any of these calibers can be found in most any gun store, even the smallest and most remote.

.223

Some states allow the hunting of deer with the .223. Most do not. Most states confine its use to varmints and small game.

.243

This is, in most places, the entry level for deer hunting; adequate power, flat shooting, and, easy on the ears and shoulder.

.270

A necked down 30-06, the .270 shoots with a flatter trajectory than any of the 30-06 leadings. Some consider this a good elk cartridge, while others think it's too light for the big guys.

30-30

The 30-30 in a lever action carbine is the All-American deer cartridge and gun. Easy to handle, easy to shoot with good terminal ballistics, this one will work as well today as it has for decades.

.308

The .308 is our former service round (NATO 7.62) and still in use in various specialized roles. It is a good choice for an all-around big game cartridge. The same caliber as the 30-06 it is essentially a shorter case version of that round.

30-06

The 06 was first developed in that year, 1906. It was used in the Springfield, the M1 Garand, and a hundred different sporting rifles. It is still an excellent all-around cartridge.

.300 WINCHESTER MAGNUM

This is an accurate round with a flat trajectory commonly used for long range and large game hunting. It is very popular for elk and kicks like a Missouri Mule. Remington makes some ammunition they call Managed-Recoil that recoils less, but at some loss in performance.

Author's Advice

There is an entire range of rifle cartridges more powerful than those I have listed. However, in my view, none of them are a good choice for a beginning shooter.

BIG GAME HANDGUNS

Many people, even veteran shooters regard handgun hunting as a stunt or as something beyond the reach of any normal shooter. It is not. Handguns are perfectly good tools with which to harvest game. The only caveat is that they must, like all weapons, be used within their effective range and limits of power, and according to the abilities of the individual shooter.

Elmer Keith (a famous shooter and writer who is no longer with us) said he made a 600-yard killing shot on an elk with a Smith and Wesson four-inch barreled .44 Magnum. Some folks do not believe Elmer made that shot. I do. But that does not mean I could make that shot or that you could.

However, I do believe that if you can't hit a small paper plate every time at fifty yards with your weapon of choice, you have no business being afield. That's a pretty minimal level of marksmanship, but it will get you game if you can get close to your quarry. Any decent handgun will meet that standard and many will far exceed it. I have an ancient Walther .22 that will reliably hit beer cans at seventy five yards. I had

Smith & Wesson Model 29 44 Magnum

a 9mm HK P7 that would bang steel plates at a hundred yards every time, wish I hadn't sold it. Like Elmer, I have a S&W four-inch .44 Magnum that makes me look good when I shoot it. The unschooled think I'm (insert hero's name here) when I blow up tomato juice cans balanced on the range markers at 100 yards. But I'm not. Lots of people can shoot those particular guns (not my guns, but models like them) as well or better, some much better.

If the notion of handgun hunting intrigues you, give it a try. After, of course, you've established a minimum level of marksmanship with that .22 target pistol. That same .22 is also the best pistol to make your hunting bones with. Start with squirrels and bunnies and see where it goes. It might go all the way to a big pistol and big game. States have regulations governing the taking of game with pistols, as they do with all other weapons. Check the local regulations before taking to the field.

COMMONLY USED HANDGUN CALIBERS FOR HUNTING

There are handgun calibers with more power than those I have listed. However, I do not think a new shooter will derive any benefit from them. The calibers I've listed have been used successfully for many years. They will do the job within their limits, as long as the shooter does his and hits a vital spot on his game.

Walther PPK .22

Smith & Wesson 44 Magnum

Photo courtesy of manufacturer

.22 RIMFIRE

As you now know, the .22 is every beginner's caliber and every expert's caliber. The automatics I recommend in *A Case for the Twenty-Two* chapter are a good place to start.

.357 MAGNUM

How times change. The .357 Magnum was once touted as "The World's Most Powerful Handgun." Advertising copy said you could take everything that walked, crawled, or flew with it. Today it's considered barely adequate for rabbits. A four-inch Smith & Wesson Model 19 in .357 Magnum was my first centerfire hunting handgun. I took my first elk with it. I don't think today's wild critters are any tougher than they used to be. If you like the .357, it'll do the job. Smith, Ruger, and a bunch of others make good revolvers for this caliber.

.10MM

The ten-millimeter is the only common auto pistol round that's legal to use to hunt large game, and that, only in some states. As of this writing, there are only a few pistols chambered for it, with the Colt Delta Elite and the Glock 20 and 29 coming to mind. The Glock 29 is the lightest weight of the small group and more accurate than you might think. Banging steel plates rapid fire at fifty yards is no trick at all. (I carry the little Glock as a trail gun in areas where creatures roam that are sharp of tooth and claw.)

.44 MAGNUM

Smith & Wesson, Ruger, and others, make excellent .44 Magnum revolvers. The four-inch Smith is my personal favorite. Almost twice as powerful as the .357, it kicks like a short changed customer at an enlisted man's beer bar.

Beretta U22 Neos   Photo courtesy of manufacturer

Browning Buckmark 22   Photo courtesy of manufacturer

Smith & Wesson M22A

Smith & Wesson Model 19

Ruger single action .357 preparing to fire

Glock 20/20C 10mm   Photo courtesy of manufacturer

Glock 29 Auto 10mm   Photo courtesy of manufacturer

But I don't mind it, probably because I don't try and fight the recoil. I just ride with it. No way can I shoot it as fast as, say, the Glock 10mm. Maybe someone can, but not me. I only use it for hunting, not for self-defense.

I have hunted bear and wild boar, both of which are somewhat dangerous. Both can be taken with a bow, using the right methods. Nevertheless you might want a more powerful weapon than what you use for deer. Brother Bear can get very angry with someone who puts a bullet in his bottom. Better make that first shot a good one.

A useful guide might be to go up a caliber from what you use for deer. However, if you're shooting anything in the thirty-caliber range and you're comfortable with it, I would suggest that you stay with what you know instead of trying to change up to an unfamiliar caliber and a new gun before a hunt. My little Mannlicher in 6.5x54 sent a good sized Pennsylvania black bear to his ancestors before he knew he had been shot.

Ruger Redhawk .44 Magnum

Smith & Wesson Model 29 44 Magnum

Photo courtesy of manufacturer

SMALL GAME

Rabbit, squirrels and such are generally considered small game. In most jurisdictions they can be legally taken with twenty-two's or shotguns.

VARMINTS

Coyotes, groundhogs, ground squirrels, and prairie dogs are generally speaking, not protected by law and are legal to take by various methods in various states. Check your local Fish and Game authority to make sure. In the West, many prairie dog hunters set up at long range from a dog town with a flat shooting scoped rifle and a spotting scope. An outdoorsman I know practices for deer season by stalking marmots. He won't take a shot over fifteen to twenty yards. (If you've ever been around marmots you'll know how difficult it is to get that close.)

In certain areas, coyotes have become a menace to domestic pets and small children. This is mainly due to loss of habitat. I've seen many coyotes taken with the twenty-two. The .223 is also a good coyote cartridge, allowing more range and having much more effect. Many coyote hunters prefer the .243 or even the .270. There is a wide range of newer cartridges, some of which you may prefer.

WATERFOWL

There are places in Latin America where Indians hunt ducks by wearing helmets on their heads designed to look like ducks, a disguise that allows them to wade or swim among the flocks resting on the water. They then grab a bird by the feet, snatch it underwater, sort of like picking apples, and wring its neck. Then the bird is stuffed into an underwater basket worn around the waist and the hunter (gatherer?) goes on to his next selection. (This is not how ducks are commonly hunted here in the United States.)

We usually use twelve gauge shotguns, ordinarily using number 2 to number 4 shot, and shoot the bird while in flight (or at least we try to do so). Usually as the bird is coming in to land on water—ideally where the hunter has cleverly placed his decoys to attract the birds and reassure them (deceitfully) that it's safe to land. The successful hunter has concealed himself and lain in wait for the ducks arrival, often for hours—often while wet and cold.

Everyone I know who hunts waterfowl does so with a twelve-gauge shotgun, usually a pump, sometime a semi-auto or an over and under double. I can't remember the last time I saw a side-by-side double in a duck blind, but I'll bet there is still a bunch of fellows out there using them.

UPLAND GAME

There is little in the shooting sport that is more enjoyable than taking to the fields on a fine, crisp autumn day in pursuit of pheasant or quail. However, I consider the pursuit of upland game to be more of a shooting activity than actual hunting. In many countries, the activity is in fact referred to as shooting, rather than hunting—and the participant as a shooter or a gun, rather than a hunter. True, birds must be located, but that's mostly left up to the dogs, or in some places, the beaters.

In England for example, a line of beaters drive up the birds from hedgerows and underbrush while the shooters take the birds as they come. Shooters usually proceed in a sort of skirmish line or wait in line, with each man's field of fire invisibly marked out by agreement, so as not to shoot one's fellow shooter. It is not unusual in England for a gun to bring down thirty birds in an afternoon's shooting. Each bird must be paid for. I'm told that today's going rate is sixty pounds a bird. At the current exchange rate, that amounts to one hundred and twenty dollars for each pheasant.

The approach in the U.S. is roughly the same, although somewhat more democratic in terms of cost; and, we don't use beaters. We do progress across fields in lines with fields of fire agreed on or understood between shooters. Sometimes, in the heat of the moment, mistakes are made. In combat such mistakes are called "friendly fire." I don't think such accidents in upland shooting are considered particularly friendly.

A FEW GUNS AND LOADS FOR WATERFOWL AND UPLAND GAME

My friend and I both shoot Remington 870s in 12 gauge, a shotgun that has served legions of hunters for many years, and still does so today. The venerable 870 is probably the most popular shotgun in America. Winchester also makes an excellent slide action shotgun, as does Mossberg. All the aforementioned companies also make automatic (semi-auto) shotguns. With today's ammunition, the autos are equal to the pump guns in reliability. We mostly used number four shot, but conditions vary and you might want to go to number two.

I have known men who would no more pursue upland game with a pump gun than they would serve rotgut moonshine to their guests in place of single malt scotch whiskey. In truth, a slide action Remington, Winchester, or Mossberg will bring home just as many birds as the finest Beretta or Browning double—in the right hands. Just because the birds are put up by dogs doesn't mean you don't have to be a good shot to get them.

The over and under doubles used by many upland game shooters are not cheap. The least expensive doubles from Beretta, Browning, or Benelli, will set you back a couple of thousand dollars; the more expensive models—two to three times as much. Brands such as Perazzi are in the, "if you have to ask you can't afford it" range.

SLIDE ACTIONS & AUTOS

Virtually all the shotgun makers build both pumps and automatics that can be used for waterfowl. Today's automatics are as reliable as the slide actions. Benelli, Browning, Remington, Mossberg, Savage, Winchester all make good guns in a range of finishes.

Browning Citori 525 Sporting

A few traditionalists use doubles for water-fowl. I would encourage you to do so if you are attracted to the graceful lines and incomparable handling of the double. (If you would like an in depth look at shotguns, rifles, or handguns I recommend that you buy *Gun Digest*, an exhaustive listing of guns with prices and specifications.)

THE TAO OF THE HUNT

With the exception of upland game or waterfowl, when I go in search of game I go alone. In fact I often also go after upland birds alone. True, I've many times been hunting with groups, but I consider those to be social events, not serious hunting. I may travel to a hunting area with friends, but when we reach our grounds, I go alone.

I also practice The Tao of The Hunt. I wrote in the marksmanship section that Taoist techniques have nothing whatever to do with religion. These are methods used by native peoples in many parts of the world and codified centuries ago. What follows is only a thumbnail description of this process.

ENTERING

First, go to your chosen hunting grounds. Of course you have selected a location where there actually is game or at least the possibility of game. There is no point in attempting to hunt elk in the Florida Keys or wild boar above treeline. You must know your quarry, its habitat, and its habits.

Second, when you reach your chosen hunting grounds, let the patterns of thought you have used to get there slip away as you walk from your vehicle. Forget about the highway and the traffic. Forget about work. Let the familiar constrictions of mind slip away as you move into the natural world.

Find a spot that feels right to you and stop. Sit or stand, as long as you're comfortable. I generally find it best to sit or even lie down, when doing an entry. I often choose a place just inside a treeline where I can see, but without being seen. You've already done your homework. You don't have to endlessly review details regarding your quarry's habits. Thoughts will bubble up. Let them go. Direct your attention to the immediate environment. See what there is to see—pine cones, rabbit dropping, a blue jay's feather. But don't analyze these details. Just note them.

Close your eyes and extend your awareness as far as you can—across meadows, through woods, up the mountainside. Wherever you happen to be, extend your awareness. Feel the wind moving; smell the cold granite, musty leaves, or the tannin from the dark swampy stream behind you. Hear the skittering of dry leaves, the breathing of the fox that's watching you, the drip of early morning dew from the limbs above you. Become part of everything around you.

SEEING AND CALLING

Now visualize your quarry, deer, rabbit, boar or bird. See the creature as if was standing in front of you. Retain awareness of your surroundings, but focus on seeing your quarry in your mind's eye. Then ask your quarry to come to you. (Yeah, yeah, I know. It sounds all woo woo, new age crystal stuff and all that. But it works.)

When you have become part of the field or swamp and when you have seen your quarry, move to a place where you will await your quarry or begin your slow stalk. Continue to watch and see and feel everything around you, above you and under you. If you're on a stand—don't move. You might think you're not moving, but if you haven't practiced the art of stillness, you are probably moving something. A deer can spot the flicker of an eyelid at fifty yards. If you are stalking, move with the forest. Move slowly. No that's too fast. Move even more slowly. Move upwind. You're not on a sidewalk; nor in a city.

When I sat with my back against an aspen waiting for my first elk, I had brought a folded space blanket to sit on. But the cold came up through it. At first I was cold, but after a while, cold wasn't cold. At first my nose itched. Then it didn't. Or if it did, I didn't mind it. I sank back into the tree and became the tree. I sank my roots deep into the ground and stretched my limbs wide and watched the days and nights pass.

Of course I didn't really, in consensual reality, sit there for weeks and become part of the tree. Nor was I doing drugs. I am not and never have been a devotee of Castaneda. I used age-old methods, well understood and codified by monks and shamans and used by hunters and warriors, and passed down over the generations. I imagined becoming the tree. I visualized it. In doing so, I subsumed my consciousness into the tree and stopped radiating hunter's energy. In effect, I created a cloak of invisibility. After some time I wasn't there. There was only the mountain and the tree. That's why the elk passed me by.

CHAPTER 8

Care and Cleaning of Your Gun

Cleaning your gun isn't just something you do so it will look nice. You clean your gun because failing to do so might result in your gun failing at a time when you need it to be in perfect working order. Think about a large, angry, hungry bear charging you, fangs bared, eyes red, claws tearing up the earth as he comes closer and closer until he's so close you can smell his rank order and feel the heat of his breath. You keep your cool and aim for a vital spot and squeeze off a round and…your gun jams.

The two most common causes for gun failures are:

1. Failing to clean the gun, resulting in gummed up and inoperative working parts.

2. Over lubrication. Too much lubrication can cause as many problems as not cleaning it at all.

CLEANING YOUR GUN

I actually like the smell of Hoppe's #9. I guess that makes me a gun nerd or a gunny; on second thought, no guessing to it. Hoppe's #9 solvent and bore cleaner has a distinctive scent. Anyone who's been shooting more than a couple of decades is familiar with the smell. It has been as much a part of shooting as the smell of cordite. That's because cleaning guns was a ritual carried out after each time the guns were fired. Not much has changed.

There are a number of new cleaning solutions and some of today's firearms (Glocks for example) have finishes that will withstand a lack of care better than the traditional blued steel. But you still should clean your guns after you shoot them. It's the right thing to do. Besides you don't want a failure to fire due to a gummed up and stuck firing pin just when you squeeze off a round at that moose you went all the way to Alaska for, do you?

The old way to clean your gun was to first unload it and put the ammo away.
Then:

1. Fieldstrip the firearm according to the manufacturer's directions.

2. Slather Hoppe's #9 over all metal parts.

3. Scrub the bore with a brass brush dipped in the solvent.

4. Dip a toothbrush in the solvent and scrub every steel surface you could find.

5. Let everything sit for a while to give the solvent time to dissolve all powder residues.

6. Run patches of cloth down the bore until they come out clean.

7. Wipe down every part of the gun to remove the solvent and powder residues.

8. Lightly oil all steel parts of the gun.

9. Reassemble the firearm.

You can still do it exactly like that today and your gun will work just fine. However, you can also use one of the modern cleaners like those listed. They all work. Some of them are "one step" cleaners. The one-step cleaners will make the process somewhat easier, but you won't get to smell Hoppe's #9.

Hoppe's #9

Photo courtesy of manufacturer

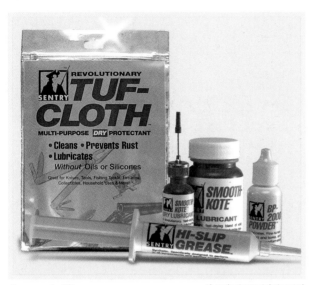

Armorer's Kit — Photo by Sentry Solutions Ltd.

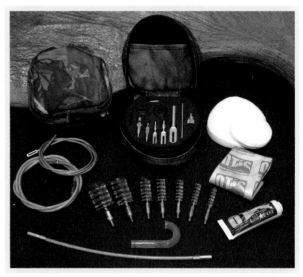

Otis' Hard-Core system — Photo by Otis Technology, Inc.

All kidding aside, keeping your gun clean is serious business. More than one person has lost his life due to a dirty gun. Not because their guns blew up, although that could happen. The more likely problems are a failure to fire or a jam at a critical moment, like when a platoon of bad guys is coming through the wire or Brother Bear decides he is really angry and isn't going to let you shoot him again.

MAKING SURE YOUR GUN IS PROPERLY LUBRICATED

Proper lubrication is particularly important in tropical and desert environments. In dry, sandy areas grit and sand blow with the wind and get into everything. Grit and sand will stick to gun oil or any of the modern lubricating substances and gum up the mechanism causing it to fail to function. In wet tropical areas, everything is attracted to oil, including many bugs. The best thing is to run slightly dry. A thin film of lubricant on moving parts is what you want. Unless all the finish has worn off of your firearm exposing bare steel there is no need to oil external non-moving parts. (I have seen more problems of the kind I mention here from over lubrication than from under lubrication.)

Some like to use various kinds of synthetic gun grease on moving parts. I have found the various greases to work OK for the shooting range, but I prefer not to use them in the field because they seem to attract debris even more so than gun oil. I do not recommend using household or auto lubricants for any firearm.

I am not an advocate for any particular brand of gun oil or lubricant and have found that any of the dedicated products such as Hoppes or Kleenbore or even the military surplus gun oil found in many shops work equally well.

Various gun finishes handle lubricants slightly differently. The best advice is to always follow the manufacturers' recommendations. They know what's best for their product.

Too much lubricant, especially some of the highly penetrative substances, can seep into your ammunition and render it useless. Keep your ammo dry. It does not need to be lubricated.

Author's Advice

1. *Always, always, always UNLOAD YOUR GUN AND PUT THE AMMO AWAY BEFORE YOU START TO CLEAN OR LUBRICATE YOUR GUN. We've all heard the stories about the guy who shot himself while cleaning his gun. Don't be that guy or girl.*

2. *Clean your gun. If you want the gunnies to respect you, keep your gun clean. Rust loves steel and all gunnies hate rust worse than a preacher hates sin on Sunday morning. A filthy, rusted gun is a disgrace to its owner, an insult to its maker, and to civilization itself.*

SECTION 3

GUN SAFETY

CHAPTER 9

Personal Responsibility for Your Firearms

Gun safety begins with the acceptance of personal responsibility for your firearm and ammunition. I'll repeat that. *Gun safety begins with the acceptance of personal responsibility for your firearm and ammunition*. This is the most important statement that can be made on the topic of gun safety. Read it, understand it, let it soak into your bones and live by it. It may one day save your life or the life of another.

My grandfather gave me my first rifle, a Remington single-shot twenty-two, which was a popular choice in those days for a first gun due to its inherent safety. A single shot has no magazine and it is a simple matter to see if the chamber has a round in it. My grandfather told me that responsibility accompanied privileges

and that I would always be held accountable for my rifle.

I remember his words after he handed me my rifle, "You now possess an instrument that gives you the power to take life. Take heed and behave in a responsible manner. Never take any life by accident, not the life of any human, friend or enemy, and not the life of any creature. Take no life by accident and by intention only for food or if your life is threatened." (My grandfather really did talk that way.)

He also instructed me in the following simple rules:

- **ALWAYS** know if your rifle is loaded or not, and loaded or not you must always handle it as if it was loaded.

THE COMPLETE GUN OWNER

- **ALWAYS** know where your rifle is pointing.
- **NEVER** point your rife at anything you are not prepared to shoot.
- **NEVER** place your finger on the trigger until you are ready to fire.
- **NEVER** fire until you are sure of your target.
- **YOU ARE RESPONSIBLE** for your rifle at all times, whether or not it is in your immediate possession.
- **NEVER** allow your rifle to be handled by anyone who you are not sure of.
- When your rife and ammunition are not in your immediate possession, **YOU MUST LOCK THEM** in your trunk.

In more than fifty years of shooting I have never yet found anything wrong with those instructions. There was more. He showed me how to safely handle my rifle so that the muzzle was always pointed towards the ground or to a place where there was no danger of hitting anyone. He also taught me marksmanship. He explained that when hunting, I must shoot to kill cleanly so as not to cause unnecessary suffering and that I should not take the shot unless I was sure of a solid hit.

Although we live in a very different world, now some things do not change. When you purchase your first firearm, you must accept personal responsibility for your firearm and ammunition. Aside from the morality of the matter, the law requires it. You must have control of your firearm and ammunition at all times. If they are not in your immediate possession they must be secured. You must also acquire the knowledge you need to handle and use your firearm responsibly, safely and effectively.

READ YOUR MANUAL

Although we will cover basics, a responsible gun owner will read the manual that comes with a new firearm. This manual will explain how the safety devices on this particular firearm operate and will give directions for using them appropriately. If the firearm did not come with a manual one should be obtained by contacting the manufacturer. In the case of older guns manufacturers may no longer have manuals, or may be out of business. However, manuals for virtually all firearms can be located through various online resources.

GENERALLY ACCEPTED SAFETY RULES

Here are three simple safety rules endorsed by the National Rifle Association and responsible shooters. There is some overlap between the NRA rules; those practiced by generations of responsible gun owners, and *Gun Safety Rules According to Ayres.*

1. **ALWAYS** keep the gun pointed in a safe direction.
2. **ALWAYS** keep your finger off the trigger until ready to shoot.
3. **ALWAYS** keep the gun unloaded until ready to use.

The NRA has eight or nine additional rules, most of which are similar to *Gun Safety Rules According to Ayres.* Many organizations and local governments have formulated their version of gun safety rules. I advise you to read all the NRA rules and others you come across and consider them carefully. Safety is the first and highest priority of every responsible shooter.

SAFETY IN GUN HANDLING

STEP ONE

Develop Gun Awareness. You must know where your firearms are at all times. At first this may seem burdensome. In fact it is no more so than knowing where your car is located. Use whatever memory devices you are familiar with, but make sure to always know the location of your guns and ammunition.

STEP TWO

Develop Muzzle Awareness. Know where your muzzle is pointing at all times. At first muzzle awareness requires constant attention. After a while, it becomes second nature, and is no more difficult than being aware of the moving and shifting traffic around you when driving.

Once you have those two things firmly in memory, safe gun handling becomes straightforward.

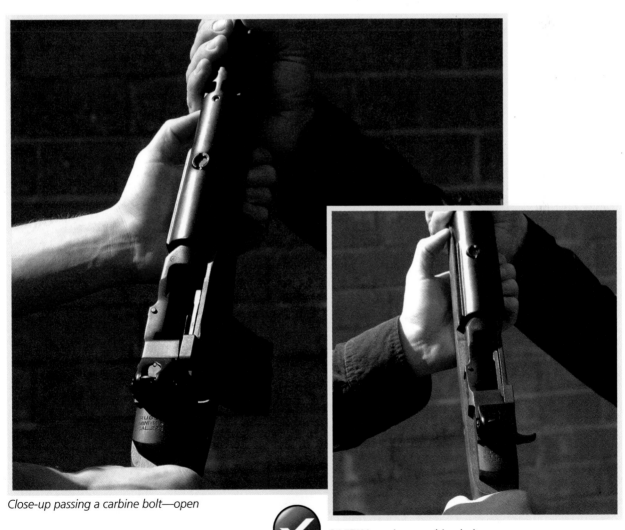

Close-up passing a carbine bolt—open

SAFELY passing a carbine bolt—open

DON'T DO this. Muzzle is pointing at a bystander

SAFELY passing the carbine muzzle pointed at the ground

X ***DO NOT*** *do this; an unsafe way to pass a firearm*

X ***DO NOT*** *do this; an unsafe way to pass a firearm*

DO NOT do this; an unsafe way to pass a firearm

Slide closed, muzzle pointing at wall, **MEDIUM SAFE**

NOT SAFE—*Muzzle pointing at bystander*

SAFE—*Pistol cleared slide open*

SAFEST—*Muzzle pointing at ground*

X **UNSAFE**—*checking chamber while muzzle pointing at another person*

SAFE—*checking chamber while muzzle pointed at ground*

SAFE—*checking chamber while muzzle pointing at ground*

SAFE—checking chamber while muzzle pointed at ground

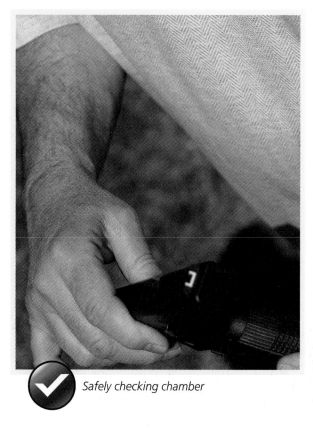

Safely checking chamber

SAFE—passing of a handgun chamber open

SAFE—*releasing the slide, muzzle towards ground*

A fellow once handed me his new, custom .45 to admire, with the muzzle pointing at me. He had removed the magazine, but had failed to retract the slide. I stepped to one side, slowly and carefully grasped his gun holding hand, and pointed the muzzle to the floor. "What's the matter?" he asked. "It's empty." He released the pistol to my hand. While still pointing it towards the floor I retracted the slide and a bright, shiny .45 cartridge flipped out of the chamber and fell to the floor. The fellow's mouth dropped open and his face went pale. "I thought..." he stammered. "Uh huh," I said.

CLEARING YOUR GUN

Clearing means to unload the gun by removing the ammunition and opening the chamber so it can be seen to be empty. The magazine of a semi-auto should be removed, even if there is no ammunition in it. All guns should be cleared and open before being passed from one person to another. However, on occasion a person might hand you a firearm with the bolt or slide closed. This might happen in a sporting goods store where clerks might be untrained or in any other situation where an untrained person is handling a gun. If this happens clear the gun as soon as you have it in hand.

When someone hands you a gun, you should automatically clear it, *even if you saw him or her clear it*. And the other way round. This may sound redundant but it's a sound practice.

Anyone can make a mistake. Assume personal responsibility and be a safe gun handler. ALWAYS CLEAR ALL GUNS.

Photos on these pages illustrate proper gun handling and improper handling.

Extracting a fired round from a Ruger single action revolver .44 Mag.

Extracting fired cases from a Smith & Wesson Model 19 double action revolver

Ruger .44 Mag. single action, loading gate open

Ruger .44 Mag. preparing to fire

SAFETY MECHANISMS

TRIGGER GUARDS

Invented centuries ago the trigger guard protects the trigger from being struck or pulled accidentally. Virtually all firearms have them, with the exception of certain small single action revolvers such as those made by North American Firearms. When using a gun with a trigger guard you must put your finger inside the trigger guard in order to reach the trigger.

Do not put your finger inside the trigger guard until you are ready to fire. Instead anchor your trigger finger on the receiver just above the trigger guard. The trigger guard is a simple piece of metal that has doubtless prevented many accidents and will prevent many more.

GUN SAFETIES

Although safety devices are particular to individual firearms, in general they work by blocking the trigger of the firing pin. Accompanying photos show various types of safeties and a variety of different guns to give you an idea what to look for. Remember you must study your owner's manual and practice with your unloaded firearms until the operation of your safety is second nature.

There is little hope for anyone who, having been properly instructed, chooses to not use safety devices and handle his firearm in a safe and responsible manner. Such persons should take a good look at themselves and their motivations. If not willing to accept the responsibility that comes with firearms recognize and accept their own limitations and not own guns.

The trigger guard is the semi-circular band of metal extending from the receiver and surrounding the trigger.

Remington 870 slide action shotgun with bolt open

FN 5.7 safety off

Shotgun safety on

Shotgun safety off

Remington 870 slide action shotgun safety on

Remington 870 slide action shotgun safety off

SAFETY WHILE SHOOTING

Always use protection for your eyes and ears while shooting. Many older shooters, myself included, have suffered some hearing loss due to inadequate or no hearing protection. Ear protection devices look like plastic earmuffs, or foam inserts that go inside your ears. Both types work well. Eye protection consists of glasses with impact resistant lenses. You can purchase good quality "eyes & ears" from any gun shop. Make sure they fit comfortably and securely. Most ranges will provide eyes & ears to those who do not have them. From what my sons tell me (as best I can hear them) you can lose a good bit of hearing at concerts also. So, maybe ear protection is second nature for some of the young.

Shooting glasses protect your eyes from the possibility of a ruptured cartridge (rare) and back splatter and general debris (common).

Safety glasses

SAFETY AT THE RANGE

Read and obey ALL range rules wherever you happen to be shooting. Aside from being safer yourself you will be respected by experienced shooters. All of us watch each other when we first meet to determine the other person's gun handling habits. No knowledgeable shooter relaxes around shooters he doesn't know until he sees how they handle firearms and themselves. Bad safety practices will earn you a friendly, or not so friendly, warning. Continued unsafe behavior might result in being requested to case your gun and attend a safety class.

Range rules vary a little from place to place, but not much at "cold" ranges, where all guns are unloaded unless they are on the firing line and guns are pointed only downrange, which is the direction of the targets. Eye and ear protection is to be worn at all times. While this may seem like just common sense it is important to always stop and read the ranges rules before entering a range. Also, as in golf, tennis and other popular sports, common courtesy is always appropriate and welcome.

Ear protection

TYPICAL RANGE RULES

- All firearms must be unloaded and cased when brought to the range. Revolvers without case will be carried by the top-strap, cylinder open. Semi-autos will have the slide locked to the rear, magazine out. Long guns when uncased must have the action open and muzzle pointed up.

- Firearms may be loaded on the range only when pointed down range, at the firing line, at the assigned stall.

- Only authorized firearms and ammunition may be used.

- Use of eye and ear protection is required at all times on the range.

- While on the range, firearms must be pointed down range at all times.

- If a misfire or other malfunction occurs, keep the firearm pointed down range and sign the range master.

- Do not fire at unauthorized targets or shoot across lanes.

- Do not move forward of the firing line. In anything falls forward of the firing line, contact the range master for assistance.

- The use of alcohol or drugs is prohibited on the range. Persons under the influence of alcohol or drugs are prohibited on the range.

- Smoking, eating or drinking is prohibited on the range.

At "hot" ranges, guns are always loaded. This is typical at "combat matches" and a somewhat different level of awareness is required. (Rules at "hot" ranges vary somewhat and so in the interest of avoiding confusion no "typical" rules are given.) Odds are you'll visit your first "hot" range in the company of someone who will guide you. If you're on your own, read the posted rules and ask someone to help you get oriented. The shooting fraternity is mostly made up of friendly folks who are pleased to help you get into shooting.

Some people simply will not follow common safety rules. There is no place for that person on a shooting range or in a hunting field with others. It's rare to see unsafe behavior with experienced shooters, but it happens.

I was once at a range where a local instructor was working with a student who was obviously new to shooting. The student walked downrange to inspect his targets with his .45 in hand. This was a "cold" range. I noticed his slide was forward, the hammer cocked, and the thumb safety down.

I politely pointed this out to the trainer. He told me to mind my own business. I thought my safety was very much my business. I spoke to the range master about the safety violation. The range master and the instructor were pals and he also felt it was OK for an unschooled shooter to be walking around with a loaded, cocked and unlocked auto.

Considering that this student had already covered the entire firing line with his muzzle I disagreed. I cased my gun and left at once, meanwhile keeping a close eye on the student. I would advise you to do the same in a similar situation. Ultimately you are responsible for your own safety.

SAFETY IN THE FIELD

Muzzle awareness, awareness of your companions, knowing where your bullet or shot will go before you pull the trigger, keeping good fields of fire, moving correctly with a firearm, all these things are fundamentals of safe gun handling in the field. Specific detail about safety in the field can be found in the *Hunting with Your Gun* chapter. However, stay alert and follow the basic rules and you should be good to go.

SECURING YOUR GUNS

GUN CASES: SOFT, HARD, AND LOCKABLE

Inexpensive good quality cases, both hard and soft are available in every local gun shop. Many jurisdictions now require hard cases for transportation of firearms. Check your local laws. Virtually all jurisdictions require guns to be in a case, hard or soft, and locked when being transported. The exception to this requirement is if you have a concealed carry permit, which is discussed in *An Approach to Self-Defense* chapter.

When traveling with guns I make it a practice to lock each gun into its individual case. I then put those cases into my locked car trunk or into another locked bag or case if traveling by air. At home a responsible shooter will unload all firearms not in use and lock them in individual cases. Locking those cases in a safe or another locked container provides another level of protection. Ammunition is always locked in a separate container. This means that an unauthorized person wanting to load a firearm would have to first locate the firearms: locate the ammunition: get through three locks and figure out how to load the weapon. Something as simple, and yet so important, as locking cases and separating ammunition could change the outcome of a situation.

Plano Shotgun Case   Photo courtesy of manufacturer

Plano Soft rifle case   Photo courtesy of manufacturer

Plano soft handgun case   Photo courtesy of manufacturer

Kalispel hard case

GUN SAFES

Formerly, gun safes were expensive propositions and only the dedicated shooter would own enough valuable firearms to justify the purchase of a safe. Not so today. Dozens of reasonably priced safes in a variety of sizes are readily available. If they are not in stock at your local gun shop, the gun shop proprietor will order one for you. Some guns safes have a quick open feature, which can be a good thing for that one gun you might wish to keep loaded and assessable in case of need.

Gardall Safe   Photo courtesy of manufacturer

Gun Vault   Photo courtesy of manufacturer

Fort Knox Safes
Photo courtesy of A.G. English

TRIGGER LOCKS

In recent years we have been deluged with requirements for the gun owner to obtain and use trigger locks. Now it seems that the gun makers are required to include them with each firearm. This may or may not be a good thing. I suspect that anyone who is responsible enough to actually engage a trigger lock will have already been using a locked case or safe.

Trigger guards, safeties on firearms, gun safes, cases and trigger locks are only tools, and useless if not properly employed. Accepting personal responsibility is the first and most important step towards becoming a safe and responsible gun owner, one who is not a hazard to his fellow citizens

Trigger lock   Photo courtesy of manufacturer

DRINKING AND SHOOTING

Don't do it. If you feel like getting liquored up and howling at the moon — lock up the guns first. Alcohol and gunpowder is an explosive mixture, not one you want to fool with. If you would like a celebratory bottle of Bollinger after bagging that moose you've chased all over Montana, or a nice glass of Lynch Bages with that duck you just shot, or a couple bottles of Budweiser after Bowser flushed those Quail, and you bagged them—case the guns first. No exceptions. Let me repeat that: ***Unload and case the guns before pulling that cork or opening that bottle.***

LOCAL STANDARDS

I once went hunting on a jungle covered island in the Southern Philippines with a bunch of Filipino guys. They loved to get red-eyed on Tuba, a particularly foul concoction made from, I think, Palm sap. We spent hours thrashing through the underbrush, well into the night. These guys were rowdy and getting pretty thirsty. But when we finally got back to their village, even these guys knew enough to unload the guns and put them away before hitting the Tuba. If they had not done so, I would have done it for them. Local standards vary, but none require me, or you to be put at risk.

WHERE DO THE BULLETS GO?

You've probably wondered where all those bullet holes in road signs on country roads come from. They come from criminally irresponsible people who have guns, cars and booze, but no common sense, or regard for others. Those bullets that make holes in road signs continue on until they hit a tree, or a cow, or a possum minding it's own business, or they go through a window and into someone's home, where folks are probably sleeping soundly and not thinking about a bullet that might come slamming through a wall and into their baby's crib. But I know none of you are the kind of person who would do that. No, not my readers. No way.

Every Fourth of July and New Years Eve some irresponsible people fire their guns into the air and others are injured or killed by those projectiles. Do not do fire your gun into the air. The bullet (or shotgun pellet) that goes up, comes down, sometimes on someone's head. Contrary to urban myth, bullets do not disintegrate in the sky. They always come down somewhere. Always.

HOW DO ACCIDENTS REALLY HAPPEN?

"It went off."

No, it did not. Guns do not "go off" by themselves. Guns are relatively simple mechanical devices and have no life or volition of their own. If your gun fired and you didn't mean for it to do so, you made a mistake. Accepting personal responsibility for your guns is both the first and last thing you must do. Accidents happen when a gun owner fails to accept his or her responsibility.

Finally, imagine this scene:

A platoon of recruits shivering in a grey dawn, an icy wind knifing through their thin clothing, a light snow on the frozen ground, a platoon sergeant who looks like he has fought in every war since the First Peloponnesian is passing along the rows of new soldiers and handing them each a rifle along with some words of instruction.

When it was my turn he took a rifle from the stack carried by the Corporal assisting him and handed me my M1 Garand rifle. I accepted it, held it at port arms and slammed the bolt back inspecting the chamber to insure that it was empty. I then stood at inspection arms. He put his face close to mine, about an inch away, and said while looking deep into my eyes, "This is YOUR rifle. YOU are responsible for it. Drunk or sober, shot up, blown up, wounded or sick, blind crippled or crazy—YOU are responsible for this rifle."

He didn't scream or bug out his eyes like a movie drill instructor. He spoke seriously, with gravity and great intensity of purpose. Then he paused for a moment, assessing me, and asked quite gently, "You got that soldier?"

"Yes sergeant," I said, "I got it."

And I did get it. I hope you get it too.

CHAPTER 10

Gun Cabinets, Cases and Safes

GUN CABINETS

In frontier times few homes had locked gun cabinets, and gun safes were virtually unknown. The average homeowner hung his rifle on wall-mounted hooks, ready to hand. Handguns were kept on the person or next to the bed at night. Later on, gun cabinets came into common usage and were often placed in the parlor with the guns on display for visitors who cared to admire them. Such cabinets were made as well any other piece of furniture and often an object of pride.

My grandfather's gun cabinet was made of thick, polished walnut with beveled glass inlaid into the upper doors so the rifles and shotguns in vertical racks could be easily seen. There was a divider at about waist level and the doors below were solid walnut, behind which were shelves holding ammunition and handguns. Sturdy brass locks secured both sets of doors and the keys were kept in an undisclosed location (at least undisclosed to me.)

One of the finest gun cabinets I have ever seen was in the study of a friend's father. It was a handsome piece of work occupying an entire wall, at least fifteen feet long and almost ceiling height. Inside the cabinet Browning and Perazzi shotguns, Wetherby rifles, and two Purdys were racked in green velvet cushioning. The whole thing, cabinet and guns, probably cost about as much as the average suburban home.

Times have changed. Guns are rarely on open display in homes and you don't often see gun cabinets these days.

GUN SAFES

Safes seem to have taken the place of cabinets for many gun owners. Most people have their safes located in a closet, bolted to the floor and walls, or in a basement or other inconspicuous location. Today, for about the price of a nice cabinet, you can buy a gun safe that will protect your firearms from all but the most determined thief. For a little more money, you can get a "fireproof" safe said to protect against home fires.

Back when I had an extensive collection of firearms I bought the largest, strongest safe I could find. Then I had a portion of the large walk-in closet in the master bedroom walled off and the safe installed behind the wall with only a hidden latch to open the swinging door that looked like part of the wall. That may seem a little extreme, but my insurance agent was very pleased with the arrangement and agreed to increase the value of my policy to the actual replacement value of the guns, which was considerable.

That was during a period of my life when I was spending time at home in the U.S., more than I had in many years. Then my working obligations changed again and made me a nomad for the next decade or so. I sold my collection and the safe, keeping only my working firearms. If you decide to collect guns you'll want a good safe.

CASES, SOFT AND HARD

I used to see quite a few beautiful saddle leather cases at the range, and at the hunting fields when wing shooters took out their engraved doubles. Various synthetics have replaced some of the leather cases, but hard cases, mostly plastic, seem to be the most common these days, even in England, where tradition is more important than it is here in the former colony.

A couple of years ago, I went with some English "guns" in Devonshire when they were shooting pheasant. At the end of the day most of the shooters went to their Range Rovers or Land Rovers to put up their guns. I expected to see an array of tan saddle leather. But no, when the tailgates swung open black plastic waterproof cases were revealed.

This is understandable. A good hard case offers a level of protection that leather cases cannot match, and for less money. Not only are hard cases more secure against prying fingers, good quality hard cases provide the best protection against water. (Still, I do miss the smell of that leather.)

CHAPTER 11

Kids and Guns

I grew up around guns. I never saw or heard of an accident involving guns in my family. In addition to the hunting rifles and shotguns we had at home, my grandfather carried a S&W Bankers Special in a slip holster in his pocket. Each day when he got ready for bed, he took his revolver in its holster from his pocket and put it on the nightstand next to his bed. When I was about four or five I asked my grandfather if I could see his pistol.

He took it from his pocket, unloaded it, and explained to me that he was doing so, and handed it to me. He explained the parts of a revolver. He also told me why he carried it, and that I was never to touch his pistol—all in terms I could understand at that age. He promised

that when I was old enough, he would show me how to fire it. (Which he did.) My grandfather treated me with respect and taught me about responsibility and honesty. I would no more have touched his revolver than I would set my dog Brownie on fire.

FAMILY TRADITIONS

My sons have grown up around guns. None of them have ever once, even as children, done anything stupid or unsafe with a gun. I credit this to proper education and a firm and clear understanding of a gun's potential. As was I taught by my grandfather, I taught my sons.

When my sons first developed curiosity about guns, my wife and I opened a dialogue with each of them. We explained that guns, like cars, were for adults and that when they were older, and if they wanted, we would teach them how to shoot as we would teach them how to drive a car.

If they asked to see my handgun, I would unload it and let them examine it. There was nothing to hide or to be secretive about. Then I would put it away and reinforce previous explanations: guns were for adults, they were not for kids because kids could get hurt.

Guns were private family business not to be discussed with friends. Above all, they were not to ever try and locate any of the family firearms, to play with them, or to allow friends to do so. Later, when they were old enough to understand, I demonstrated to each of my sons the potential power of a gun.

At a very early age, different for each one, they were instructed in the following simple rules:

- A gun cannot hurt you by itself.

- You can hurt another person with a gun.

- Another person can hurt you with a gun.

- Do not touch any gun you might see.

- The family guns were not to be touched or discussed with any friends.

- If you see a gun, go directly to an adult and tell him or her.

- If a friend wants to play with a gun, do not do so. Leave at once and get an adult.

In addition, all guns in our home, except for my personal handgun, which is always under my immediate control, were always under lock and key.

When the boys were old enough to understand consequences and accept responsibility, *and when they said they were ready and I thought they were ready*, I taught them gun handling and marksmanship—one step at-a-time. My youngest had little interest in guns until he was fourteen. My oldest and middle sons were ready at ten. When they were ready for their first rifle, I taught them what my grandfather taught me about safety and responsibility—all of which is discussed in detail in the *Personal Responsibility for Your Guns* chapter.

In addition, I had one rule that could not be compromised—a tough one for ten year olds, not so much for a fourteen year old. Before they could have their first rifle, they had to give up all of their toy guns and make a commitment to never again play with toy guns. No exceptions. I drew a clear and unwavering line. To add weight to the moment, I also had them read and copy down the following:

When I was a child, I spake as a child, I understood as a child, I thought as a child: but when I became a man, I put away childish things.

Tough stuff for kids. But not as tough as a foolish accident and a dead kid.

BOY SCOUTS AND THE NATIONAL SHOOTING SPORTS FOUNDATION

When I was ten or eleven, I joined in the Boy Scout Marksmanship program. On Friday, I would take my rifle to school with me. This was well understood and accepted by school authorities. After school, I pedaled to the local city park that had a small-bore range where the Boy Scout program was held. (My sons look at me in disbelief when I tell them things like this about my childhood. Understandably.)

I recently met a man who is doing his part to give some kids a lot of fun, while teaching them valuable skills and responsibility. Brian Dillon runs the Southern California Boy Scout Marksmanship program. When Brian told me about his activities I said that I thought that whole thing had been blown way with the sixties. It was. But Brian brought it back to this one place. Basically, Brian is the Southern California Boy Scout Marksmanship program—along with a bunch of kids.

If you have kids and you want them to learn how to shoot and to learn the core responsibility that should be attached to guns, contact your local Boy Scouts. If they don't have such a program, ask them to revive the old Boy Scout Marksmanship program. If the Boy Scouts aren't interested, there is always the National Rifle Association's Youth Program. My youngest son honed his rifle skills with the NRA and so have thousands of other kids.

Boy Scout Troop 104 at a troop-to-troop rifle competition. Scout Master Brian P. Dillon bottom left.

Photo courtesy of Brian P. Dillon

THE NATIONAL SHOOTING SPORTS FOUNDATION

The NSSF is a non-profit organization devoted to promoting shooting sports. It has a wide range of safety and education programs, plus printed material, some of which is designed for kids. This organization suggests these safety rules for kids:

1. Don't go looking for firearms in your house or a friend's house. Don't let other kids look for firearms in your house.

2. If you find a firearm in your house—or anywhere else—leave it alone. Don't touch it! Don't let anyone else touch it! Tell an adult.

3. Even if a firearm looks like a toy—don't touch it. Some real firearms look like toys. Don't take a chance. Tell an adult.

Author's Advice

In general these rules sound pretty good. However, the most important thing is dialogue. When kids and parents are talking openly and freely and when kids have clear boundaries and understand that boundaries are not arbitrary, it's less likely they will get into trouble.

Kids and guns? Sure, they go together just fine.

SECTION 4

GUN SELF-DEFENSE

CHAPTER 12

An Approach to Self-Defense

The subject of armed self-defense is one of the utmost seriousness; one that is too often treated lightly. Doing violence to another person in the real world has nothing in common with ballet-like, choreographed movie violence. Violence is an ugly thing. It is a thing that will remain in your memory, especially if you have the misfortune to witness or take part in a particular event.

I will discuss this subject based on my experience and observations and will do so in a realistic manner. Therefore, some of the language that follows will be of necessity, a little rough, and in some cases graphic, but no more so than is needed to make certain points. It in not my intention to shock and I do not pander to those who enjoy vicarious bloody "war stories." I recount certain events to instruct and do so only in consideration of the possibility that such instruction might save the lives of good people.

When Native Americans first encountered Europeans with guns, they concluded based on their observations, that the European's guns killed by producing a loud noise that killed by shock. The Indians were incorrect in their conclusions. Although good observers, they simply didn't have enough information or experience to reach the correct conclusion. That came later.

Many people today have beliefs about firearms that are equally erroneous. Few peaceful civilians in our culture have witnessed someone being shot. Fewer still have taken part in a gunfight. Most people get their impressions from movies and television. Based on these fictional depictions, many seem to think that a handgun functions as some sort of paralytic device. The actor pulls a trigger, the movie gun seems to make a loud noise and someone falls down; often with no evidence of injury, but perhaps a small smear of fake blood. In more graphic films there may be a lot of movie blood. There may even be some simulated effects and some acting that simulates real-world wounding.

We all know that movies and TV are fiction. We may even know that the movie gun is a prop incapable of firing live ammunition and that the noise is stripped in when the sound track is added. But repetitious viewing creates the unconscious belief that this is how guns work in the real world. They do not. This belief is as incorrect as the one held by first contact Native Americans. Guns are basically, highly-sophisticated rock throwers. They are not instant paralytic rays.

REALISTIC CONSEQUENCES

When a person fires a handgun at another person, he usually misses. If he does hit another human target, the bullet makes a hole in the person. This usually results in a great deal of pain and much blood, more than you might imagine if you haven't witnessed such an event. When someone is wounded, he often thrashes around, screams, curses, cries, runs away, or perhaps falls down, depending on a universe of variables. Various body tissues are sometimes exposed or ripped from the body. An expression which

seems to be popular these days in movies about criminals is, "brains on the wall." This is not just a metaphor. When a powerful bullet breaches the cranial vault, brains do get splattered on walls, and elsewhere, along with bits of bone and other body tissues.

It is far more traumatic to witness this sort of thing in real life, than to watch a sanitized, choreographed movie. If you do have such an experience, the odds are you will experience a post-traumatic psychological effect, whether you are the person who pulled the trigger, the one who got shot or a bystander. If you are the agent of such violence, you will find that the only way to live with having brought this to a fellow human is if you were totally justified in your actions. If you have fired to save your life or the life of a loved one or to prevent rape or other violence, you will have the consolation of knowing you acted righteously. But—you will still carry the weight and the memory.

As a moral person trying to defend yourself, you do not shoot with the intention to kill. But it is impossible to shoot with the certainly you will only wound. No matter how much skill you have, once the bullet leaves the muzzle it can bring death to another. Your intention should be to simply stop the assailant, but things happen fast in violent encounters and there are no guarantees. Moreover, it is virtually impossible to affect such a stop without risking a lethal result.

I often hear rough and casual talk about shooting and killing. This talk usually comes from people who have no experience of being shot at, shooting at another person, or in fact, of any violence other than the schoolyard variety. Such talk grates on my sensibilities, as it should on yours. Soldiers objectify their enemies in order to function and do what their duty requires of them. Rough dehumanizing talk is sometimes part of a soldier's life. It should be no part of being an armed civilian.

Five hundred years ago John Donne wrote:

No man is an island, entire of itself...
any man's death diminishes me... and
therefore never send to know for whom
the bell tolls; it tolls for thee.”

This comes down to us as literature and like much great literature, it contains a simple truth. If you have the great misfortune to be placed in a situation where you must take another's life in order to survive, the experience will change you and not in any movie macho way. It will diminish you.

We live in a random and sometime violent world. Any of us might be forced to violence to protect a loved one or ourselves. The only thing worse than being forced to do violence, is to witness the death or violation of a loved one or to have such done to oneself. The decision to arm or not to arm yourself is yours alone. It is not mine.

I am neither an advocate nor an opponent of armed self-defense. Arming oneself is a moral issue with legal consequences; an issue that each must decide for himself. If you have made your decision, and if the decision is to arm yourself, the following information may be of some value to you.

Author's Advice

I am not a lawyer. I offer no legal counsel. You are responsible for your own actions. Learn the laws that govern violence and self-defense and abide by them.

ALTERNATE MEANS OF DEFENSE

There are means of self-defense other than the gun. Pepper spray, impact weapons such as sticks, canes, heavy flashlights, and edged weapons all come to mind when one is threatened. Discussion of all of these defensive alternatives is beyond the scope of this book, as is a discussion of martial arts. However, a less than lethal defense is always to be desired.

Over the years, I have traveled in dangerous places and encountered threatening circumstances when I was not armed with a firearm. Yet, like many others in tight spots, I found a way to prevail. Sometimes "thinking out of the box" is enough. Other times not.

If faced with an armed assailant or a group of assailants, a gun may be your best tool since the gun is a more effective weapon than anything else readily available. However, if your only tool is a hammer, you tend to see all problems as nails. Try to have an alternative to the gun in place. (Personally, I eagerly await the invention of the temporary paralysis ray.)

In the much loved trilogy, *The Lord of The Rings*, J.R.R. Tolkien's character, Frodo, tells Gandalf the wizard that Gollum deserves to die for his deeds. Gandalf counsels Frodo, agreeing with him that Gollum does so deserve death, but tells him, "Do not be anxious to take that which you cannot give."

THE USE OF A GUN FOR SELF-DEFENSE

Many people immediately think of a gun, most often a handgun when they think of defending themselves from criminal assailants. This is understandable. There are good reasons why Samuel Colt's invention (the first reliable, easily portable, repeating handgun) was called an "equalizer." A good handgun combined with sufficient skill can enable a small, physically weak person to defend his or her life against larger and multiple assailants. *Sufficient skill* is the key point. Mere possession of a firearm will not make you a world-class gunfighter, anymore than buying a saxophone would allow you to play like Chet Baker.

You must learn to use your firearm as a self-defense tool, in order for it to be effective. This should be self evident, but based on my experience and observations—it is not. Ranges today are packed with people banging away with a variety of handguns and wrinkling their brows in confusion when they fail to hit their targets. Yet, as their conversation indicates, these same folks leave the range convinced their new 9mm or .45 will protect them. It will not.

Guns are inanimate objects. They are not talismans or amulets with magic powers to protect you from evil doers. The gun will not protect you from anything. You, yourself, must assume the obligation of protection, or assign it to another. I also hear new gun owners talking about how they will shoot better when "they" are coming at them. Probably not. Odds are that they will not "rise to the occasion," but will fall back in frozen panic, or worse, spray rounds everywhere—perhaps hitting bystanders.

During the 1992 Rodney King riots in Los Angeles, I was besieged by emotional requests from a few non-gun owning close friends for the loan of a firearm. Outside of my family, only close friends, fellow professionals, or sporting friends, have ever known that I possessed firearm or had any expertise with them (as an adult, that is). When I was a kid, everyone had guns. Today's climate is different. Also, many years of professional discretion have created certain habits. I received similar emotional requests from two friends in Washington D.C. during the riots of 1968 that followed the assassination of Dr. Martin Luther King. On both occasions I refused to provide firearms to my friends. *Why? Was my refusal cold hearted and callused? No, it was not.*

In a Central American capitol city, during a civil disturbance in which hundreds were killed during the first night, I received a similar request from an associate with whom I had spent the evening the night the violence broke out. We were holed up in the bar of an international hotel. I gave him my backup pistol without question. *Why would I arm this friend but not the others?*

I did so because my friend in Central America knew how to defend himself with a firearm. He was not a danger to himself or to the innocent. The friends who asked for guns in Los Angles and Washington D.C did not know how to shoot; had no knowledge of basic gun handling and had never fired or owned guns. Being able to actually use one in personal defense was a skill as remote to them as playing that saxophone like Chet Baker. I was not willing to arm an untrained person who might shoot innocents, themselves, or me by mistake. It would have been irresponsible to do so.

It would be equally irresponsible for you to arm yourself and go forth thinking you are prepared to defend you and yours before you have acquired a minimum level of competence. That competence might well be self-taught. Although it is preferable to get capable instruction, many have taught themselves to shoot well. Others have learned the basics from books and then practiced until competent.

But what about those friends I left unarmed? Were they left to the mercies of the mob? Certainly not. I did not, and would not leave my friends to fend for themselves. I offered to personally defend any and all who wanted to move into my home for the duration of the disturbance and any who were in my company while out and about. I also offered to provide basic armed defensive training when time permitted.

No one is immune to error, professionals included. We can all miss our mark and send a lethal round screaming down a city street. But we can avoid the obvious pitfalls of arming inexperienced, untrained, frightened people.

STOPPING POWER

Most experts in this field advise the novice to choose the most powerful handgun that he or she can control, the minimum being one of the service calibers. The argument is that you need all the "stopping power" you can get and that less powerful cartridges, sometimes scornfully called "sub-calibers" or "mouse guns," are inadequate for self-defense in that they have marginal "stopping power." This point of view has merit but ignores certain realities having to do with the definitions of "control" and "stopping power." It also ignores other realities regarding daily carry for civilians. Service calibers tend to come in handguns that are either too large or too heavy or both for civilian carry.

The argument about what constitutes "stopping power" is one that has a long history.

It continues today with more heat than light and will likely rage on until the invention of the paralytic ray. Among experts, there is much disagreement. Entire books are devoted to this ongoing discussion. For our purposes, let's stipulate that modern service calibers are more or less up to the job required of them (if the shooter does his part), but that none of them are the hammer of Thor. However, I do not think that a service caliber is always the best choice for self-defense by the average civilian who is not a gun enthusiast.

DIFFICULTY OF USE

Service handguns have considerable recoil and are difficult to shoot accurately without training and practice. Few civilian novices who are not planning to go into a career requiring professional level shooting are going to obtain the training or do the practice required to master a service handgun. Notice I said master—not control. Mastering a handgun means that you know that you can hit your mark under field conditions—every time—fast.

Of course, a .45 ACP, a .357 Magnum, 10mm, a .40, or a 9mm will deliver more power on target than say, a .32. The question is, will it do so in your hands, in rapid fire, in poor lighting, when you're under extreme stress and everything is moving fast? If you can't claim this level of expertise, you might be better served with a less powerful caliber. One that you can master with the amount of training and practice you can and will devote to the pursuit.

Oh, by the way they're called handguns, not *handsguns* for a good reason. Two-handed fire, such as we now see in movies, is good when possible. Many trainers only teach two-handed shooting. Shooting with both hands is more accurate and is preferred at longer ranges when possible. But what about when you're using your off arm to hold your child behind your back while returning fire? How about if one arm has been injured? What if your assailant is only three feet away from you and closing fast or already on you?

One fellow I know has been to a school of "combat handgunnery" where he was taught to always shoot with two hands. With a firm two-handed grip he can, more or less control his .45. That is, he can get most of his shots on a silhouette target, most of the time. When he shoots one-handed, the muzzle flips up—way up—and it takes him a long time to get back on target. In one-handed rapid fire, he's lucky if his shots go downrange. Yet he's convinced he can control his .45. He might be able to better control a less powerful handgun, but he is also convinced that it is the .45 he must use—nothing else will stop a bad guy. This sort of thinking simply will not do. If you want to defend yourself with a handgun, learn to shoot your handgun of choice with one hand, as well as two.

THE FLINCH

The most common cause for misses that I have observed is the anticipation of recoil and muzzle blast leading to jerking the trigger, pushing, pulling or "heeling" the gun, which moves the handgun out of alignment. This is commonly called a "flinch." I've had occasion to shoot with many armed professionals, including uniformed police officers, undercover agents, covert operators and active duty armed service people. Some of them have had flinches the size of Mt. Rushmore. (I'm sorry if that disillusions you, but most armed professionals are just regular folks who work at acquiring their skills.)

There are few geniuses of the gun like Bill Jordan or Jelly Brice, and even they practiced a great deal, more than most non-professional civilians ever will. I have no knowledge whether either of those great shooters ever developed a flinch. But take a look at Bill Jordan shooting a .44 Magnum in his excellent book, *No Second Place Winner*. In one very clear photo, Bill Jordan demonstrates the folly of choosing a weapon more powerful than you can master. Although his service weapon was a .357 Magnum and he was a consummate master of it, he wrote that a pocket-sized, alloy-framed revolver loaded with .22 Magnums was a good hideout gun and superior to the same revolver chambered for the .38 Special. Jordan thought that the .22 magnum was a highly effective round, faster in rapid fire than the .38 and that savings in weight over a .38 was a significant matter for everyday carry. And these assertions are from one of the finest shooters of all time—a man who was a master of highly powerful weapons.

A flinch is no disgrace. I've had one. Like the measles, I got over it. The cure is more training. With proper training and practice, a dedicated person can overcome a flinch; it takes time and work. (More time and work than most non-professionals are willing to commit to the process.)

The basic technique of diagnosing a flinch is to have a coach load a dummy round in your magazine without telling you which is the dummy round. When you squeeze the trigger on a dummy round it will become immediately apparent if you have a flinch. The diagnosis is also part of the cure, which I detail in the *How to Shoot* chapters. However, some people simply cannot get over a flinch induced by a powerful gun. For them, a less powerful gun is a better choice than a gun they cannot control.

Every time I go to a public range, I see people banging away with two or three different 9mm, .40 or .45 pistols that someone told them to buy, usually on the grounds that these were what they had to have to stop an assailant. These folks are always shooting at silhouettes and they are always missing them. At best, they get a few rounds somewhere on the silhouettes at a range of about seven yards. They're thrilled if they manage to get a cluster of shots the size of a basketball anywhere on the target. The concept of a "group" doesn't seem to exist for them. They switch from handgun to handgun, presumably thinking that one or another will provide the magic required for them to consistently hit the target. All of them—not some—all of them are flinching like Mel Gibson in *Lethal Weapon*. Will this sort of shooting serve to save them and their loved ones in a lethal encounter? Maybe. If they fire enough rounds at their assailant, they might get lucky, again forgetting about who else might get hit with those stray rounds. On the other hand, maybe not.

Eighty-five to ninety-five percent of the

effectiveness of any shot is determined by shot placement. Under stress, you will be more likely to hit your target, a vital spot with a gun you are comfortable with, rather than with one that you are not. You'll see this again because it's of utmost importance. Hitting a vital spot is the most important part of the entire process—not the caliber. If you can hit a small paper plate at twelve feet, while drawing and shooting fast, ten out of ten times with a .32, and two out of ten times with a .45, with which gun do you think you're better armed?

ABILITY TO CONCEAL AND TO CARRY

If you obtain a Concealed Carry Permit, which you must apply for with your local police, you will learn that one of your obligations as a legally-armed citizen is to keep your weapon concealed from public view. The larger the gun, the more difficult this is to accomplish. Most service handguns are for many people, too large and too heavy to carry totally concealed all day.

That may not apply to you. You may find no problem with daily carry of a service handgun. However, the odds are that unless you are in a high threat environment or an armed professional, you will eventually leave your service weapon at home. Why? Because service weapons are heavy and not especially comfortable to carry. Most police officers I know are relieved to get home and take off their guns at the end of their duty shift. Not one uniformed police officer I know carries his service weapon off duty. They choose something smaller and lighter. Do you

think a civilian shooter will behave differently? Odds are that big gun will stay home.

I once read a comment that a highly regarded trainer, a shootist of the first order, supposedly made in reference to carrying a service handgun, "It's supposed to be comforting, not comfortable" or something like that. That's a clever zinger. But it does not change the reality that even with a good holster, you're still toting a couple of pounds of steel on one side of your body—not the best prescription for avoiding the orthopedist and chiropractor. And it isn't comfortable, even with a good holster. It's a price professionals must pay. Is it one you are willing to pay?

PROFESSIONAL TRAINING

Professional instruction can be a significant shortcut to the acquisition of armed defensive skills. The National Rifle Association will refer you to a local instructor who has been certified to teach basic skills, which is where a new shooter really should start. This basic instruction will give you a foundation, but it won't make you a gunfighter.

There are schools available to private citizens where they can obtain training from highly qualified professionals. But there are also obstacles to attending a shooting school, including cost. Most schools appear to offer a fair price, considering the attention given and the potential skills that can be acquired. However, it's a price that many cannot afford. In addition to the cost in money, there is the cost in time. I've heard the argument that anyone who is serious about armed self-protection should make the time and find the money to get proper professional training. The reality is that few of us have time stretchers or trust funds. Most will not or cannot manage to attend a shooting school.

Besides, there isn't room for everyone. Based on the number of training facilities in the country, the average class size and the number of classes that are offered each year, it would appear that less than 1% of those who buy handguns for self defense would be able to take such a course—even if it were free.

There are eight million new gun owners in the United States each year. About half of them are buying guns for self defense. The U.S. Army couldn't train four million people each year. Throw in the Marines and we still couldn't do it. This is far more people than all of our armed services and all the civilian training schools combined could train each year. Further, based on the available numbers, most people who buy handguns for self-defense don't even join a local gun club or get basic NRA instruction.

What do the other 99% plus percent do—the ones who get no formal training? They might buy books like this one and others written on the topic. They get some instruction from a friend or a family member or someone they meet at a range. They practice a little, maybe a box of ammo or two and call it a day. Is this enough to enable persons to defend themselves with any handgun, let alone a.45 or a 9mm, both of which clearly require more work to master than say, a target .22? Maybe. Maybe not. The universe is a chancy place. They might get lucky.

Note that I said, "defend themselves." I'm not discussing "combat hand gunnery, tactical hand gunnery" or any variation of these activities, which are the topics many of the shooting schools appear to be focused upon. Simple self-defense is entirely different than clearing a room filled with hostages and terrorists. By self-defense, I mean engaging one or more hostiles who have the intent to do you or yours mortal harm, at close range. According to available statistics, the distance between contact and twenty feet takes in the great majority of assaults on persons.

To expect the average citizen to reach a level of expertise with a service pistol only achieved by highly trained professionals and to task him to do so without the weeks of training and the thousands of service caliber rounds professionals expend—is to set him up for failure. Many of those who do minimally qualify with the skills taught at some schools, don't continue to practice and their skills degrade over time.

The first handgun I ever formally trained on was the Government Model 1911 .45ACP. I loved it. I shot distinguished expert with it after a few days of training and practice. But there were others, healthy, strong, young men who were headed for combat and highly motivated, who could not and did not qualify with the .45. Why? The training was certainly adequate. I think the answer is simple. Some people, even soldiers just aren't into guns. They don't particularly like them. They have no talent for the gun and won't put in the work required for competence. And make no mistake, it takes work to become accustomed to the muzzle blast and recoil of a service pistol, to master trigger control and the other skills that go into defensive marksmanship.

What then do we say to these folks? "Oh well, if you can't handle the right gun, too bad for you. There's always pepper spray and prayer. Go forth and hope for the best." No. I don't think so. There's an alternative for them—less powerful handguns. Handguns are easy to shoot, and to shoot, well.

SHOT PLACEMENT

As I stated earlier, studies carried out by various government organizations indicate that between eighty-five percent and ninety-five percent of the effectiveness of any shot is determined by shot placement. Understanding this is of the highest possible importance. Not caliber; not "stopping power;" bullet placement is the most important determinant of effectiveness.

Bullets work by striking the central nervous system or the blood circulation system and interrupting the flow of blood or neural impulses. Shocking power is a factor in the more powerful cartridges. But how much shock it takes to put down a particular assailant and how much is delivered by a given cartridge is subject to much debate.

What we know is that if neural impulses stop, the person stops. Quickly. If the blood supply is stopped, the assailant also stops—but more slowly. Again, the details of all this are beyond the scope of this book. For our purposes, let's take it as a given that a less powerful round placed in a vital spot is more effective than a powerful round in a less effective location or a miss. And a miss is what most untrained people shooting a service weapon under highly stressed defensive conditions will achieve. Many trained people do the same under real-world conditions.

No number of powerful misses will stop an assailant as well as one well-placed round of moderate or low power. And, let's not forget that those misses are going somewhere—maybe into an innocent bystander. Aside from the moral implications of wild fire and stray rounds, there are also legal liabilities. Remember, you are responsible for every round you fire.

I see that many now consider an area about the size of two legal pads in the center of a static silhouette to be the critical zone and state that there is no need to be any more accurate. Further, we are told that you must use your sights and both hands to achieve this level of accuracy; this at seven yards. If you can hit this area most of the time, in daylight while standing still and shooting with both hands and getting a good sight picture—you're supposedly competent in defensive shooting. Maybe so.

But when I was learning to "shoot to live," our instructor pinned playing cards to the silhouettes, face out, and told us to focus on the pips. We started with single shots at about three yards, using one hand. The idea was to focus on a small part of the target, thereby better insuring that we would get a good hit on a vital spot, or if we missed, we would miss by a small margin.

After we could hit the playing cards with regularity, we took a giant step to the rear and started over and so on until we found the distance at which we needed to use our sights—mainly our front sight.

We were told that in combat we should focus on say, a button, or (rough as this sounds) an eye, rather than the whole person. This is similar to advice given hunters to not "shoot at the whole animal." The point of all this was to make us understand that the only way to stop an assailant for sure was to hit a vital point. We were training to do exactly that.

Low light shooting, with so little light you couldn't see your sights, and shooting in full darkness, was another topic, one that occupied about a third of our training. At night, you cannot of course see the pips on a playing card and so our focus was to shift to the center of mass of our target and to fire "bursts"—two or three rounds fired rapidly.

FIGHT, FLIGHT, FREEZE, OR FLAP

All of us have heard of the fight or flight syndrome, the response coded into our species at the level of DNA. We perceive a threat and our bodies shift into fight or flight mode and we do one or the other. That's what we're told. There are two other responses that I have observed that are equally common. I think the fight or flight syndrome could be more accurately called the fight, flight, freeze, or flap syndrome.

People don't only flee or fight. They freeze. This is also known as the "deer in the headlights" effect. It often happens to people who don't have a clue as to how to deal with a situation or have any frame of reference for it. It also happens to people who get stuck in many different choices and can't decide which action to take before it's too late. My training sergeant used to say, "Don't just stand there. Do something—even if it's wrong." The idea being to get out of the way of the oncoming train, even if you have to jump into a ditch and maybe twist your ankle.

People also flap. This is a term I first heard from a British SAS trooper. To "flap" means to move fast and frantically do irrelevant things, but nothing that will help the situation, kind of like a hog on ice—lots of squealing, legs and hooves every which way—but no forward motion. Too many choices, complicated training methods and too little practice to get reactions into reflex can be just as deadly as not having a clue.

FIGHT LIKE YOU TRAIN

I've often heard the statement, "You'll fight like you train." Maybe. Maybe not. If your training has been too complicated; if you haven't had time to absorb it, and if you haven't continued the practice required to retain the skills, there is an excellent chance you'll forget everything and freeze or flap. Unless you have spent a few weeks training as a fulltime job with excellent professional coaches, you're probably not going to be able to run that M-4 Carbine at the same level as an Army Ranger running and gunning in Mosul. And it's unlikely that a weekend seminar in "combat hand gunnery" will serve your needs if armed assailants attack you.

What's the answer? How can you acquire life saving skills without joining the military or spending a fortune at private training schools, many of which will still not provide you with the simple, effective, durable training you need?

DEFENSIVE SHOOTING

If you want to become a well-rounded marksman, go to the *How to Shoot* chapters and learn the fundamentals first. Also, as suggested there, contact your local NRA instructor for some hands-on training. If you are only concerned about self-defense and are looking for the maximum ROI (Return On Investment), go with the combat masters: Fairbairn & Sykes, Applegate, and Jordan. The methods I was trained in can be found in *Shooting To Live* by Captain W.E. Fairbairn and Captain E.A. Sykes, in *Kill or Get Killed* by Colonel Rex Applegate and in *No Second Place Winner* by William H. Jordan. I do not have the level of experience that these men had, but I have used these methods in life-threatening situations and they have proven effective for me.

The skills these men advocate are relatively easy to learn and easy to retain. There are some variations in method from one to the other, but basically they're all singing in the same choir. My personal methods are drawn from these sources and adapted to my needs. Once learned, a relatively modest amount of practice (about 1000 fully-focused live fire rounds) will get them coded in to reflex. Another 1000 rounds of dry fire will help to embed those reflexes so that they become part of you.

A key point in this training is that these methods follow natural reflexes that humans revert to when threatened. Therefore, if the new reflexes you develop follow the ones you have as original equipment, you are less likely to freeze, flap, or have your training fall apart under life-threatening stress. This has been proven in combat many, many times.

A deep cover civilian "consultant" I once knew, I'll call him Jesse (not his real name), had been retained by a U.S. agency and was working solo in a Latin American country during an extended armed conflict. While there, he contracted typhoid and was laid up recovering for a couple of weeks in a remote village. There were guerillas operating in the nearby countryside but Jesse's cover held and he was not bothered—until he tried to leave.

Thinking he could make his way to a road where he could catch a "chicken bus" into a town, he set out on foot, and alone. While walking through the mountainous countryside he discovered that he was still sick and weak and was afflicted with dizziness and various unpleasant and debilitating symptoms of typhoid

It was late evening when Jesse arrived at the dirt road where he expected to catch the bus. Four armed men were waiting for him. They were smoking and talking and were as surprised by Jesse's quiet approach as he was to encounter them. The guerillas quickly recovered, brought their weapons to bear, and got off a few rounds narrowly missing him as he leaped sideways into a thicket of bushes, drew his handgun and returned fire.

Jesse reflexively dropped into a deep crouch in the bushes pointed his pistol at the armed men and emptied his magazine. He quickly reloaded and continued firing. The armed men retreated with much yelling and wild shooting. Jesse ran in the other direction, eventually working his way back to the road a few miles away where he hitched a ride into town with a Catholic priest driving an old pickup truck.

Later he learned that he had wounded two of the guerillas and confirmed that they had intended to ambush and kill him because they thought he was an American spy—which in fact he was.

A moment before the encounter, he had been doubled over with cramps—his entire body trembling and shaking. He was staggering and stumbling and near the end of his rope. He had lost over twenty pounds during the previous two weeks. In spite of his condition or perhaps because of it, he reacted at his most basic and durable level of training and survived.

No one can guarantee how you, as an individual, will perform under stress. But Fairbairn & Sykes and Applegate trained large numbers of men and women in these methods in a relatively short period of time. These same men and women then faced our enemies in World War II. As many accounts show, the methods worked and saved lives. They have been passed on as methods that still work today.

The point of the story? Jesse had served with an elite military unit and had trained extensively as a civilian in various combat and shooting arts, including the "new technique," that was at that time just coming into vogue. When he was under extreme stress the new technique, including the Weaver Stance (a shooting method) disappeared. Jesse had more than a passing acquaintance with the new technique, yet he reverted to the simple "Shooting to Live" method.

CHAPTER 13

Defensive Shooting Skills

(If you have read the How to Shoot a Handgun chapter, some of this material will be familiar.)

TARGET IDENTIFICATION

For the purposes of this book, let's take it as a given that you can identify a threat and make your own decision to respond with gunfire. This is a serious responsibility and one that no one but you can make at the critical moment. (Advanced perceptual skills for threat identification are beyond the scope of this book.)

FIELD STANCE

In the *How to Shoot a Handgun* chapter, I also called this position the field stance. Although many use terms such as combat stance, let's stay with field stance. It is basically the same for the rifle and the pistol—from the waist down. It is a dynamic and powerful position from which the shooter can see, shoot, and move. It provides secure footing and balance for movement over broken terrain and away from an immediate threat.

The feet should be at least shoulder width apart, with the front foot about a step ahead of the rear foot. The rear foot points slightly to the outside. Both knees are bent. This stance is similar to what Fairbarin & Sykes call a "crouch." It is a powerful and mobile position that allows the shooter to swivel at the waist to engage threats over an arc of about 180 degrees. Have a friend push your shoulder while in this stance. If you are firmly grounded, he or she should not be able to move you without undue force. This is a basic fighting stance that many will go to instinctively.

Basic field stance

Basic field stance

Basic field stance

GRIP

Ideally, the handgun becomes an extension of the hand and arm. With a firm and consistent grip, the handgun can point as well as your index finger. About the only difference between the grip for defensive shooting and ordinary shooting is that you should practice gripping the pistol very strongly. The idea being that this is what you will normally do when threatened.

ONE-HANDED GRIP

Grasp the handgun first with the V formed by the thumb and index finger. This V should be placed as high as possible on the back of the grip and in alignment with the barrel and sights. Wrap your lower three fingers around the grip and grasp firmly, placing most of the pressure toward the rear of the grip. Too much sideways pressure from the fingers can torque the gun out of alignment and lead to missing your target. When practicing, grasp the handgun with as much strength as you can. Continued practice will strengthen the grip.

Gripping the handgun correctly

One-handed grip

Arm fully-extended, one-handed grip

Author's Advice

Learn the one-handed grip before the two-handed grip. It is foundational to learning the two-handed grip and, since the great majority of encounters take place at close range, is critical to your defense.

TWO-HANDED GRIP

The two-handed grip, correctly applied, provides more support and stability for the firing hand, thus more accuracy. In defensive shooting, the two-handed grip is best used at distances over three to four paces.

Aside from the fact that the accuracy required at six to nine feet does not require a two-handed grip, you may not have your other hand available; it may be engaged in fending off your assailant or in pushing a loved one behind your body and out of the line of fire. Also, it takes slightly longer to acquire the two-handed grip and you may not have the extra tenth of a second if a hostile is upon you.

Two-handed grip

AIMING AND SIGHT PICTURE

In close-range, defensive shooting—keep your eyes on the threat, not your weapon. At close range and under immediate threat, there is no time to acquire a sight picture. If you can bring your handgun to shoulder level, you can aim simply by looking down the barrel. At very close range, you aim by pointing. At longer ranges, use the sights as explained in the *How to Shoot a Handgun* chapter.

Two-handed grip

TRIGGER SQUEEZE

The trigger squeeze should be essentially the same as described in the *How to Shoot a Handgun* chapter, with the only difference being that you do it quickly.

DRY FIRING PRACTICE

Dedicated and concentrated dry fire practice is even more important in defensive shooting than for sporting use. (Details on dry fire practice are in the *How to Shoot a Handgun* chapter.)

SPEED

Smoothness brings speed. Practice slowly and be aware of each part of every movement. Practicing in front of a mirror is a good way to make sure you are moving correctly. Speed will come after you have the skill in muscle memory.

THE HANDGUN SHOOTING POSITIONS

HIP FIRING POSITION

Many experts deride hip shooting as being totally useless. They feel that no one can hit anything from this position. Perhaps they are setting their sights incorrectly. No one who knows what he is doing, except a legend like Ed McGivern or Jelly Brice, should consider shooting from this position at any distance beyond a couple of paces. However, within that range, the technique is useful and effective.

If attacked at close range, the defensive shooter will almost certainly begin to return fire as soon as the muzzle of his weapon clears the holster, or wherever the handgun is carried—whether he has trained to do so or not. Therefore, you should practice actually getting hits from this position.

Good hits from the hip can be obtained at about two paces with a minimum of training. Getting hits from the hip at longer ranges will

Hip 1

Hip 2

require considerably more practice for most. Shooting from this position as a deliberate choice at any distance over two paces is not a good tactical move and will likely result in a miss.

Another reason for using this firing position is that it protects your handgun from an assailant at arms reach. Extending your weapon will make you vulnerable to disarming. At one time, disarming methods were closely held and not taught to the general public. This is no longer so. Anyone with an Internet connection can view videos demonstrating disarming methods—some of them quite effective. Stick your gun in your assailant's face and he just might snatch it from you and use it against you. (Yes, the bad guys watch those videos, too.)

PARTIALLY-EXTENDED ARM

Bill Jordan refers to this firing position as the "gun throwing" method. This position is more of a true pointing position and superior to the hip position for getting good hits.

Partially-extended arm, Hip level

FULLY-EXTENDED ARM

This is the most desirable position if your target is more than ten to twelve feet from you. With this position, you can look down your arm and over your handgun, which greatly improves accuracy. To check if you have a solid position, have a friend push on your hand while your arm is extended. He should not be able to move you without applying a fair amount of force.

Fully-extended arm

TWO ARMS, FULLY-EXTENDED

If you can look down your arm and over your handgun with one arm extended you might be able to do so with both extended, if your other arm is not occupied. This position provides more stability, greater accuracy, and facilitates transition to aimed fire. This is a good position to use if you have time and the distances are longer than fifteen feet.

LIVE AMMUNITION PRACTICE

Start your practice between six and nine feet from your target with your gun hand at your side. The distance does not need to be exact. Bring your gun hand up with your arm fully extended towards your target. Shoot each round with total concentration, as if each shot was the only one you had. Focus tightly on a small spot on your silhouette target, bulls-eye or informal target while looking down the barrel of your gun. Fire one shot at a time noting where each one goes. Lower your gun after each shot. The idea is to eventually make the process—acquiring the target, raising the gun, and firing—a smooth continuing motion.

If your shots are more than six inches from your focus spot or spread out over the target, check your position and continue to shoot one round at a time until you are getting a group about the size of a small paper plate around your focus spot. Then take a giant step to the rear and start over. Once you achieve your group at

Two arms, fully-extended

this new range, step back again. Continue until you reach the maximum distance at which you can get that paper plate-sized group.

A six-inch group will serve your purpose, but if you wish to improve (which I recommend), go back to a closer range and shoot until you get a three-inch or smaller group. You might surprise yourself. Many people learn to shoot at this level within a few hours. Some can do this within one magazine. Others may require a couple of days. Do not be discouraged if you don't get groups right way. You will if you continue. Do not over tire yourself. Take breaks at least once an hour. Few can shoot with full concentration for more than a few hours each day.

A tight, 3-inch group

After achieving groups with your arm fully extended at three or four paces, move closer to the target, say about six feet. Bring your gun hand up from your side to the partially-extended position. Fire one round and continue to practice as you did with full-arm extension. After getting your group, step back and begin again. Then do the same from the hip position. You will probably find that you cannot get groups as good from the hip position or the partially-extended position at the same distances as the fully-extended position. This is normal. Exact distances will vary from person to person.

Rest when you find your concentration wavering. It may take you an hour to fire fifty rounds if you are concentrating on your focusing point and body position. Shoot slowly and deliberately. Speed will come with practice.

After you can shoot three-inch to six-inch groups in single shots in all positions at your maximum distances, start on shooting doubles and bursts of three rounds. To shoot a double, trigger your second round as soon as you have triggered your first round. If your grip, position, and other factors are correct, you will see two holes in your target very close to one another. If your hits are more than three inches apart, check your technique and focus more tightly. This may require a fair amount of practice. Or not. Some get it right away.

Once you can shoot consistent doubles, do the same with three-round bursts. When you can hold a group with three round bursts, you can probably do the same with rapid fire strings of five or more shots. Try it. Then go to multiple targets.

Start over with single shots and traverse from one target to another as shown in accompanying photos. It's best if your targets are at varying ranges and heights, rather than exactly the same. When you begin to get good hits with single shots, go to doubles and bursts. When you

Traversing to the right from basic field stance

Traversing to the left from basic field stance

can get your six-inch or three-inch group from all positions on multiple targets at your best distance for each position, it's time to increase your speed. Do so gradually and smoothly. With good concentrated practice, you will find that you can shoot about as well fast, as you do slowly.

Next, do the same practice in poor lighting conditions, uneven footing, rain, snow, or whatever conditions you are likely to encounter in your environment. If you are getting good groups fast in various conditions, you have reached a minimum level of competence in self-defense shooting. I have seen many students achieve this in one weekend. Others required more time. No matter the speed of your progress, do not become discouraged. Remember, thousands of ordinary people, not super athletes, have been trained this way and later prevailed against their enemies.

MOVING WHILE FIRING

The accompanying photos show an advanced student training to move towards assailants while firing, often called "running and gunning." The details of how to do this while insuring that your shots do not go astray, and that you are moving safely, are part of advanced instruction and can not be covered here. The photos are included to give you an idea of correct movement and why the field stance is fundamental to defensive skills. If you decide to try this on your own, DO NOT consider attempting this kind of movement with a loaded firearm before you are fully competent in the basic skills. Then, if you want to try this, start on level ground and do a good deal of dry practice before attempting this with live ammunition.

Pistol run & gun sequence 1

Pistol run & gun sequence 2

Pistol run & gun sequence 3

Pistol run & gun sequence 4

Rifle run & gun sequence 1

Rifle run & gun sequence 2

Rifle run & gun sequence 3

CHAPTER 14

Guns for Self-Defense

It is vital to have a gun you are comfortable with and that you can rely on to perform as needed. A firearm that malfunctions at a critical moment can be worse than no firearm at all. Pick a gun with a good reputation, but do not trust it until you have done the drills in the previous chapter and fired a thousand rounds with that particular firearm.

Author's Advice

Clean and maintain your defensive firearm as if your life depends on it. It might one day.

THE CARBINE

Generally speaking, the carbine is not a self-defense weapon that a civilian can keep close at hand during his daily routine. I mention the carbine only because it can be of use in massive civil disturbances which unfortunately seem to be common. At distances of over say, twenty yards, it is much easier to hit your target with a carbine than with a handgun. Whether you would be legally justified in shooting an assailant at that range is a question I cannot answer. Finally, moral justification is a matter for your own conscience.

The techniques in the *How to Shoot a Rifle* chapter are similar to those for carbines; there is no difference in their function. Snap shooting or point aiming is the preferred technique at ranges to about fifty yards or to whatever range you can score reliable hits. Use the same dry fire and live fire practice recommended for the handgun but at longer ranges. Start at the maximum range you can shoot groups with a handgun, arm fully- extended. Then move back step-by-step, as in handgun practice, until you reach the maximum distance you can successfully get a three-inch or six-inch group without aiming and using the sights. You should use your sights at longer ranges.

Correct body alignment

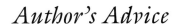

Author's Advice

- *Keep your eyes on the threat, not on your gun.*
- *Point your handgun as if pointing your finger.*
- *Look down your arm and to the pistol barrel, if at shoulder height.*
- *If using a carbine, look down the barrel.*

PRACTICE TO IMPROVE YOUR SKILLS

When you begin to get good hits, pause after each shot and focus on your body alignment—how it feels when you hit where you want. The approach I explain in *The Tao of Shooting* chapter is particularly important in this application. (I recommend that you read that section closely and apply it.)

Silhouettes showing vital points are available from gun stores and on-line. It's a good idea to start with these targets. If you only have standard silhouettes available, use a marker to make dots about an inch in diameter in vital spots. After you have some success with silhouettes, start with smaller targets, such as paper plates placed at irregular intervals. Then go to moving targets such as explained in the *How to Shoot* chapters.

Although you can achieve a basic level of competence in a few days, continual practice will hone and improve your skills. If you don't have time to go to a place where you can do live fire, visualization and dry fire will do a great deal towards maintaining and sharpening your skills.

A video will reveal that each of the mentioned firing positions is a point on a continuum, starting with the handgun in one hand at or below waist level and ending with the handgun at eye level for the most accurate fire. The defensive shooter should, after mastering the static positions, practice firing from all of these positions as he or she brings his handgun to bear on the target in one smooth, flowing motion. When I first learned these methods, we were taught to shoot a burst during this continuum—as many as five or six rounds—with the impact point rising with the gun. This was referred to as "running a zipper" because on a silhouette target, the bullets would strike from below the belt to the head. The idea being that you did not stop shooting until your assailant was neutralized.

When we could hit the playing cards every time with single shots, we were trained to fire two and three shot "bursts" per target—as I suggest you do in your practice. The reason is that in reality, no handgun has a great deal of power and none can be relied upon to stop an assailant without perfect shot placement. This is difficult and sometimes impossible in real-world conditions, thus tight focus and rapid bursts may be necessary until your assailant is stopped.

We were also taught to move while firing or under fire, sometimes advancing towards the enemy sometimes getting out of the line of fire, depending on the situation. We were also trained to go to cover if any, in order to shoot multiple targets. But most importantly, we were trained to *fight*—not just shoot—with a gun.

You might note that some of the accompanying photos show "protector and principal" drills. I cannot teach these skills within the limits of this book. But I have included the photos to give you a general idea of how to approach the problem of protecting your loved ones when confronted by armed assailants. (These photos also illustrate a major reason one-handed shooting is a critical skill.)

Protector & Principal

Protector draws and aims toward threat

Protector steps in front of principal to shield from incoming fire

Protector controls principal by holding his arm and guiding him to stay behind protector

Front view of protector shielding and guiding principal while aiming at threat

The ranges discussed earlier may seem very short. Many choose to not practice at these ranges at all, thinking that if they can score hits at, say, twenty-five yards, they can hit an assailant at two yards with no practice at all. Such has not proven to be the case. This has been shown in hundreds of real-life encounters in which people who had been trained for target range shooting missed their assailants at close range. If learning defensive shooting is your primary goal, you should invest more time in practicing at close range than at extended range.

I recommend that you begin your practice with a .22 target pistol for all the reasons mentioned in the chapter on twenty-twos. I also recommend that you master your pistol by following the procedures outlined in the *How to Shoot a Handgun* chapter. Shoot your 1,000 conscious and considered rounds. Remember, quality counts more than quantity. Accuracy and smoothness first—speed second. You can't miss fast enough to hit your target. Have some fun with balloons and other moving targets. After this, you will have a firm grounding in the basics.

If you can't commit that much time, follow the methods I outline here. Once you're confident you have mastered these skills with your twenty-two, progress to a more powerful weapon and start over. If you find yourself missing your mark, go back to your twenty-two and check yourself. Remember, your twenty-two target pistol is your "no excuses" handgun. If you miss with this one, it's you, not the gun. You learned to analyze your shooting while learning the basics. You'll know if you develop a flinch.

You'll know how to overcome it. Or you may elect to stay with a less powerful handgun.

SMALL CALIBER WEAPONS

Many competent defensive shooters decide to stay with a small caliber. When I was still active in our martial arts school, we worked with organizations such as the Los Angeles Police Department and the Rape Crisis Center. (Our work with the RCC was pro bono, our effort to give something back to the community.)

One of our referrals from the RCC was a woman who had been violated in her own home. Clara (not her real name), took our Rape Prevention class, and went on to mainstream martial arts and then into combat classes. Clara was about 5' 7', athletic, and hardly a shrinking violet. She worked out with guys who weighed in at well over 200 lbs and were serious fighters and good martial artists. Yeah, they cut her some slack, who wouldn't? But they worked her hard, knowing that giving her a free pass would be doing her no favor. After some months, Clara came to me after class one day and said that she had come to realize that if a large male with ill intent and similar training attacked her, she probably could not defeat him.

Clara decided to arm herself. After shooting various handguns at a rental range, she bought a HK P7 9mm (an excellent small, powerful, accurate and easy to shoot handgun) and acquired competence with it. She could hit playing cards on multiple silhouettes at about twelve feet—seven out of seven times—fast. Then she decided to sell the P7 and buy a smaller pistol.

Given her nightmarish experience, she intended to be armed at all times. The P7 was more gun than she could carry in *total* concealment. She worked in films as a crew member. Her job was physical and often other crewmembers were in physical contact with her while they together lifted heavy props and lighting. She could not allow anyone to learn that she was armed with a pistol. Aside from the general alarm and gossiping such a discovery would cause, it might also result in the loss of her job.

She settled on a .25 Beretta as her daily carry and trained with it until she could hit balloons blowing in the wind, tennis balls hanging from string, and tin cans rolling on the ground. She could draw from deep cover and put two rounds into about two inches on the heads of each of three silhouette targets from contact range to about twelve to fifteen feet, every time—fast. I've heard many gun shop commandos say that .25s bounce off heads and are completely useless; that if you shoot anyone with a .25 or a .22 it will just make them mad. Such has not been my experience. And I doubt that any of these

bulletproof fellows would care to stand in for Clara's targets. (Another factor in Clara's decision was that it was impossible for her, a regular citizen, to get a permit to legally carry a concealed firearm.)

In Los Angeles, only Hollywood stars and the politically connected can get permits to carry. If she was going to carry, she had to make sure her pistol was never seen by anyone. She chose to break the law rather than risk a repeat of the most horrific experience of her life. **(I do not advocate breaking any laws or carrying a firearm without a permit.** I'm only recounting the decision of one person who decided to protect herself from violation as best she could.)

Some professionals, for example many covert operators and intelligence officers, are also armed with small calibers. There are good reasons for this. First, the gun isn't central to their mission. Unlike an infantryman whose job it is to engage his enemy with his weapon, a clandestine operator's mission may be to obtain critical information or an intelligence officer's to recruit an agent of a foreign power. Their orders are often to not engage an enemy with violence unless he or she is threatened and has no choice. Second, they may be placed in greater danger if their enemy learns that he or she is armed, which in many cases would violate their cover. In this instance, deep concealment is as important as being armed.

The deep cover civilian "consultant" I previously wrote about, "Jesse," was armed with only a pocket sized .22 in a holster of his own design which suspended his handgun near his groin, an area sometimes overlooked in first level searches. He also kept ready-cash in his pockets and successfully bribed his way out of danger more than once, preferring the expenditure of a couple of hundred dollars to violence. However, there was more than one occasion when he was forced to use his little pistol in self-defense.

One evening at the entrance to his hotel, four men who he knew were members of an urban terrorist group, approached him with the intention of kidnapping and interrogating him, an experience he would not survive. One of the men openly carried an automatic weapon. The others had handguns, but only one had his pistol in hand—the other two men's pistols were holstered. The men were just short of arm's reach when Jesse acted decisively and aggressively, quickly drawing his .22 from deep cover and without hesitation firing, hitting each of them in the face or head and dropping all four men instantly. He then fled.

Jesse was successful for a number of reasons. He acted without hesitation. He trusted his training and his weapon. Also acting in his favor was the fact that his assailants assumed he was not armed and approached him with the confidence that he would be an easy victim.

Jesse had no desire to take anyone's life, nor did he want to get into a full-on firefight. While he was not equipped for that type of confrontation, a firefight would not have aided his mission in any way. He was tasked with information acquisition and was armed for the sole purpose of enabling him in an emergency to break contact, escape, and evade—which he did, successfully. Although his little pistol was decisive in this encounter, his situational awareness and his decisive response were instrumental in his survival.

It is popularly believed that only assassins use .22 pistols against their "enemies." I suspect this is mostly because mob assassins are known to use .22s and perhaps because many have seen the movie Munich, where a fictionalized Israeli kidon (assassination) team hunts down the Black September terrorists who were responsible for the deaths at the Munich Olympics in 1972. In fact, Israeli intelligence officers (katsas) are often armed with .22 pistols, just like certain U.S. operatives are. Why?

There are four reasons. First, the round is more effective than its size would indicate. Second, the caliber is easy to learn how to shoot well. These are highly trained and skilled professionals, but their profession is not armed conflict. They might only receive a few days training and practice with a handgun, whereas they might well study a foreign language for years and their cover for weeks in preparation for their duties. Third, the small, lightweight handguns they use are concealable from all but a body search. Fourth, the small firearms are not a burden to carry and so the operative will most likely have the weapon with him when and if it is needed..

Does Jesse's experience and Clara's decision mean we should all arm ourselves with .22s or .25s? No. Clara's decision was a personal one. Jesse prevailed due to making the best use of his equipment and training. These two examples show that small caliber weapons are not always the handicap that some experts would have us believe.

One night when we were getting close to the bottom of a bottle of bourbon I asked him why he didn't carry a .45. He said, "The .45 is over-rated and too heavy. I killed Nazis with this little pistol all over Europe. What counts son is where you shoot them."

Sergeant Poleaski had also been armed with an M1 Carbine, a weapon often criticized to-

day as being underpowered. But he thought his weapons were adequate for his needs and he survived to tell about it. Maybe today's bad guys are tougher and more formidable than the dedicated, World War II veteran soldiers, many of whom had years of combat behind them. But I don't think so. Do you? Really?

Yes, I've heard the stories about the pumped up, steroid popping, amphetamine-driven weight pile monsters. I even have one of those stories myself. But so far, I haven't seen anyone who can flex his pectoral muscles and deflect a bullet. And all the "roid monsters" I have ever seen have had hearts (well blood pumps anyway), brains, and need their neurological and circulatory systems to function. As such, they will be subject to hits to vital areas, just like lions and tigers and bears.

You don't buy that? Are you worried about coming home one night and finding Godzilla in your driveway? OK, maybe you need to get a Godzilla Gun. But if you do, make sure you master that fire breather so that when you touch it off, you hit Godzilla, not some mom walking with a baby carriage three blocks away. And no, I don't think being able to hit a static target the size of two legal pads at three paces five out of ten times, using both hands, in broad daylight will do it. You'll probably be trying to get out of Godzilla's way and he's going to be coming at you fast. Why else would you be shooting at him? You can't shoot the old lizard just because he's eating your shrubbery. It wouldn't be right.

Sergeant Poleaski taught me some blood truths about staying alive, at least one of which

One of my training sergeants, Sergeant First Class Poleaski, carried a Colt Model 1908 Pocket Hammerless .380 ACP in a shoulder holster during his service with the 82nd Airborne Division in World War II. He jumped into Italy and fought his way up the boot. Then he was pulled out and sent north. He jumped into Normandy before the D-Day landings and later at Nimagen (A Bridge Too Far).

later saved my life. And I haven't yet met the expert who has convinced me that power is more important than the ability to hit a vital spot.

If you can master, and I mean master (not just hit a silhouette occasionally) a service pistol and choose to carry one, then, as the Aussies say, "Good on ya mate." If, for whatever reason you choose to use a less powerful weapon for self-defense and you have mastered it, then you are as adequately armed as some professionals.

But don't think you have an instant paralyzer ray; no handgun is that. Anything can, and does happen during violent encounters and your choice of firearm might prove to be the least important factor in the encounter. Do not fall into the trap of believing a powerful gun will save the day. All the noise about stopping power and caliber choice is mostly sound and fury—signifying not much at all.

"COMBAT" COMPETITION

More than one practitioner of the sport of "combat shooting" has told me that their sport is "just like the real thing" and that the stress of "combat" competition is like that of an actual firefight. No it is not. It is not in same zip code, not in the same city, and not in the same country. In the country where death is coming at you, some people scream and cry and void their bowels and bladders, and those are the ones who haven't been shot. Others trance out and empty their guns into the air. Some people revert to lizard brain and shoot everything that moves. I haven't seen much of that kind of behavior at "combat matches." However, I've seen all of that and worse in real firefights. So no, the stress is not comparable and the events are not "just like the real thing."

To have it be like the "real thing," the shooter would have to be under return fire, which would result in considerable reduction in the number of participants in the sport. I do not foresee such events being organized in the near future. Even the military, which does everything it can to prepare its soldiers for actual combat does not have its soldiers fire upon each other, nor does it represent that their training is the "real thing." In fact, their instructors are quite clear that their training is not the real thing or even close to it. It is however the best they can do to train soldiers for actual combat.

Some "combat" competition can be a good way to acquire specific skills that might be useful in certain kinds of armed encounters. Other "combat" competitions are organized as challenging contests, requiring a high level of specialized skills and have little or nothing to do with any realistic simulation of armed encounters. Shooting sports can be great fun. They provide the opportunity to meet people who share your interest. They can bring with them the stress and pressure of any competitive sport, much like that with golf or tennis—the desire to win and so forth. Such sports, if practiced in the right spirit and with the right mindset, can be useful in skill development.

If you would like to participate in these events with the intention of developing skills that would serve you in a "real-life" encounter, do so with whatever handgun you have chosen to use for self-defense. Do not allow sports enthusiasts to talk you into buying a specialized firearm unless you find that you enjoy the sport and would like to more fully participate. Also, do not be persuaded to buy more gun that you can handle, unless you are committed to work up to it. If you discover that you enjoy the sport, then go for it. You'll almost certainly become a better shooter.

There are many local organizations and shooting clubs that offer such competitions. If you are interested, inquire at your local range. The best known national organizations are:

UNITED STATES PRACTICAL SHOOTING ASSOCIATION

USPSA bills itself as providing a sporting activity, which although focused on pistol shooting, is similar to golf, in that it's a relaxing weekend activity. Its players commonly use highly specialized "race guns" and fast-draw holsters. The association can be contacted through their website at www.uspsa.org.

INTERNATIONAL DEFENSIVE PISTOL ASSOCIATIONS

IDPA presents itself as a shooting sport that simulates self-defense scenarios and real life encounters Shooters competing in IDPA sanctioned events are required to use handguns and holsters that are suitable for self-defense use. For more information on this organization, contact them at www.idpa.com.

REAL-WORLD DEFENSE

You can do everything right in a gunfight, be armed with the best possible weapon, and still get killed. In the events I relate, the good guys won and their tactics and weapons worked for them. That time. Will those same weapons and tactics work the next time? Maybe. Maybe not. Nothing is certain.

There are too many factors in play during any armed encounter to be able to predict the outcome with certainly. An armed adversary may be shot in the heart and continue fighting for some time. Buying a gun and developing good defensive skills does not create a bubble of invulnerability.

Biochemistry, individual physical and psychological makeup, training and determination all play a part. Perhaps more important than guns and shooting abilities are skills such as:

- awareness
- perception
- the ability to detect intentions and sense a potential dangerous situation
- the ability to avoid or deflect a critical situation before it rises to the level of violence

The decision to go to the gun is one that should only be arrived at after careful situational analysis, which may take place in a split second. (I call these skills The Tao of Combat, but further details are beyond the scope of this book.)

CENTERFIRE RIFLES

Centerfire rifles in thirty caliber and above (or any variant such as .270, 25-06 etc) have little or no place in self-defense, in an urban environment. That .308 that your neighbor uses to hunt deer, can perforate an intruder, the walls of your

THE ARMORY

Springfield M14 chambered for .308 a military battle rifle too powerful for urban self defense

Photo courtesy of manufacturer

The First Name In American Firearms
SPRINGFIELD ARMORY USA.

neighbor's house, and continue on through your walls and strike anyone in its path. In general, large caliber centerfire rifles are far too powerful to be used in the city or a suburban neighborhood.

A rifle does not make a good interior home defense weapon, being too awkward to maneuver in close quarters. Some excellent rifles are made in short versions, but the cartridges are still too powerful for this kind of use. Do not confuse a short rifle with a carbine. Generally speaking (there are always exceptions) carbines chamber a less powerful cartridge than centerfire rifles.

CARBINES

In the United States, civilians do not normally go about their daily business with rifles, shotguns, or carbines in hand. That said there have

been occasions in recent memory when the possession of a carbine would have been most welcome for an armed citizen.

Chambered for less powerful rounds, carbines are safer than rifles in areas where there may be innocent bystanders. They are more powerful than handguns by an order of magnitude and far easier to shoot accurately at longer ranges. Although most civilian self-defense needs are at ranges under fifteen feet, there have been recent civil disturbances when law and civilized behavior broke down and criminals ran wild.

Millions of television viewers witnessed the societal breakdown and the 1992 violence in Los Angeles during what has become commonly referred to as the Rodney King riots. Many also witnessed

199

storekeepers and other residents protecting their lives with carbine fire from the roofs and windows of their homes and businesses.

I was in downtown Los Angeles the day the riots started and during the following days. People panicked. Drivers ran their cars up onto sidewalks, endangering pedestrians and in some cases, actually running over people to escape traffic jams that confined them to the danger zone. Unarmed people ran to their armed neighbors for protection. And some of those armed neighbors sent out for more ammo for their carbines after they had expended their basic load. Few who saw the firefight between armed citizens and rioters, whether on television or in person, doubt the effectiveness of the carbine.

Similar disorder and violence followed Hurricane Katrina in New Orleans, although much of it was not captured on television as the severity and the extent of the devastated area prevented access by news crews.

There are a variety of carbines currently available. The ones I mention below are those with which I have personal experience.

M-16

The M-16 series has proven its value over the past forty years of use by our armed forces and by the militaries of many other countries. Regardless of what you may hear around your local gun shop or range, the .223 (5.56x45mm) round is an effective anti-personal round when used within its limits. It is not a 1000-yard round. Used within urban ranges it will do what it is supposed to do—if the shooter does his part.

More than one version of the round has been issued for armed forces duty, all of them FMJ, which is required by the Geneva Convention. For various technical reasons there have been problems with some of the duty rounds, all of which have been corrected. As a civilian, you are not limited to FMJ and may choose to use hunting rounds, which are... let's just say, they're adequate for defense. If you've seen what one of these rounds can do, you don't need me to describe it. If you've never seen what they do, you don't want me to describe it. (Trust me on this one.)

The longer-barreled models in this series may be a little unwieldy in urban areas, houses, and cars. One of the short-barreled versions would be a better choice for this application. A problem you may encounter with using a weapon from this series is it may be viewed as an "assault rifle" and as such, be restricted in some jurisdictions. The civilian version is semi-auto only and does not meet the definition of an assault rifle, that is, it fires both full automatic and semi-automatic.

Another possible problem is that these guns are black in color and as the dreaded "black gun" may incite unwarranted fear in the unschooled. On the other hand, that may be a good thing if

Ruger Mini-14

you're facing a mob bent on violence. In fact, the M-16 ballistics can be duplicated in a number of handy carbines in more traditional dress— wooden stock, blued steel, and so on; the Ruger Mini-14 is one of them.

RUGER MINI-14 SERIES

The Ruger Mini-14, in many variations has been with us for well over thirty years and has been proven to be a reliable and reasonably accurate carbine. It fires the same round as the M-16 series and is equally effective. With a wooden stock it looks like an ordinary sporting rifle (which in fact it is) and is less likely to cause alarm among the clueless. The Ruger is also available in a version called the Mini-30, which chambers the Russian 7.61x39 round used in the AK-47. (Many states prohibit hunting deer with anything smaller than 6mm, thus the Mini-30, can be used to hunt deer in most states.)

AK-47

The Kalashnikov automatic rifle of 1947 is the world's most widely distributed weapon of its type. In military versions it can be fired either full automatic or semi-automatic. In the United States, only the semi-automatic version is readily available and legal. The standard chambering is 7.61x39.

The AK-47's ruggedness and reliability are well established. Its generous clearances between moving parts enable the gun to function even when fouled, uncleaned, or covered with mud and rust. However, due to those loose tolerances, it is not an especially accurate weapon, at least not in the versions I have fired. I am told that some current commercial versions are made with tighter tolerances and are therefore more accurate, and so less tolerant of poor maintenance.

There are many today who like this gun and use it in the semi-auto only version. I saw a number of them deployed effectively in Los Angeles in 1992. If you decide to go with an AK, make sure you zero it carefully and understand its limits of accuracy.

TWENTY-TWO RIMFIRE CARBINES

Twenty-two carbines can be effective self-defense weapons in an urban civil disturbance scenario and they offer many advantages. Nothing is easier to shoot accurately, and nothing is less likely to send wild rounds zinging down city streets and through walls. Twenty-two rimfire bullets can do considerable damage to soft tissue and be effective at stopping assailants. However, they have little penetration through hard surfaces and are unlikely to go through walls, thus making the possibility of hitting bystanders in their homes less likely. Any of the guns mentioned in *A Case for the Twenty-Two* chapter will do.

SHOTGUNS

In defensive work, shotguns are sometimes referred to as "The Hammer" because a load of twelve-gauge buckshot will, *sometimes*, hammer an assailant to the ground. However, this is a result of massive pain and neural overload, not as many think from the energy of the projectiles. If you fired a gun powerful enough to knock someone across a room, the recoil would also knock you an equal distance across the room.

For police and defensive use, the twelve-gauge with double ought (00) or single ought (0) buckshot is the most common shotgun load. A twelve-gauge double ought (size 00) shotgun shell contains eight lead balls with a diameter of .33, which is to say, .33 caliber. A single ought shell contains nine balls of .32 caliber. Firing one of those rounds is sort of like firing eight rounds of .33 caliber or nine rounds of .32 caliber—with one squeeze of the trigger.

The question arises: Can you get the same effect by firing a very rapid burst of nine rounds from a .32 pistol? Probably not. The massive neural overload from all the projectiles hitting at once produces a more extreme effect. (I will note that the Czech Skorpion machine pistol in 7.65 (.32) is much more effective than its caliber would seem to indicate. According to an associate of mine, a Croatian national who fought in the Croatian War of Independence [1991 to 1995], and had more than one occasion to use this weapon in street fighting—a short burst from a Skorpion will reliably drop an armed and determined hostile.)

However terminally effective the shotgun may be, it does not make a good interior home defense weapon. Like the rifles, they are difficult to maneuver in close quarters. More importantly, unless you have a good bit of trigger time with some kind of twelve gauge (the usual antipersonnel shotgun), it will probably be too much gun for a new shooter to handle, especially for a person of small stature. Even some police departments are recognizing this and allowing smaller officers to qualify with the twenty-gauge, which is a cartridge with much less recoil.

Also, if you fire at a target more than a few yards away, you must concern yourself with stray pellets. A shotgun's pattern spreads as the distance from the muzzle increases. This can result in wounding or even killing bystanders if you were, say, returning fire from your window at urban rioters. If you want to use a shotgun for self-defense, you'll want a short barrel about 18", which is available on most of the popular guns. Any short-barreled, semi-auto, or pump will do the job. Some military units are using Mossbergs. Many police departments select the Remington 870. Personally, I have found the

Benelli semi-auto to be reliable, to handle well, and to cycle quickly.

Author's Advice

For all but specialized situations, I think anyone is better armed with a carbine then a shotgun. Every women I know who has any experience with both the carbine and the shotgun prefers the carbine.

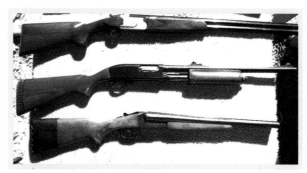

Center shotgun is a Remington 870

SELF-DEFENSE HANDGUNS

Obviously, single-shot handguns are not a good choice for defense. Repeating handguns are available in automatics and double action revolvers. From least powerful to most powerful, the line-up looks like this: .22 or .25, both of which are at the floor of available power, .32, .380, .38 Special, 9mm, .40 caliber, .45 ACP caliber, .357 Magnum, 10mm .44 Magnum. Actually, I don't consider the .44 Magnum to be a defensive caliber for anyone except the most highly trained and skilled. Anything more powerful is a hunting cartridge.

Which to choose is the question? Generally speaking 9mm, .40, 10mm, .357 Magnum and .45 ACP calibers are considered service cartridges and the best compromise between power and controllability. However, as I think I've made clear in previous pages, I think the smaller calibers not only have their place, but are sometimes a better choice.

I offer somewhat more detail on certain hand-guns and their use, than on shoulder weapons because there has been considerable development in handguns in recent years. In addition, handguns, by their nature, are more personal devices and people are often given to placing too much faith in them.

SERVICE HANDGUNS AND REVOLVERS

Revolvers are virtually obsolete for service use, but they may be a useful choice for the civilian who only wishes to acquire the minimum level of skill for self-defense and has trouble with understanding mechanical functions.

Many old timers still like revolvers for self-defense, but for a new shooter, there is little reason to get one other than if you happen to be severely challenged, mechanically. This is not to say that a well-used and familiar handgun used for hunting cannot be used for self-defense. But as a service handgun, the revolver's day has passed.

The automatic is easier to learn to shoot well and is much faster to shoot, thereby allowing more rounds on target—faster. It also holds more rounds and is so much faster and easier to reload, that the revolver is not even in the game. The automatic is also more durable, less subject to damage from being banged against a hard object or being dropped, and easier to maintain under field conditions. All of these reasons, and more, explain why automatics are the handguns of choice for every military organization I am aware of and for the vast majority of police departments. The universal caliber choice for virtually every military organization on the planet, other than a few specialized units, is 9mm. The majority of U.S. police departments use 9mm, .40, or .45. In Europe the 9mm is now standard for police, and in many cases has replaced such rounds as the .380

Two service pistols deserve to be treated in separate discussions. Both are single action automatics and have been around since Moses sent Caleb and his buddies to spy out the land of Canaan—or almost that long.

GOVERNMENT MODEL 1911 .45ACP

"Old Slabsides" as the Government Model 1911 .45 Automatic is affectionately known by thousands of veterans (and not so affectionately by thousands of others), has been in service for almost a century. Designed by John Browning, a firearms genius, it has served generations of servicemen and civilians. It's available in a hundred variations, some of which offer match-grade accuracy. It is popular with many professionals for good reasons which include: a clean, smooth-breaking trigger, comfortable ergonomics, reliability, accuracy, and good power. But part of the reason many choose this old warhorse is its

Colt XSE
A variation on the venerable Colt 45 ACP 1911 Government Model

mystique. It's got major mojo going for it; more than maybe any other handgun.

The 1911 is also available in .38 Super, which I prefer to the .45ACP. But the .45ACP is it. Many worship at the altar of the .45 ACP 1911, and will have no other handgun. Its devotees will tell you it's the best "manstopper" ever developed and "the best handgun ever invented." It is neither.

One round from the .45 in the foot or arm will not render every one shot, immediately unconscious. It will not "put a man down faster than a blast of twelve gauge buckshot in the chest." It is not a light saber or a deathray. It has serious mojo, but no real magic. It is simply a good handgun—nothing more or less. But members of the .45 cult will not listen to reason; it's a matter of faith with them.

It's a great gun, but if you decide to get one, be sure and learn its manual of arms. I've seen more accidental discharges with the 1911 than with any other firearm. Just getting dialed in on the safeties and getting them into muscle memory takes training, attention, and application. Yeah, I know the gunnies tell us anybody can master the 1911. I've said it myself many times. But many won't. If you're not going to put the work into it, do yourself a favor and choose another handgun.

BROWNING HI-POWER

Browning Hi-Power   Photo courtesy of manufacturer

Also designed by John Browning, chambered for the 9mm and with its magazine holding thirteen rounds, it was the first high capacity automatic pistol. The 1911 has good ergonomics—the Browning's are excellent. Most people who handle this pistol say that it's more comfortable in the hand than any other handgun. The Hi-Power's manual of arms is somewhat simpler than the 1911, but in general, the same comments apply.

FORTY-FIVE VERSUS NINE MILLIMETER

For the benefit of the new shooter, I will address an argument that has been carried on for years and still goes on in gun stores and at ranges. The members of the Cult of the Forty Five often ambush new shooters and ask, "Why buy a puny little 9mm when the more effective manstopper, The Hammer of Thor, the all powerful, the all mighty .45 ACP, is available?" Nine-millimeter users vociferously proselytize for their chosen caliber with various arguments, often aimed at newcomers to shooting.

The two handguns mentioned above, the 1911 and the Hi-Power, were for many years the icons of the opposing camps. Although I have addressed the issue of "stopping power," more detail is warranted to forewarn the new shooter. Here in the U.S., this notion of the .45 as the ultimate handgun caliber has taken on absurd proportions, to the point that a new shooter may well be influenced to purchase a 1911 .45ACP or a 9mm, when neither is a good choice. In my view, the controversy is one that accomplishes nothing but the consumption of much paper that could be put to better use. I address it only because it is a heated topic of discussion at virtually every range I have visited in the past few years, with much of the heat coming from those who have never heard a shot fired in anger. If I could lay this non-issue to rest, I suspect I would be doing many new shooters a favor.

At Smoke Bomb Hill (the home of Special Forces-the Green Berets) in the early sixties, most of us selected the Browning Hi-Power over the Colt .45 for our primary personal handgun. We did so for a number of reasons.

There was the feedback from the many men who had much combat experience, both in uniform and in non-uniformed service going back to World War II. The consensus was that there was little difference in terminal results in the two calibers. There were also, at that time, a number of engagements in progress that provided immediate information. This feedback was considered particularly pertinent because some missions required personnel to deploy in civilian clothing and to not be visibly armed. Therefore, much weight was given to the importance of the handgun, a weapon normally of little concern on a battlefield.

Further, those deployed in civilian clothing much preferred the Hi-Power due to its large magazine capacity and the fact that an individual could carry and conceal more rounds on his person. There were also the results from medical research that strongly indicated that there was little difference in wounding between the 9mm FMJ and the .45 FMJ. In other words, caliber was a non-issue.

"But wait," I hear someone saying. "That's old school. What about now? Everything's different now." OK, let's talk about now. Now the nine-millimeter is our current handgun service cartridge, as well as that of dozens of other countries. In fact the nine-millimeter is virtually the universal handgun caliber choice of military services worldwide. (You think all those guys all over the world who do this stuff for a living are stupid?)

I am in communication with people currently serving in military and civilian service in Iraq, Afghanistan, and other conflict areas. Most of them have been issued 9mms. A few have been issued .45s. None of them have said a word to me about either round being ineffective. A handgun is not a particularly important weapon to a frontline solider, as he is armed with a rifle, carbine, machine gun, hand grenades, and other war weapons. However, a handgun is of utmost importance to those in non-uniformed service in that it may be their only weapon if they are confronted with a situation where armed enemies grossly outnumber them. Therefore, I consider the conclusions reached at Smoke Bomb Hill back in the sixties, which are also congruent with those in similar service today, to be of considerable importance.

I suspect this so-called *controversy* is one that started in the pages of hobbyist gun magazines. But wherever its genesis, the discussion has reached the point of absurdity. I was buying some 9mm ammunition in a gun shop recently, when another customer said to me, "You better not rely on that nine millimeter stuff. Get yourself a forty-five. Everybody knows that nine millimeter just slips right on through your body without causing any damage."

I did not engage this gentleman in conversation. It seemed hopeless. But my thoughts ran like this, "Slip through my body without damage? Excuse me? Slip through what—my liver, heart, lungs, bladder, spleen, a kidney, through muscles and blood vessels, or maybe it would just slip through my breastbone? Ask yourself this: just what part of your body would not be damaged by a nine millimeter or a twenty-two, slipping right on through it? (I don't want any bullet slipping through any part of my body. Nuff said.)

Author's Advice

I have personally used handguns (although not all models), from all but two of the companies mentioned. They all make good serviceable, reliable guns. Your personal selection should be influenced by how the gun feels in your hand, how well it points for you, and how well you can shoot it.

SERVICE AUTOMATICS

The pistols in this category are those used by our armed forces, police departments, and many specialized units. Many non-uniformed professionals also choose handguns in this category for the obvious reasons of superior performance. Service pistols are more powerful, generally have a greater practical range, and carry more ammunition than smaller handguns. These pistols may not be the best choice for concealed carry, but they are the best choice in terms of overall performance. They really are not all that hard to master, if you make the commitment to do the work and then carry through.

BERETTA

The Beretta 92 double action automatic is our current military service sidearm. It has also been chosen by many police departments. It's reliable, accurate, and an excellent handgun in almost every respect, although a little large for some hands.

Beretta 92FS Photo courtesy of manufacturer

BROWNING

Browning continues making its Hi-Power along with a number of more modern designs, all with the exceptional Browning quality.

Browning Hi-Power Photo courtesy of manufacturer

SIGARMS

I don't think I've ever seen a Sig that was anything other than accurate, well-made, and reliable. The 226, an excellent 9mm service pistol, is in use by a number of government agencies, as are the smaller models, such as the 228, in this series. The 220 is probably the most accurate .45 ACP I've fired, other than specialized custom pistols.

Sigarms 220 Elite Carry Blk   Photo courtesy of manufacturer

Sigarms P226 Beauty   Photo courtesy of manufacturer

HECKLER & KOCH

H&K is known for making durable, innovative, and reliable guns. The USP is a robust example of the H&K approach and is in use by certain units in our armed forces.

H&K Universal Service Pistol   Photo courtesy of manufacturer

The H&K P7 is out of production, but it is well worth searching out a used one. Its unique squeeze cocker is about the simplest to use and has the safest cocking and safety mechanism I've ever seen. Other than the Sig 210, this is far and away the most accurate 9mm I've ever fired, with one hundred yard hits on steel plates being common. The P7 is easy to shoot, and with its flat profile easy to carry.

GLOCK

Everyone who has been to a shoot 'em up movie knows that Glock makes plastic pistols. Many, if not most police departments in the U.S. have adopted Glocks. The G17 9mm was the first Glock, followed by the slightly smaller G19, and much later by the (sort of), pocket-sized G26.

The Glock manual of arms is simplicity itself. I have given Glock 19s to one of my sons and one of my brothers-in-law, and recommended them to at least a dozen friends, most of who were not into guns. Glocks are, in some ways, the gun for the person who doesn't care much about guns. They are reliable. They require minimal care. They are reasonably accurate.

Glock 19   Photo courtesy of manufacturer

SPRINGFIELD

In addition to their all-steel 1911s, Springfield offers a number of very well-made and designed polymer-framed pistols. All that I have fired have worked well and been fairly accurate. The grip of the ones I have fired is thinner, and therefore for some people more comfortable than the rather fat handled Glock.

SMITH & WESSON

S&W was a pioneer is U.S.-made, double action automatics. They continue production in both steel and alloy-framed pistols, and have introduced a range of polymer-framed guns. Smith is still in production on some of the finest revolvers ever made. Although revolvers may not be service handguns today, if you are not comfortable with an automatic and want a powerful handgun, you might want to take a look at the Model 19. I know of no better revolver.

Springfield EMP 1911-A1   Photo courtesy of manufacturer

FN HERSTAL FIVESEVEN

The 5.7X28 caliber was developed by FN some years ago and is the foundation of their FiveSeveN system. This round and the weapons that use it have generated considerable controversy, more in the U.S. than in Europe due

S&W Model 19   Photo by Justin Ayres

FN5.7 in case

to its radical approach. In a sense, this round and the FiveSeveN pistol redefine the handgun performance envelope, which is something the militaries of many countries have been searching for. The handgun is now in use with some U.S. police departments, a number of federal agencies, and various European special operations groups.

The FiveSeveN uses a small caliber projectile with a muzzle velocity in excess of 2000 feet per second (faster than any other handgun round) and has a flat trajectory. It is easy to shoot due to the lack of recoil, a little more than that of a .22 pistol. From reports I have heard and read, the round produces severe wounds, well beyond those of standard service rounds.

I have spoken with people who have used them in action, including SWAT team members, covert operators, and one clandestine agent, all of whom stated that it is highly effective, even devastating in terminal effect. I have read one second-hand report from a police officer who said the round did not perform for him. But the majority opinion, based on a very limited amount of respondents, is that this round and pistol is everything it's said to be. Quite a few police officers have privately purchased FiveSeveNs for off-duty use.

There have been two topics of some controversy attached to this pistol and its round. The first is that the military duty round (which is FMJ and not available to the public), will penetrate body armor and therefore is a "cop killer." This is, of course, nonsense. There are many standard rounds that will defeat body armor. If someone has the criminal intention of murdering a police officer, he doesn't need a specialized round to do so. The second point of controversy has to do with the terminal effect of the round. Some simply don't think a small caliber round can be effective—regardless of velocity. We saw the same argument when the 5.56 was adapted in place of the 7.62 and have seen the results. The 5.56 has proven effective in over thirty years of service.

From my point of view, the round and the pistol appear to have much promise. Although the pistol is about the same size as a Glock 17, it is even lighter in weight and therefore easier to carry. It is more accurate at long range than any current service pistol I have fired, and not only in the hands of experienced shooters. Three of my friends, none with more than basic handgun abilities, were able to consistently hit large paper plates at 150 yards, which is exceptional, extraordinary in fact, and does indeed change the performance envelope of the standard service pistol.

While at a range trying out the FiveSeveN, I was approached by another shooter who asked if he could try the pistol. I agreed. After firing three rounds he put down the handgun and said, "It don't have any kick. How can it hurt anyone?"

If you've been reading the previous pages you know the answer to that question. I explained certain basic concepts to my fellow shooter. He said, "I don't know. That's like a little ol twenty-two. It won't do no more than poke a hole in somebody like an ice pick. That ain't nothin to stop a man." I thanked the gentleman for his input and resumed shooting.

Two Walther PPKs one .380 & one .22

Walther P38   Photo by Justin Ayres

The FiveSeveN system might be the greatest thing since the invention of the repeating firearm or not. Time will tell us more. But one thing we can be certain of is that any metal projectile that strikes you while traveling at 2000 feet per second will purely mess you up. (Sorry if that sounds rude. Of late my patience has been worn thin by willful ignorance.)

WALTHER

I have had no personal experience with any of the newer Walthers, but am told by friends in the shooting business that they are good guns. I have used older models for over forty years.

P-38 and P-5

Much vilified by certain experts, the P-38 is, in its better versions, a good handgun. The war surplus models required a trigger job to correct its heavy, rough pull; however, those manufactured later did not. The P-38 was the first double action automatic in a service caliber pistol. Most that I have fired have been quite accurate. The P-38 is no longer in production, but good used examples can be found.

The lineal descent of the P-38, the P-5, is an excellent service pistol—highly accurate, compact, and has good ergonomics. The Walther P-88, also out of production, is one of the finest services pistols ever made.

DOWNSIZED SERVICE PISTOLS

There is an ongoing effort to downsize pistols that shoot the service cartridges. This is one approach to the "more power, less gun" problem. I doubt this is really the solution and I suspect that the answer will come from an unexpected technical development.

POCKET PISTOLS IN SERVICE CALIBERS

KAHR P9

Kahr pistols appear to be well made. I have never fired one. I mention them here because a number of shooters whose skills I respect have told me they are accurate, reliable, and that they like them very much. I am also informed that the smaller ones, especially in .40 caliber, kick like a Missouri mule.

Shown K9, Matte stainless steel (K9093C)

Kahr K9093

Photo courtesy of manufacturer

BABY GLOCK

The first "baby" Glock was the G26 in 9mm; others have followed in larger calibers. I find the G26 to shoot as well as the G19. It is shorter in both dimensions, as thick as the larger pistols, and so, for me, not particularly concealable.

Kimber, Springfield, Colt and others also make excellent quality pocket-sized (if you have really big pockets) versions of their service pistols. If you can handle them and carry them, they might be a good choice. (However, they are more difficult to control than the full-sized service pistols.)

POCKET PISTOLS

Pocket pistols tend to be considerably thinner than even downsized service pistols, sometimes lighter in weight, and therefore easier to carry concealed. Being of less power, these pistols are as easy to shoot as they are to carry. Excellent accuracy can be obtained from many of them. All of this taken together makes them a good self-defense choice for a civilian who chooses to not carry a larger gun.

This category of handgun is extremely popular, not only with civilians, but with armed undercover or off-duty professionals. Even some gunnies would be embarrassed for their fellow gun enthusiasts to learn that they carried a "mouse gun." (There's a saying in the shooting community, "Everyone talks .45, shoots 9mm, and carries .380. That's about right, if you include .32, .22 and .25 in the carry category.)

BERETTA CHEETAH

The Cheetah, available in .22 and .380, appears to be the double action descendant of the 70 series. Double action is a good thing, especially in a pocket pistol. It offers a greater level of safety and requires more deliberation to squeeze off that first round. As far as I can tell, Beretta doesn't make any bad guns. I have fired a friend's Cheetah. It worked well with no malfunctions and very good accuracy.

Beretta 80 Cheetah :22   Photo courtesy of manufacturer

BERETTA MODEL 70 SERIES

The Beretta Model 70 series was offered in .22, .32 and .380. A single action auto once popular with the covert and clandestine community (and still is with some), the Model 70 in .22 caliber became famous or infamous, as the weapon of choice for Israel's Kidon (assassination) teams. Less known is that the Model 70, in .22 caliber, was issued to Israel's katsas (intelligence officers) as a self-protection handgun. A number of katsas overcame a team of Palestinians armed with fully automatic weapons during an attempted bombing at Rome's airport armed with only their .22 pistols. Clearly tactics and aggression were the deciding factors. Hardware rarely is.

One of my best friends who I served with for two years, chose the Model 70 in a .22 caliber as his personal piece and got excellent service from it. No longer in production, used ones are sometimes available. Beretta makes similar models today in double action.

BERSA

This Argentine company produces, among other firearms, pocket pistols modeled on the Walter PP PPK series. Available in .22 and .380, the ones I have fired were reasonably accurate and reliable. The prices and the general quality make these guns a bargain.

Bersa Thunder   Photo by Justin Ayres

SIGARMS

The Sig 232 is a top quality pocket pistol. Available in .380, it fits most people's hands. The ergonomics make the recoil hardly noticeable, even for a small woman with little training. I trained a small-framed woman on the Sig 230, the 232's immediate predecessor. She fired a total of fifteen hundred rounds. There were no reliability issues and it was as accurate as my personal Walther. It pointed well for her and fit her hand comfortably. Not once did she experience sore hands. This may well be the best .380 on the market today. You can occasionally find one of the old Sig 230s around, but not very often. Those who have them tend to keep them (and for good reason.)

S&W M67FC   Photo courtesy of manufacturer
A variation on the basic Model 36

Walther PPK .22

Walther PPK .22

SMITH & WESSON MODEL 36 ET AL

There are other companies making small-framed, short-barreled revolvers besides S&W, such as Tauru. But I am most familiar with the S&Ws. Smith makes about 100 variations on this theme. I can't keep track of them all, but they seem to be cut from the same cloth, so to speak. Back in the day (as my sons say), I used one and it worked as advertised, but I haven't used a revolver for anything other than hunting for at least thirty years. The small autos offer too many advantages. However, if you're that person who cannot deal with an auto, these little handguns will serve you well—within their limitations.

WALTHER PP &PPK

I bought my first Walther PPK a couple of years before I ever heard of James Bond, and before any of the movies were actually released. Many think of the PPK as The James Bond Gun, but in fact, Ian Fleming equipped his fictional hero with a pistol that was in common use in the covert and clandestine community since before World War II. A double action automatic offered in calibers .22, .32, and .380 the PP and PPK, a shorter version of the PP, has been in production since 1929.

The pocket-sized Walther was first recommended to me by a Hungarian Freedom Fighter who had fought Russian tanks with bottles of flaming gasoline in the streets of Budapest. Gabor (not his real name) had also accounted for a number of Russian soldiers with his 7.65 (.32) Walther PPK. I shared a barracks at Smoke Bomb Hill with him and some of his friends who had escaped the Iron Curtain in the late fifties.

One night when we were talking weapons and tactics for urban guerrilla warfare, Gabor said, "I know, I know, in America everything must be jumbo. It is a, what…a cultural thing. Cars are jumbo, beefsteaks are jumbo, even women's breasts must be jumbo, and especially guns must be jumbo. But you should understand that it's not only the cowboys with their blazing .45s that know how to employ guns. In Europe, we have seen more war, more fighting, more death, than Americans can imagine. There are many of us who have done much fighting and know a great deal about firearms from using them in battle."

According to Gabor and his friends, he had killed at least four Russian soldiers in pitched battle, the Russians being armed with assault rifles and backed up by tanks. How did he do that with his miserable little .32, which most experts today agree isn't enough gun to reliably put down possums at ten paces? Was it simply that Russian soldiers, circa 1956, were a bunch of weaklings ready to drop at a loud noise? (I've known a few Russian soldiers. None of them were that. And I don't think the ones in Budapest were either.) Gabor did what he did the same way hundreds of other unnamed and hard-pressed men and women have survived and triumphed, with marksmanship, tactics, discipline and a cool head. He didn't panic. He used what he had and used it within its limits.

Walther PPK .380 & pocket litter

Walther PPK .22 & other working tools

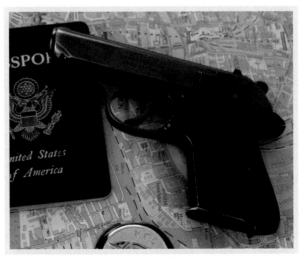
Two Walther PPKs, one in .22 and one in .380

I've owned a dozen or so Walthers in the PP and PPK series over the years. The German and French-made pistols were reliable and extraordinarily accurate. Those made in the U.S. by Interarms suffer from uneven quality control and are generally inaccurate, unreliable, and will need the attention of a gunsmith before they can be relied upon.

PALM PISTOLS

Many of the fellows who hang out at shooting ranges and gun shops love to poke fun at these little pistols. You might hear comments like, "Shoot me with that and I'll get mad and kick your ***," and similar witty remarks. Make no mistake; these little pistols can be deadly.

Intuitively, many people unfamiliar with guns, will chose one of these little pistols for self protection. They do so because they know they will actually carry it every day and will have it when the unexpected occurs. They figure that the little gun will, maybe, do enough damage to stop an assailant, and they aren't wrong.

I am willing to bet that if I could somehow magically shake down everyone across the country, I would find more of these tiny pistols than any other type of handgun (and that's including the cops). More police officers than want to admit carry one of these or a pocket pistol as an everyday backup or as an off-duty gun when the backup becomes the only gun. Are all of these people mentally challenged? No, they are not. They made their choice for good reasons. Don't they know these popguns are useless? Actually, they know these guns are not useless. These pistols are appropriate for their environment and threat level.

None of the people who choose the palm or pocket pistols expect to get into running gun battles on their way home from work. Yes, it could happen. But you gotta figure the odds. We live in America. Remember? We have some areas that are dangerous. We have armed criminals. Muggers and rapists are out there. But get a grip; we don't live in downtown Mosul or Kabul. When was the last time you saw a firefight at your local mall? Mostly what people want is to be able to STOP a criminal who is attacking them. At arms length, a fast three round burst of .25 or .22 in the face will have a pretty good chance of doing just that.

BERETTA 950

Variations of this model have been in production for fifty years. A single action auto formally available in .25 (6.35) and .22 Short the current production is only in .25. Used ones in .22 short can be found but they are not reliable. The .22 Short does not feed reliably in these pistols. If you choose a 950 get it in .25.

BERETTA 21

This is an updated, double action descendant of the 950 and the discontinued 20 (also a double action) and is the standard by which other palm pistols are judged. I have owned both .22 and .25 caliber 20 and 21 Berettas and they never failed to do what they were supposed to do. The .22 wants to be fed high-speed rounds, at least mine did. In over 3000 rounds of high-speed .22, I never had a malfunction. The .25 would handle anything from frangible Glaser or MagSafe to pre-war stuff and current productions.

.22 Beretta Bobcat Model 21A Photo courtesy of manufacturer

KEL-TEC

The K32 and the Kel-Tec Company are relatively new to gunmaking, at least compared to Beretta, which has been in business since 1520. I include them here because two of my experienced friends think highly of them and because the K32 is a polymer-framed palm sized .32 weighing only six ounces. You can even get it with a clip on the side, like a Spyderco pocketknife. I haven't fired one yet; but I'm told they are good little guns, although some of them seem to need a bit of after-purchase care. The company has the reputation of taking immediate care of all customer complaints. If you get one of these, be sure to fire a few hundred rounds with it before relying on it.

NORTH AMERICAN FIREARMS

The NA Guardian is offered in both .25 and .32. Both are palm sized; both of high quality. They come without sights, which is fine for 99% of the projected uses of the pistol. However, I suspect that these guns are capable of pretty good accuracy at longer ranges.

North American PR25 Photo courtesy of manufacturer

WALTHER TPH

I've owned six TPHs. Two of them were German-made, the other four were made in the U.S. by Interarms, under license. Unfortunately, the German guns cannot be imported due to legislation. I say unfortunately, because my German TPHs have been the best palm pistols I've ever owned, ever seen, or ever heard of. They have been totally reliable with high-speed ammo. On a good day with my German TPHs, I have outshot friends with target pistols. One-inch groups at twenty-five yard were doable (on a really good day,) which means hitting button-sized targets at twelve feet was a piece of cake.

None of the Interarms TPHs functioned properly or shot to point of aim. One of them shot twelve inches high at twenty-one feet. Interarms seemed not to be interested in correcting the problems. I dumped them with fair warning to a guy who wanted to try his hand at gunsmithing.

TARGET PISTOLS FOR SELF-DEFENSE

What about that twenty-two target pistol you bought to practice and learn with; can't it be used for self-defense? If you've read everything up to here, you probably know the answer. It's the size of a service pistol, so it's no easier to drag around with you. But if you've been practicing, you can probably put ten rounds into a circle the size of a teacup at, say, fifteen or twenty feet in a couple of seconds. What do you think?

BACK-UP GUNS

Few civilians are going to go about their affairs toting two guns. Nor do I recommend you do so. I do however recommend that once a person finds a gun he is comfortable with, he buy another one of the same model for a back-up in case the first gun goes missing or your pet pit-bull wolverine crossbreed eats it, or whatever. If one gun goes down, then you will still be armed.

RELIABILITY

Whichever gun you choose, it's gotta go bang every time you pull the trigger, if it's loaded. If it doesn't, it isn't fit for self-defense. It's generally agreed that if you can't fire at least two hundreds rounds without any kind of jam or misfire, the particular gun and ammo combination you're using is not reliable. If I get a malfunction that I cannot immediately explain, I retire the gun until the problem is solved. You may need to have a gunsmith take a look if you're having problems, although sometimes simply changing ammo will do the trick. Either way, correct the problem or get another gun.

Author's Advice

There is an oft-repeated rule, which is said to be the first rule of gunfighting: Have a gun. *It's a good rule, but I don't think it should be the first rule—maybe the second. Here's the first rule of gunfighting according to Ayres:* Don't get into a gunfight.

The only thing worse than doing violence to another person, is to become a victim of violence. There is no moral justification for anyone who would victimize another. However, self-defense and the defense of others is not only morally justified and righteous, it's basic to our humanity. Now, do us both a favor and go back to the beginning of this section and read again my opening comments about the nature of real- world gunfighting. Trust me, this is the first rule: Don't get into a gunfight. *Self-defense and the defense of others is the only reason to break that rule.*

SECTION 5

APPENDICES

Guns and Federal Laws

The National Instant Criminal Background Check System (NICS) is designed to prevent the legal purchase of firearms by criminals and others who are not allowed to legally purchase a firearm. Below is a summary of the actual wording of the federal law. If you would like to know more about this law, or if any part of it is unclear, you should consult with an attorney.

The laws governing the transportation of firearms in checked luggage by airline passengers are also below. In addition to the regulations laid down by the Federal Government, each airline has its individual regulations which are subject to change, as are the Federal regulations.

You should always check with the airline before any flight to determine the regulations in effect at that time. It is also advisable to contact the Transportation Security Authority (TSA) before a flight to determine if any regulations have been changed since this book has been printed.

NICS PROGRAM SUMMARY
DETAILED NICS PROGRAM INFORMATION

In November 1993, the Brady Handgun Violence Prevention Act (Brady Act) was signed into law. The Brady Act requires Federal Firearms Licensees (FFLs) to request background checks on individuals attempting to receive a firearm. The permanent provisions of the Brady Act, which went into effect on November 30, 1998, required the United States Attorney General to establish the National Instant Criminal Background Check System (NICS) so that any FFL may contact for information to be supplied immediately as to whether the receipt of a firearm by a prospective transferee would violate Title 18, United States Code (U.S.C.), Section 922 (g) or (n) or state law.

The NICS Section, located at the FBI's Criminal Justice Information Services Division in Clarksburg, West Virginia, provides full service to FFLs in 30 states and five U.S. territories, and the District of Columbia. Upon completion of the required Bureau of Alcohol, Tobacco, Firearms and Explosives (ATF) Form 4473, FFLs contact the FBI NICS Section, via a toll-free telephone number or electronically through the NICS E-Check System via the Internet, to request a background check with the descriptive information provided on the ATF Form 4473. The NICS is customarily available 17 hours a day, 7 days a week, including holidays (except for Christmas).

Thirteen states have agencies acting on behalf of the NICS in a full Point-Of-Contact (POC) capacity. These POC states, which have agreed to implement and maintain their own Brady NICS Program, conduct firearm background checks for FFLs' transactions in their respective states by electronically accessing the NICS. Upon completion of the required ATF Form 4473, the FFLs conducting business in the POC states contact a designated state agency to initiate a NICS background check in lieu of contacting the NICS Section.

Additionally, eight states are currently sharing responsibility with the NICS Section by acting as partial POCs. Partial-POC states have agencies designated to conduct checks for handguns and/or handgun permits, while the NICS Section handles the processing of the states transactions for long gun purchases. The NICS Participation Map, as illustrated below, depicts each state's level of participation with the NICS.

Record information that would exhibit and/or clarify an individuals prohibitive status pursuant to the Brady Act is vital to the NICS in order to determine subject eligibility to receive and/or possess a firearm. Records contained within the databases searched by the NICS include those of the Interstate Identification Index (e.g., millions of criminal history records), the National Crime Information Center (e.g., protection orders and active felony or misdemeanor warrants) and the NICS Index, a database created solely for the use of the NICS which contains information provided by local, state and federal agencies pertaining to persons prohibited under federal law from receiving or possessing a firearm. Additionally, a fourth search of the applicable databases via the Department of Homeland Security's United States Immigration and Customs Enforcement will be conducted for background checks initiated on all non-United States citizens.

The federally prohibitive criteria outlining the reasons an individual may be precluded from the transfer/possession of a firearm or firearm-related permit, pursuant to Title 18 U.S.C., §§ 922 (g) and (n), are as follows:

- A person convicted in any court of a crime punishable by imprisonment for a term exceeding one year, whether or not sentence is imposed. This includes misdemeanor offenses with a potential term of imprisonment in excess of two years, whether or not sentence was imposed.

- Persons who are fugitives of justice; for example, the subject of an active felony or misdemeanor warrant.

- An unlawful user and/or an addict of any controlled substance; for example, a person convicted for the use or possession of a controlled substance within the past year, or a person with multiple arrests for the use or possession of a controlled substance within the past five years with the most recent arrest occurring within the past year, or a person found through a drug test to use a controlled substance unlawfully, provided the test was administered within the past year.

- A person adjudicated mental defective or involuntarily committed to a mental institution or incompetent to handle own affairs, including dispositions to criminal charges pertaining to found not guilty by reason of insanity or found incompetent to stand trial.

- An alien illegally/unlawfully in the United States or a non-immigrant who does not qualify for the exceptions under Title 18 U.S.C. Section 922(y); for example, not have possession of a valid hunting license.

- A person dishonorably discharged from the United States Armed Forces.

- A person who has renounced his/her United States citizenship.

- The subject of a protective order issued after a hearing in which the respondent had notice that restrains them from harassing, stalking, or threatening an intimate partner or child of such partner. This does not include ex parte orders.

- A person convicted in any court of a misdemeanor crime which includes the use or attempted use of physical force or threatened use of a deadly weapon and the defendant was the spouse, former spouse, parent, guardian of the victim, by a person with whom the victim shares a child in common, by a person who is cohabiting with or has cohabited in the past with the victim as a spouse, parent, guardian or similarly situated to a spouse, parent or guardian of the victim.

- A person under indictment or information for a crime punishable by imprisonment for a term exceeding one year.

This is a transcript of the laws covering transportation of firearms by air.

TSA
TRAVELING WITH SPECIAL ITEMS
FIREARMS & AMMUNITION

You may only transport firearms, ammunition and firearm parts in your checked baggage. Firearms, ammunition and firearm parts are prohibited from carry-on baggage.

There are certain limited exceptions for law enforcement officers who may fly armed by meeting the requirements of Title 49 CFR § 1544.219. Law enforcement officers should read our policies on traveling with guns.

The key regulatory requirements to transporting firearms, firearm parts or ammunition in checked baggage are:

- You must declare all firearms to the airline during the ticket counter check-in process.
- The firearm must be unloaded.
- The firearm must be in a hard-sided container.
- The container must be locked.
- We recommend that you provide the key or combination to the security officer if he or she needs to open the container. You should remain present during screening to take the key back after the container is cleared. If you are not present and the security officer must open the container, we or the airline will make a reasonable attempt to contact you. If we can't contact you, the container will not be placed on the plane. Federal regulations prohibit unlocked gun cases (or cases with broken locks) on aircraft.
- You must securely pack any ammunition in fiber (such as cardboard), wood or metal boxes or other packaging that is specifically designed to carry small amounts of ammunition.
- You can't use firearm magazines/clips for packing ammunition unless they completely and securely enclose the ammunition (e.g., by securely covering the exposed portions of the magazine or by securely placing the magazine in a pouch, holder, holster or lanyard).
- You may carry the ammunition in the same hard-sided case as the firearm, as long as you pack it as described above.
- You can't bring black powder or percussion caps used with black-powder type firearms in either your carry-on or checked baggage.

We and other authorities strictly enforce these regulations. Violations can result in criminal prosecution and civil penalties of up to $10,000 per violation.

Airlines may have their own additional requirements on the carriage of firearms and the amount of ammunition that you may have in your checked baggage. Therefore, travelers should also contact the airline regarding its firearm and ammunition carriage policies.

Also, please note that many other countries

have different laws that address transportation and possession of firearms. If you are traveling internationally, please check with the authorities at your destination about their requirements.

AIRLINE TRANSPORTATION OF FIREARMS

To answer questions new airline security procedures have raised for NRA members transporting firearms in their checked baggage, NRA-ILA staff contacted the Office of Security Regulation and Policy at the Transportation Security Administration (TSA).

You can transport a firearm in your checked baggage subject to state and local restrictions, but you should first check with your airline or travel agent to see if firearms are permitted in checked baggage on the airline you are flying. Ask about limitations or fees that may apply at this time. NRA-ILA is working toward achieving uniformity and fairness in the rules and regulations that law-abiding gun owners face in their travels.

While surely few NRA members could forget this, the Transportation Security Administration (TSA) wants to remind all travelers that attempting to bring firearms onto a plane in carry-on luggage is a serious federal violation. This is a "strict liability" offense, and TSA says violators can be, and have been, convicted regardless of criminal intent, or even if they simply forgot they possessed a firearm. TSA is obliged to enforce all the existing laws within its jurisdiction and will do so vigorously.

Firearms carried as checked baggage must be unloaded, packed in a locked hard-sided container and declared to the airline at check-in. Only the passenger may have the key or combination. Small arms ammunition must be placed in an appropriate container: "securely packed in fiber, wood, or metal boxes, or other packaging specifically designed to carry small amounts of ammunition. " Under TSA regulations, ammunition may be packed in the same locked container as the unloaded firearm, but airline rules may differ.

Some airlines, as private businesses, have imposed additional restrictions or requirements, such as limiting the number of guns that can be transported in a single case, or providing different standards under which gun cases may or may not be exempt from excess baggage limitations. Especially for international flights, many airlines follow industry guidelines that limit ammunition to 11 lbs. per passenger. Again, NRA-ILA is working to secure fair and uniform rules.

Following Congress's mandate that all checked baggage must be screened for explosives, many travelers have become concerned by announcements that passengers should leave bags unlocked to allow hand inspection. This suggestion, the TSA made clear, does not apply to baggage containing firearms. All gun containers must still be locked after they are declared at the ticket counter.

Checked bags—including those containing firearms—will then be screened for explosives by various means. Depending on the airport, methods may include high-tech "sniffers" that analyze chemical vapors, X-ray machines, trained bomb detection dogs or a combination of these systems. Not all of these methods can differentiate explosives from the gunpowder residues on a fired gun or in loaded ammunition.

If the screening detects explosive materials other than those associated with ammunition, or if screeners can't determine the exact nature of the alarm, and if all means available (such as X-rays) cannot rule out the possible presence of explosives, TSA screeners, working with airline representatives, will make every effort to contact the passenger so that the passenger can supply the key or combination to open the case, eliminating the need to break locks.

Cases will not be labeled as containing firearms. That practice was outlawed almost 10 years ago. Federal law now states: "No common or contract carrier shall require or cause any label, tag, or other written notice to be placed on the outside of any package, luggage, or other container that such package, luggage, or other container contains a firearm." [18 USC Sec. 922(e)] TSA will warn any airline that is marking cases that it is in violation of the law.

As always, since some airline counter clerks may have little training or experience in these procedures, gun owners should contact the airline in advance, obtain a written copy of the airline policy from a reservation clerk or the airline's website, and bring it to the airport in order to answer any questions that arise at check-in. For further information, see: www.tsa.gov.

State Laws on Firearms

From coast to coast, our gun laws are a thicket of thorns and confusion. What is perfectly legal in one state is often considered illegal in another state. Gun laws also vary from county to county and city to city. Concerning firearms there is no way to know what is legal and what is illegal without reading the actual laws in force, and even then, you may need the services of an attorney to decipher them.

If all you want to do is buy a firearm, your local gun store will probably be able to inform you of what you must do in order to legally purchase it in that locale. If you want to shoot a firearm, you will need to know where and under what conditions you can legally do so.

Carrying a firearm is a whole other thing. There are states that have "shall issue laws" that require the regulatory agency to issue a Concealed Carry Permit. There are also states they make it virtually impossible to get a CCP. It is entirely possible to get a CCP in one county of a given state, and then learn that the permit in not good in another county. There is no uniformity in firearm law from state to state.

Contact your state Attorney General's office and request a copy of the statutes covering firearm ownership. The contact information for each state is in this appendix.

You must contact your local authorities to determine local laws and ordinances.

Alabama

Office of the Attorney General
State House
11 South Union Street
Montgomery, AL 36130
(334) 242-7300

Alaska

Office of the Attorney General
Post Office Box 110300
Diamond Courthouse, 4th Floor
Juneau, AK 99811-0300
(907) 465-3600

Arizona

Office of the Attorney General
1275 West Washington Street
Phoenix, AZ 85007
(602) 542-4266

Arkansas

Office of the Attorney General
200 Tower Building
323 Center Street
Little Rock, AR 72201-2610
(800) 482-8982

California

Office of the Attorney General
1300 I Street, Suite 1740
Sacramento, CA 95814
(916) 445-9555

Colorado

Office of the Attorney General
Department of Law
1525 Sherman Street, 5th Floor
Denver, CO 80203
(303) 866-4500

Connecticut

Office of the Attorney General
55 Elm Street
Hartford, CT 06106
(860) 808-5318

Delaware

Office of the Attorney General
Carvel State Office Building
820 North French Street
Wilmington, DE 19801
(302) 577-8500

District of Columbia

Office of the Corporation Counsel
1350 Pennsylvania Ave., NW
Suite 409
Washington, DC 20004
(202) 727-3400

Florida

Office of the Attorney General
The Capitol
PL 01
Tallahassee, FL 32399-1050
(850) 414-3990

Georgia

Office of the Attorney General
40 Capitol Square
Atlanta, GA 30334-1300
(404) 656-3300

Hawaii

Office of the Attorney General
425 Queen Street
Honolulu, HI 96813
(808) 586-1282

Idaho

Office of the Attorney General
P.O. Box 83720
Boise, ID 83720-0010
(208) 334-2400

Illinois

Office of the Attorney General
James R. Thompson Center South
100 West Randolph Street
12th Floor
Chicago, IL 60601
(312) 814-3000

Indiana

Office of the Attorney General
Indiana Government Center
302 West Washington Street
5th Floor
Indianapolis, IN 46204
(317) 232-6201

Iowa

Office of the Attorney General
Hoover State Office Building
1305 East Walnut
Des Moines, IA 50319
(515) 281-5164

Kansas

Office of the Attorney General
120 S.W. 10th Avenue, 2nd Floor
Topeka, KS 66612-1597
(785) 296-2215

Kentucky

Office of the Attorney General
State Capitol, Room 118
700 Capitol Avenue
Frankfort, KY 40601
(502) 696-5300

Louisiana

Office of the Attorney General
Department of Justice
Post Office Box 94005
Baton Rouge, LA 70804
(225) 326-6000

Maine

Office of the Attorney General
Six State House Station
Augusta, ME 04333-0006
(207) 626-8800

Maryland

Office of the Attorney General
200 Saint Paul Place
Baltimore, MD 21202-2202
(410) 576-6300

Massachusetts

Office of the Attorney General
One Ashburton Place
Boston, MA 02108-1698
(617) 727-2200

Michigan

Office of the Attorney General
Post Office Box 30212
525 West Ottawa Street
Lansing, MI 48909-0212
(517) 373-1110

Minnesota

Office of the Attorney General
State Capitol
Suite 102
St. Paul, MN 55155
(651) 296-3353

Mississippi

Office of the Attorney General
Department of Justice
Post Office Box 220
Jackson, MS 39205-0220
(601) 359-4279

Missouri

Office of the Attorney General
Supreme Court Building
207 West High Street
Jefferson City, MO 65101
(573) 751-3321

Montana
Office of the Attorney General
Justice Building
215 North Sanders
Helena, MT 59620-1401
(406) 444-2026

Nebraska
Office of the Attorney General
State Capitol
Post Office Box 98920
Lincoln, NE 68509-8920
(402) 471-2682

Nevada
Office of the Attorney General
Old Supreme Court Building
100 North Carson Street
Carson City, NV 89701
(775) 684-1100

New Hampshire
Office of the Attorney General
State House Annex
33 Capitol Street
Concord, NH 03301-6397
(603) 271-3658

New Jersey
Office of the Attorney General
Department of Law and
Public Safety
Box 080
Trenton, NJ 08625
(609) 292-8740

New Mexico
Office of the Attorney General
Post Office Drawer 1508
Santa Fe, NM 87504-1508
(505) 827-6000

New York
Office of the Attorney General
Department of Law -The Capitol
Room 220
Albany, NY 12224
(518) 474-7330

North Carolina
Office of the Attorney General
Department of Justice
9001 Mail Service Center
Raleigh, NC 27699
(919) 716-6400

North Dakota

Office of the Attorney General
State Capitol
600 East Boulevard Avenue
Bismarck, ND 58505-0040
(701) 328-2210

Ohio

Office of the Attorney General
State Office Tower
30 East Broad Street, 17th Floor
Columbus, OH 43215-3428
(614) 466-4320

Oklahoma

Office of the Attorney General
State Capitol, Room 112
2300 North Lincoln Boulevard
Oklahoma City, OK 73105
(405) 521-3921

Oregon

Office of the Attorney General
Justice Building
1162 Court Street NE
Salem, OR 97301-4096
(503) 378-4732

Pennsylvania

Office of the Attorney General
1600 Strawberry Square
Harrisburg, PA 17120
(717) 787-3391

Rhode Island

Office of the Attorney General
150 South Main Street
Providence, RI 02903
(401) 274-4400

South Carolina

Office of the Attorney General
Rembert C. Dennis Office Bldg
Post Office Box 11549
Columbia, SC 29211-1549
(803) 734-3970

South Dakota

Office of the Attorney General
500 East Capitol
Pierre, SD 57501-5070
(605) 773-3215

Tennessee

Office of the Attorney General
2nd Floor
Cordell Hull Bldg.
Nashville, Tennessee 37243
(615) 741-3491

Texas

Office of the Attorney General
Capitol Station
Post Office Box 12548
Austin, TX 78711-2548
(512) 463-2100

Utah

Office of the Attorney General
P.O. Box 142320
Salt Lake City, Utah 84114-2320
(801) 538-9600

Vermont

Office of the Attorney General
109 State Street
Montpelier, VT 05609-1001
(802) 828-3171

Virginia

Office of the Attorney General
900 East Main Street
Richmond, VA 23219
(804) 786-2071

Washington

Office of the Attorney General
P.O. Box 40100
1125 Washington Street, SE
Olympia, WA 98504-0100
(360) 753-6200

West Virginia

Office of the Attorney General
State Capitol, Room E26
1900 Kanawha Boulevard East
Charleston, WV 25305
(304) 558-2021

Wisconsin

Office of the Attorney General
114 East State Capitol
Post Office Box 7857
Madison, WI 53707-7857
(608) 266-1221

Wyoming

Office of the Attorney General
123 State Capitol Building
Cheyenne, WY 82002
(307) 777-7841

Fish and Game Agencies

The fish and game folks are good guys. I've often heard complaints about the "Possum Police," as the game wardens are sometimes called. These complaints often come from uninformed hunters who think that hunting or fishing regulations are unduly burdensome or should not apply to them. In all cases, such complaints are inappropriate. Without game wardens and all the scientists and administrators who back them up, there would likely be no game to regulate or hunt and no habitat for wild animals to live in.

Fish and game regulations vary from state to state and from region to region because local conditions vary. These regulations are determined by the state fish and game agencies, administered by them and enforced by them. The regulations are designed (after considerable study by qualified scientists) to insure that the population of game animals is protected and allowed to flourish to the extent that there is habitat, and to insure that there will be future stocks for hunters and fishermen.

Many agency employees are scientists who apply their knowledge and work in the lab and in the field to the betterment of the environment, as well as the animals that live in the wild. Without a sound understanding of environmental conditions and the needs of wildlife, the resource management that has preserved our wild places would not have been possible.

Education is one of the most important jobs for these agencies. They generate informative materials explaining the reasons behind the regulations, as well as the regulations, themselves. As a new hunter, you should make it your business to obtain and read everything your state prints on this topic. I suggest that it would be a good idea for non-hunters to do the same in order to be better informed about the condition of our wild places.

The frontier days are over. The buffalo are gone, as are passenger pigeons. They are gone because they were over-hunted and driven to the point of extinction. At one time there were flights of migrating ducks in flocks so big they blotted out the sun. We will probably never again see such a spectacle. Loss of habitat is a prime contributor to the reduction in ducks and all other game animals. Every time a developer builds another suburb, another population of wild animals is threatened. Fish and game agencies work closely with environmental organizations and builders to try and preserve what wild country we have left.

These agencies really do know how many animals can be taken from an area without endangering the population. Having made it your business to learn the regulations, you should also abide by them. Don't be a poacher – one who hunts or fishes illegally. We all benefit by doing the right thing and following the regulations laid down by the people who know what's best for the wildlife. There are those who persist in taking more than the legal limit or in using illegal hunting methods. Sometimes, those who hunt illegally style themselves as rugged individualists. They may be that, but they are also criminals who harm all of us who care about the wild. Be thankful the Possum Police are on the job.

Alabama Department of Conservation and Natural Resources
64 N. Union Street
Montgomery, Alabama 36130
COMMISSIONER'S OFFICE
(334) 242-3486
www.outdooralabama.com

Alaska Department of Fish and Game
P.O. Box 115526
1255 W. 8th Street
Juneau, AK 99811-5526
(907) 465-4100
 www.adfg.state.ak.us

Arizona Game and Fish Department
5000 W. Carefree Highway
Phoenix, AZ 85086
(602) 942-3000.
www.azgfd.gov

Arkansas Game and Fish Commission
2 Natural Resources Drive Little Rock, AR 72205
(800) 364-4263
www.agfc.com

California Department of Fish and Game
1416 9th Street
Sacramento, CA 95814
(916) 445-0411
www.dfg.ca.gov

**Colorado Department of
Natural Resources
Division of Wildlife (DOW)**
6060 Broadway
Denver, Colorado, 80216
(303) 297-1192
www.dnr.state.co.us

**Connecticut Department
of Environmental Protection**
79 Elm Street
Hartford, CT 06106-5127
(860) 424-3000
www.ct.gov/dep/site/default.asp

**Delaware Department of Natural
Resources and Environmental Control**
Division of Fish & Wildlife
89 Kings Highway
Dover, DE 19901
(302) 739-9910
www.fw.delaware.gov

**Florida Fish and Wildlife
Conservation Commission**
Farris Bryant Building
620 S. Meridian St.
Tallahassee, FL 32399-1600
(850) 488-4676
http://myfwc.com

**Georgia Department of
Natural Resources**
Wildlife Resources Division
2065 U.S. Hwy. 278, S.E.
Social Circle, GA 30025
Hunting and Fishing Licenses:
(706) 557-3597
http://georgiawildlife.dnr.state.ga.us

**Hawaii Department of Land and
Natural Resources**
1151 Punchbowl Street, Rm 325
Honolulu, Hawaii 96813
(808) 587-0166
www.dofaw.net

Idaho Fish and Game Department
600 S. Walnut
Boise, ID 83712
(208) 334-3700
http://fishandgame.idaho.gov

Illinois Department of Natural Resources
One Natural Resources Way
Springfield, IL 62702-1271
(217) 782-6302
http://dnr.state.il.us

**Indiana Department of
Natural Resources**
4850 S. St. Rd. 446
Bloomington, IN 47401
(812) 837-9536
www.in.gov/dnr

Iowa Department of Natural Resources

Henry A. Wallace Building

502 E. 9th Street,

Des Moines, IA 50319-0034

(515) 281-5918

www.iowadnr.com/wildlife/index.html

Kansas Department of Wildlife & Parks

512 SE 25th Ave.

Pratt, KS 67124

(620) 672-5911

www.kdwp.state.ks.us

**Kentucky Department of
Fish and Wildlife Resources**

#1 Sportsman's Lane

Frankfort, KY 40601

(800) 858-1549

www.kdfwr.state.ky.us

**Louisiana Department of
Wildlife and Fisheries**

2000 Quail Drive

Baton Rouge, LA 70808

(225) 765-2800

www.wlf.state.la.us

**Maine Department of Inland Fisheries
and Wildlife**

284 State Street

41 State House Station

Augusta, ME 04333-0041

(207) 287-8000

www.maine.gov/ifw

**Maryland Department of
Natural Resources**

580 Taylor Avenue

Annapolis, Maryland 21401

(877) 620-8367

www.dnr.state.md.us

**Massachusetts Department of
Fish and Game**

Commissioner

Department of Fish & Game

251 Causeway St., Suite 400

Boston, MA 02114

(617) 626-1500

www.mass.gov/dfwele

**Michigan Department of
Natural Resources**

Mason Building, Fourth Floor, P.O. Box
30444, Lansing MI 48909

(517) 373-1263

www.michigan.gov/dnr

**Minnesota Department of
Natural Resources**

500 Lafayette Road

St. Paul, MN 55155-4040

(651) 296-6157

www.dnr.state.mn.us/index.html

Mississippi Department of Wildlife, Fisheries, and Parks

1505 Eastover Drive

Jackson, MS 39211-6374

(601) 432-2400

http://home.mdwfp.com

Missouri Department of Conservation

2901 W. Truman Blvd.

Jefferson City, MO 65109

(573) 751-4115

www.mdc.mo.gov

Montana Department of Fish, Wildlife, and Parks

1420 E 6th Ave.

PO Box 200701

Helena, MT 59620-0701

(406) 444-2535

http://fwp.mt.gov/default.html

Nebraska Game and Parks Commission

2200 N. 33rd Street

Lincoln, NE 68503

(402) 471-0641

www.ngpc.state.ne.us

Nevada Department of Conservation and Natural Resources

Headquarters / Statewide Contacts

1100 Valley Road

Reno, NV 89512

(775) 688-1500

www.ndow.org

New Hampshire Fish and Game Department

11 Hazen Drive

Concord, NH 03301

(603) 271-3214

www.wildlife.state.nh.us

New Jersey Division of Fish, Game and Wildlife

Department of Environmental Protection

P. O. Box 402

Trenton, NJ 08625-0402

(856) 629-0552

www.state.nj.us/dep/fgw

New Mexico Game and Fish Department

P.O. Box 25112

Santa Fe, NM 87504

(505) 222-4731

www.wildlife.state.nm.us

New York State Department of Environmental Conservation

625 Broadway

Albany, New York 12233-0001

888-HUNT-ED2

www.dec.ny.gov

North Carolina Department of Environment and Natural Resources

1751 Varsity Drive

Raleigh, NC

(919) 707-0031

www.ncwildlife.org

North Dakota State Game and Fish Department

100 N. Bismarck Expressway Bismarck, ND 58501-5095

(701) 328-6300

http://gf.nd.gov

Ohio Department of Natural Resources

2045 Morse Rd., Bldg. G, Columbus, OH 43229-6693

800-WILDLIFE

www.dnr.state.oh.us

Oklahoma Department of Wildlife Conservation

1801 N LINCOLN

OKC OK 73105

(405) 522-4572

www.wildlifedepartment.com

Oregon Department of Fish and Wildlife

3406 Cherry Avenue N.E.

Salem, OR 97303-4924

(503) 947-6028

www.dfw.state.or.us

Pennsylvania Department of Conservation and Natural Resources

2001 Elmerton Avenue

Harrisburg, PA 17110-9797

(717) 787-4250

www.pgc.state.pa.us

Rhode Island Department of Environmental Management

Stedman Government Center

4808 Tower Hill Road

Wakefield, RI 02879

(401) 789-3094

www.dem.ri.gov/index.htm

South Carolina Department of Natural Resources

Embert C. Dennis Building, 1000 Assembly Street, Columbia, SC 29201

(800) 277-4301

www.dnr.sc.gov

South Dakota Game, Fish and Parks

523 East Capitol Avenue

Pierre, SD 57501

(605) 773-3485

www.sdgfp.info

Tennessee Wildlife Resources Agency

200 Lowell Thomas Drive

Jackson, TN 38301

(731) 423-5725

www.state.tn.us/twra

Texas Parks and Wildlife

4200 Smith School Road

Austin, TX 78744

800-792-1112 X63

www.tpwd.state.tx.us

**Utah State Department of
Natural Resources**

Utah Division of Wildlife Resources

1594 W. North Temple

Salt Lake City, Utah 84116

(801) 538-4700

http://wildlife.utah.gov/index.php

Vermont Agency of Natural Resources

Vermont Fish & Wildlife Department

10 South

103 South Main Street

Waterbury, VT 05671-0501

802-241-3720

www.vtfishandwildlife.com

**Virginia Department of Game
and Inland Fisheries**

4010 West Broad Street, P.O. Box 11104,

Richmond, Virginia 23230

(804) 367-1000

www.dgif.virginia.gov

**Washington Department of
Fish and Wildlife**

1111 Washington St. SE

Olympia, WA 98501

(360) 902-2200

http://wdfw.wa.gov

**West Virginia Department of
Natural Resources**

State Capitol

Building 3, Room 812

1900 Kanawha Boulevard, E.

Charleston, WV 25305

(304) 558-2771

www.wvdnr.gov/hunting

**Wisconsin Department of
Natural Resources**

101 S. Webster Street . PO Box 7921

Madison, Wisconsin 53707-7921

(608) 266-2621

www.dnr.state.wi.us/org/land/wildlife

Wyoming Game and Fish Department

5400 Bishop Boulevard

Cheyenne, WY 82006

(307) 777-4600

http://gf.state.wy.us

Case and Safe Manufacturers

When you buy your guns, get lockable cases to protect them. By itself, a locked case won't stop a determined thief, little will, but it's the first line of defense against theft and more importantly, an effective safety device that could prevent a potential disaster by stopping an inquisitive kid.

These days, many jurisdictions require all firearms to be transported in a locked case, unless you have a Concealed Carry Permit or are in the hunting field. Both hard and soft cases are available at most any gun shops. All airlines that I am aware of require a locked hard case for the transportation of a checked firearm.

In addition to these reasons for getting a case, a good case will protect your rifle, shotgun, or handgun from getting knocked around in the truck of your car on the way to the range or hunting area. I have a case for each firearm I own, as do other gun owners I know. When not in use I store my firearms in their individual cases. I recommend that you do the same.

For additional protection you might consider getting a gun safe, which can deter even a determined thief, at least for a while, and will provide another layer of preventative protection against over curious or unschooled kids and other unauthorized persons. If you bolt your safe into the floor, you will prevent thieves from simply hoisting it on a dolly and rolling out the door while you're away. There are also small safes that are suitable for one or two firearms and can be discreetly secured inside a piece of furniture.

Ace Case Manufacturing LLC

160 N. Main St

St. Clair, MO 63077

(800) 544-0008

www.acecase.com

A.G. English

708 S 12th Street

Broken Arrow, OK 74012

(800) 251-3399

(888) GUN-SAFE

(800) 222-7233

www.agenglish.com

Americase, Inc.

1610 East Main St.

Waxahachie, TX 75165

(800) 972-2737

(972) 937-3629

Fax: (972) 937-8373

www.americase.com

Bear Track Cases

Made by:

FREEDOM ARMS INC.

PO Box 150

Freedom, WY 83120

Tel: (307) 883-2468

Fax: (307) 883-2005

www.beartrackcases.com

Boyt Harness Company

One Boyt Dr.

Osceola, IA 50213

(800) 550-2698

Fax: (641) 342-2703

www.boytharness.com

Bulldog Gun Safe Co.

Gardall Safe Corporation

Box 240

Syracuse, NY 13206-0240

Fax (315) 434-9422

Toll Free (800) 722-7233

www.gardall.com

Cannon Safe Co.

216 S. 2nd Ave. Bldg. 932

San Bernadino, CA 92408

(800) 242-1055

www.cannonsafe.com

Concept Development Corporation

14715 N. 78th Way #300

Scottsdale, AZ 85260

(800) 472-4405

FAX (480) 948-7560

saftblok@aol.com

Fort Knox Security Products

993 N. Industrial Park Dr.

Orem, UT 84057

(800) 821-5216

www.ftknox.com

Franzen Security Products, Inc.

680 Flinn Avenue Suite 35

Moorpark, CA 93021

(800) 922-7656

Fax: (805) 529-0446

www.securecase.com

Granite Security Products

Granite Security Products, Inc.

4801 Esco Drive

Fort Worth, TX 76140

(800) 561-9095

Fax: (800) 478-3056

www.granitesafe.com

Gun Vault

216 S. 2nd Ave.

San Bernadino, CA 92408

(800) 222-1055

www.gunvault.com

Heritage Safe Company

20 N. Industrial Park Rd.

Grace, ID 83241

(800) 515-7233

www.heritagesafe.com

Homak Mfg.

1605 Old Route 18 Suites 4-36

Wampum, PA 16157

www.homak.com

Hunter Co., Inc

3300 W. 71st Ave.

Westminster, CO 80030

(800) 676-4868

www.huntercompany.com

Kalispel Case Line

PO Box 267

Cusick, WA 99119

(800) 398-0338

www.kalispelcaseline.com

Liberty Safe and Security Products, Inc.

1199 West Utah Avenue

Payson, UT 84651

(800) 247-5625

Fax (800) 465-2712

www.libertysafe.com

New Innovative Products, Inc.

2180 Hwy 70A East

Pine Level, NC 27568

(877) 782-7544

Fax (919) 965-9177

www.starlightcases.com

Plano Molding Company

431 East South Street

Plano, IL 60545

(800) 226-9868

www.planomolding.com

Rhino Safe

Rhino Metals, Inc.

607 Garber Street

Caldwell, ID 83605

(208) 454-5545

(800) 701-9128

www.rhinosafe.com

Shot Lock Corp.

33 Office Park Road Suite A-172

Hilton Head Island, SC 22928

(800) 230-4784

www.shotlock.com

Sportsmans Steel Safe Co.

6311 N. Paramount Blvd.

Long Beach, CA 90805

(800) 266-7150

www.sportsmansteelsafes.com

Stack-on Products Co.

1360 N. Old Rand Rd.

Wauconda, IL 60084

(800) 323-9601

www.stack-on.com

Sun Welding Safe Co.

290 Easy St. Ste. 3

Simi Valley, CA 93065

(800) 729-7233

www.sunweldingsafes.com

The Safe Outlet, Inc.

28822 Old Town Front St. Suite 201

Temecula, CA 92590

(951) 506-6899

www.thesafeoutlet.com

Trigger Lock

Hodge Products, Inc

1410 Hill Street

El Cajon, CA 92020

(800) 778-2217

www.triggerlock.com

T.Z. Case International

1786 Curtiss Court

La Verne, CA 91750

(888) 892-2737

www.tzcase.com

Versatile Rack Co.

5232 Alcoa Ave.

Vernon, CA 90058

(323) 588-0137

www.versatilegunrack.com

V-Line Industries

370 Easy Street

Simi Valley, CA 93065

(805) 520-4987

www.vlineind.com

Winchester Safes

101 Security Parkway

New Albany IN 47150

(800) 457-2424

www.fireking.com

Zanotti Armor

123 W. Lone Tree Rd.

Cedar Falls, IA 50613

(319) 232-9650

www.zanottiarmor.com

Manufacturers' Directory

In the various chapters of this book, I have commented on some of the guns I have used, particularly those that have worked well for me. I did so with the intention of helping a new gun user to find the type of gun, if not the specific model, that will work for him or her. But no one I know, certainly not me, has used every rifle, shotgun, and handgun ever made. Nor have I been able to shoot with you and help analyze your shooting style. So, I cannot tell you exactly which gun is right for you and your circumstance. This directory, which includes virtually all manufactures that make guns currently available, will help you to find the gun or guns that are right for you. Take the time to survey the market before you visit your local gun shop, might aid you in making the right choices.

A

A Zone Bullets, 2039 Walter Rd., Billings, MT 59105 / 800-252-3111;
FAX: 406-248-1961

A.A. Arms, Inc., 4811 Persimmont Ct., Monroe, NC 28110 / 704-289-5356 or 800-935-1119; FAX: 704-289-5859

A.B.S. III, 9238 St. Morritz Dr., Fern Creek, KY 40291

A.R.M.S., Inc., 230 W. Center St., West Bridgewater, MA 02379-1620
508-584-7816; FAX: 508-588-8045

A.W. Peterson Gun Shop, Inc., The, 4255 West Old U.S. 441, Mount Dora, FL 32757-3299 / 352-383-4258; FAX: 352-735-1001

Acadian Ballistic Specialaties, P.O. Box 787, Folsom, LA 70437 / 504-796-0078 gunsmith@neasolft.com

Accuracy International Precision Rifles (See U.S.)

Accuracy International, Foster, P.O. Box 111, Wilsall, MT 59086 / 406-587-7922;
FAX: 406-585-9434

Accuracy Int'l. North America, Inc., P.O. Box 5267, Oak Ridge, TN 37831
423-482-0330; FAX: 423-482-0336

Accuracy Unlimited, 7479 S. DePew St., Littleton, CO 80123

Accuracy Unlimited, 16036 N. 49 Ave., Glendale, AZ 85306 / 602-978-9089;
FAX: 602-978-9089 fglenn@cox.net www.glenncustom.com

Accura-Site (See All's, The Jim Tembelis Co., Inc.)

Accurate Arms Co., Inc., 5891 Hwy. 230 West, McEwen, TN 37101 / 931-729-4207;
FAX: 931-729-4211 burrensburg@aac-ca.com www.accuratepowder.com

Accu-Tek, 4510 Carter Ct., Chino, CA 91710

Ackerman, Bill (See Optical Services Co.)

Action Bullets & Alloy Inc., RR 1, P.O. Box 189, Quinter, KS 67752 / 785-754-3609;
FAX: 785-754-3629 bullets@ruraltel.net

Action Direct, Inc., 14285 SW 142nd St., Miami, FL 33186-6720 / 800-472-2388;
FAX: 305-256-3541 info@action-direct.com www.action-direct.com

Action Products, Inc., 954 Sweeney Dr., Hagerstown, MD 21740 / 301-797-1414;
FAX: 301-733-2073

Action Target, Inc., P.O. Box 636, Provo, UT 84603 / 801-377-8033;
FAX: 801-377-8096 www.actiontarget.com

Actions by "T" Teddy Jacobson, 16315 Redwood Forest Ct., Sugar Land, TX 77478 /
281-565-6977 tjacobson@houston.rr.com www.actionsbyt.com

AcuSport Corporation, William L. Fraim, One Hunter Place, Bellefontaine, OH 43311-3001 / 937-593-7010; FAX: 937-592-5625 www.acusport.com

Adair Custom Shop, Bill, 2886 Westridge, Carrollton, TX 75006

ADCO Sales, Inc., 4 Draper St. #A, Woburn, MA 01801 / 781-935-1799;
FAX: 781-935-1011

Advantage Arms, Inc., 25163 W. Ave. Stanford, Valencia, CA 91355 / 661-257-2290

AFSCO Ammunition, 731 W. Third St., P.O. Box L, Owen, WI 54460 / 715-229-2516
sailers@webtv.net

Ahlman Guns, 9525 W. 230th St., Morristown, MN 55052 / 507-685-4243;
FAX: 507-685-4280 www.ahlmans.com

Ahrends Grips, Box 203, Clarion, IA 50525 / 515-532-3449; FAX: 515-532-3926
ahrends@goldfieldaccess.net www.ahrendsgripsusa.com

Aimpoint, Inc., 14103 Mariah Ct., Chantilly, VA 20151-2113 / 877-246-7668;
FAX: 703-263-9463 info@aimpoint.com www.aimpoint.com

Aimtech Mount Systems, P.O. Box 223, Thomasville, GA 31799 / 229-226-4313;
FAX: 229-227-0222 mail@aimtech-mounts.com www.aimtech-mounts.com

AirForce Airguns, P.O. Box 2478, Fort Worth, TX 76113 / 817-451-8966;
FAX: 817-451-1613 www.airforceairguns.com

Ajax Custom Grips, Inc., 9130 Viscount Row, Dallas, TX 75247 / 214-630-8893;
FAX: 214-630-4942

AKJ Concealco, P.O. Box 871596, Vancouver, WA 98687-1596 / 360-891-8222;
FAX: 360-891-8221 Concealco@aol.com www.greatholsters.com

Aldis Gunsmithing & Shooting Supply, 502 S. Montezuma St., Prescott, AZ 86303 /
602-445-6723; FAX: 602-445-6763

Alessi Holsters, Inc., 2465 Niagara Falls Blvd., Amherst, NY 14228-3527
716-691-5615

All American Lead Shot Corp., P.O. Box 224566, Dallas, TX 75062

Allen Co., Inc., 525 Burbank St., Broomfield, CO 80020 / 303-469-1857 or
800-876-8600; FAX: 303-466-7437

Allen Mfg., 2784 Highway 23, Brook Park, MN 55007

Alliant Techsystems, Smokeless Powder Group, P.O. Box 6, Rt. 114, Bldg. 229,
Radford, VA 24141-0096 www.alliantpowder.com

Alpine Indoor Shooting Range, 2401 Government Way, Coeur d'Alene, ID 83814
208-676-8824; FAX: 208-676-8824

Amadeo Rossi S.A., Rua: Amadeo Rossi, 143, Sao Leopoldo, RS 93030-220
BRAZIL / 051-592-5566 rossi.firearms@pnet.com.br

American Ammunition, 3545 NW 71st St., Miami, FL 33147 / 305-835-7400;
FAX: 305-694-0037

American Derringer Corp., 127 N. Lacy Dr., Waco, TX 76705 / 800-642-7817 or
254-799-9111; FAX: 254-799-7935

American Gunsmithing Institute, 1325 Imola Ave. #504, Napa, CA 94559
707-253-0462; FAX: 707-253-7149 www.americangunsmith.com

American Handgunner Magazine, 12345 World Trade Dr., San Diego, CA 92128
800-537-3006; FAX: 858-605-0204 www.americanhandgunner.com

American Safe Arms, Inc., 1240 Riverview Dr., Garland, UT 84312 / 801-257-7472;
FAX: 801-785-8156

American Security Products Co., 11925 Pacific Ave., Fontana, CA 92337
909-685-9680 or 800-421-6142; FAX: 909-685-9685

American Small Arms Academy, P.O. Box 12111, Prescott, AZ 86304
602-778-5623

American Target, 1328 S. Jason St., Denver, CO 80223 / 303-733-0433;
FAX: 303-777-0311

Americase, P.O. Box 271, 1610 E. Main, Waxahachie, TX 75165 / 800-880-3629;
FAX: 214-937-8373

Amherst Arms, P.O. Box 1457, Englewood, FL 34295 / 941-475-2020;
FAX: 941-473-1212

Ammo Load Worldwide, Inc., 815 D St., Lewiston, ID 83501 / 800-528-5610;
FAX: 208-746-1730 info@ammoload.com www.ammoload.com

Amrine's Gun Shop, 937 La Luna, Ojai, CA 93023 / 805-646-2376

AMT/Crusader Arms, 5200 Mitchelldale, Ste. E17, Houston, TX 77092
800-272-7816 www.highstandard.com

Antique American Firearms, Douglas Carlson, P.O. Box 71035, Dept. GD,
Des Moines, IA 50325 / 515-224-6552 drearlson@mailstation.com

Antique Arms Co., 1110 Cleveland Ave., Monett, MO 65708 / 417-235-6501

AO Sight Systems, 2401 Ludelle St., Fort Worth, TX 76105 / 888-744-4880;
or 817-536-0136; FAX: 817-536-3517

AR-7 Industries, LLC, 998 N. Colony Rd., Meriden, CT 06450 / 203-630-3536;
FAX: 203-630-3637

ArmaLite, Inc., P.O. Box 299, Geneseo, IL 61254 / 800-336-0184 or 309-944-6939;
FAX: 309-944-6949

Armi Perazzi S.P.A., Via Fontanelle 1/3, 1-25080, Botticino Mattina, ITALY
030-2692591; FAX: 030-2692594

Armi San Marco (See Taylor's & Co.)

Armi San Paolo, 172-A, I-25062, via Europa, ITALY / 030-2751725

Armi Sport (See Cimarron Firearms, E.M.F., KBI & Taylor's & Co.)

Armite Laboratories Inc., 1560 Superior Ave., Costa Mesa, CA 92627
949-646-9035; FAX: 949-646-8319 armite@pacbell.net www.armitelahs.com

Armory Publications, 2120 S. Reserve St., PMB 253, Missoula, MT 59801
406-549-7670; FAX: 406-728-0597 armorypub@aol.com www.armorypub.com

Arms & Armour Press, Wellington House, 125 Strand, London, WC2R 0BB
ENGLAND / 0171-420-5555; FAX: 0171-240-7265

Arms Corporation of the Philippines, Armscor Ave. Brgy. Fortune, Marikina City,
PHILIPPINES / 632-941-6243 or 632-941-6244; FAX: 632-942-0682 info@
armscor.com.ph

Arms Craft Gunsmithing, 1106 Linda Dr., Arroyo Grande, CA 93420 / 805-481-2830

Armscor Precision, 5740 S. Arville St. #219, Las Vegas, NV 89118 / 702-362-7750

Armscorp USA, Inc., 4424 John Ave., Baltimore, MD 21227 / 301-775-8134 info@
armscorpusa.com www.armscorpusa.com

Art's Gun & Sport Shop, Inc., 6008 Hwy. Y, Hillsboro, MO 63050

A-Square Co., 205 Fairfield Ave., Jeffersonville, IN 47130 / 812-283-0577;
FAX: 812-283-0375

Astra Sport, S.A., Apartado 3, 48300 Guernica, Espagne, SPAIN / 34-4-6250100;
FAX: 34-4-6255186

Austin & Halleck, Inc., 2150 South 950 East, Provo, UT 84606-6285 / 877-543-3256
or 801-374-9990; FAX: 801-374-9998 www.austinhallek.com

Austin Sheridan USA, Inc., 89 Broad St., Middlefield, CT 06455 / 860-346-2500;
FAX: 860-346-2510 asusa@sbcglobal.net www.austinsheridanusa.com

Auto Arms, 738 Clearview, San Antonio, TX 78228 / 512-434-5450

Auto-Ordnance Corp., P.O. Box 220, Blauvelt, NY 10913 / 914-353-7770

B

Ballard Rifle & Cartridge Co., LLC, 113 W. Yellowstone Ave., Cody, WY 82414
307-587-4914; FAX: 307-527-6097 ballard@wyoming.com www.ballardrifles.com

Ballistic Products, Inc., 20015 75th Ave. North, Corcoran, MN 55340-9456 / 763-494-9237; FAX: 763-494-9236 info@ballisticproducts.com
www.ballisticproducts.com

Ballistic Program Co., Inc., The, 2417 N. Patterson St., Thomasville, GA 31792
912-228-5739 or 800-368-0835

Ballistic Research, 1108 W. May Ave., McHenry, IL 60050 / 815-385-0037

Ballisti-Cast, Inc., P.O. Box 1057, Minot, ND 58702-1057 / 701-497-3333;
FAX: 701-497-3335

Bang-Bang Boutique (See Holster Shop, The)
Bansner's Ultimate Rifles, LLC, P.O. Box 839, 261 E. Main St., Adamstown, PA 19501 / 717-484-2370; FAX: 717-484-0523 bansner@aol.com www.bansnersrifle.com
Barbour, Inc., 55 Meadowbrook Dr., Milford, NH 03055 / 603-673-1313; FAX: 603-673-6510
Barnes Bullets, Inc., P.O. Box 215, American Fork, UT 84003 / 801-756-4222 or 800-574-9200; FAX: 801-756-2465 email@barnesbullets.com www.barnesbullets.com
Barrel & Gunworks, 2601 Lake Valley Rd., Prescott Valley, AZ 86314 928-772-4060 www.cutrifle.com
Barrett Firearms Manufacturer, Inc., P.O. Box 1077, Murfreesboro, TN 37133 615-896-2938; FAX: 615-896-7313
Battenfeld Technologies, Inc., 5885 W. Van Horn Tavern Rd., Columbia, MO 65203 573-445-9200; FAX: 573-447-4158 battenfeldtechnologies.com
Bear Archery, RR 4, 4600 Southwest 41st Blvd., Gainesville, FL 32601 904-376-2327
Bear Arms, 374-A Carson Rd., St. Mathews, SC 29135
Bear Mountain Gun & Tool, 120 N. Plymouth, New Plymouth, ID 83655 208-278-5221; FAX: 208-278-5221
BEC, Inc., 1227 W. Valley Blvd., Suite 204, Alhambra, CA 91803 / 626-281-5751; FAX: 626-293-7073
Beeman Precision Airguns, 5454 Argosy Dr., Huntington Beach, CA 92649 714-890-4808; FAX: 714-890-4808
Bell & Carlson, Inc., Dodge City Industrial Park, 101 Allen Rd., Dodge City, KS 67801 / 800-634-8586 or 620-225-6688; FAX: 620-225-6688 email@bellandcarlson.com
Bell's Gun & Sport Shop, 3309-19 Mannheim Rd., Franklin Park, IL 60131
Benelli Armi S.P.A., Via della Stazione, 61029, Urbino, ITALY / 39-722-307-1; FAX: 39-722-327427
Benelli USA Corp., 17603 Indian Head Hwy., Accokeek, MD 20607 / 301-283-6981; FAX: 301-283-6988 benelliusa.com
Bengtson Arms Co., L., 6345-B E. Akron St., Mesa, AZ 85205 / 602-981-6375
Benjamin/Sheridan Co., Crosman, Rts. 5 and 20, E. Bloomfield, NY 14443 716-657-6161; FAX: 716-657-5405 www.crosman.com
Beretta Pietro S.P.A., Via Beretta, 18, 25063, Gardone Valtrompia, ITALY 39-30-8341-1 www.beretta.com
Beretta U.S.A. Corp., 17601 Beretta Dr., Accokeek, MD 20607 / 301-283-2191; FAX: 301-283-0435
Berger Bullets Ltd., 5443 W. Westwind Dr., Glendale, AZ 85310 / 602-842-4001; FAX: 602-934-9083
Bersa S.A., Benso Bonadimani, Magallanes 775 B1704 FLC, Ramos Mejia, ARGENTINA / 011-4656-2377; FAX: 011-4656-2093+ info@bersa-sa.com.dr www.bersa-sa.com.ar
Bianchi International, Inc., 27969 Jefferson Ave., Temecula, CA 92590 / 951-676-5621; FAX: 951-676-6777 www.customerservice@bianchi-intl.com www.bianchi- intl.com
Birchwood Casey, 7900 Fuller Rd., Eden Prairie, MN 55344 / 800-328-6156 or 612-937-7933; FAX: 612-937-7979
Bismuth Cartridge Co., 3500 Maple Ave., Suite 1650, Dallas, TX 75219 214-521-5880; FAX: 214-521-9035
Black Hills Ammunition, Inc., P.O. Box 3090, Rapid City, SD 57709-3090 605-348-5150; FAX: 605-348-9827
Black Hills Shooters Supply, P.O. Box 4220, Rapid City, SD 57709 / 800-289-2506
Blaser Jagdwaffen GmbH, D-88316, Isny Im Allgau, GERMANY
Blount, Inc., Sporting Equipment Div., 2299 Snake River Ave., P.O. Box 856, Lewiston, ID 83501 / 800-627-3640 or 208-746-2351; FAX: 208-799-3904
Blount/Outers ATK, P.O. Box 39, Onalaska, WI 54650 / 608-781-5800; FAX: 608-781-0368
Blue Ridge Machinery & Tools, Inc., P.O. Box 536-GD, Hurricane, WV 25526 / 800-872-6500; FAX: 304-562-5311 blueridgemachine@worldnet.att.net www.blueridgemachinery.com
Bob's Gun Shop, P.O. Box 200, Royal, AR 71968 / 501-767-1970; FAX: 501-767-1970 gunparts@hsnp.com www.gun-parts.com
Bob's Tactical Indoor Shooting Range & Gun Shop, 90 Lafayette Rd., Salisbury, MA 01952 / 508-465-5561
Boessler, Erich, Am Vogeltal 3, 97702, Munnerstadt, GERMANY
Bond Arms, Inc., P.O. Box 1296, Granbury, TX 76048 / 817-573-4445; FAX: 817-573-5636 www.bondarms.com
Bond Custom Firearms, 8954 N. Lewis Ln., Bloomington, IN 47408 / 812-332-4519
Borden Rifles Inc., RD 1, Box 250 #BC, Springville, PA 18844 / 717-965-2505; FAX: 717-965-2328

Boss Manufacturing Co., 221 W. First St., Kewanee, IL 61443 / 309-852-2131 or 800-447-4581; FAX: 309-852-0848
Bowen Classic Arms Corp., P.O. Box 67, Louisville, TN 37777 / 865-984-3583 bcacorp@aks.net www.bowenclassicarms.com
Boyds' Gunstock Industries, Inc., 25376 403 Rd. Ave., Mitchell, SD 57301 605-996-5011; FAX: 605-996-9878 www.boydsgunstocks.com
Brenneke GmbH, P.O. Box 1646, 30837, Langenhagen, GERMANY +49-511-97262-0; FAX: +49-511-97262-62 info@brenneke.de brenneke.com
ullet Co., Inc., 3442 42nd Ave. SE, Tappen, ND 58487 / 701-327-4578; FAX: 701-327-4579
Brigade Quartermasters, 1025 Cobb International Blvd., Dept. VH, Kennesaw, GA 30144-4300 / 404-428-1248 or 800-241-3125; FAX: 404-426-7726
Briley Mfg. Inc., 1230 Lumpkin, Houston, TX 77043 / 800-331-5718 or 713-932-6995; FAX: 713-932-1043
British Sporting Arms, RR 1, Box 193A, Millbrook, NY 12545 / 845-677-8303; FAX: 845-677-5756 info@bsaltd.com www.bsaltd.com
Brooks Tactical Systems-Agrip, 279-C Shorewood Ct., Fox Island, WA 98333 253-549-2866; FAX: 253-549-2703 brooks@brookstactical.com www.brookstactical.com
Brown Precision, Inc., 7786 Molinos Ave., Los Molinos, CA 96055 / 530-384-2506; FAX: 916-384-1638 www.brownprecision.com
Brownells, Inc., 200 S. Front St., Montezuma, IA 50171 / 800-741-0015; FAX: 800-264-3068 orderdesk@brownells.com www.brownells.com
Browning Arms Co., One Browning Place, Morgan, UT 84050 / 801-876-2711; FAX: 801-876-3331 www.browning.com
Browning Arms Co. (Parts & Service), 3005 Arnold Tenbrook Rd., Arnold, MO 63010 / 617-287-6800; FAX: 617-287-9751
BRP, Inc. High Performance Cast Bullets, 1210 Alexander Rd., Colorado Springs, CO 80909 / 719-633-0658
Brunton U.S.A., 2255 Brunton Ct., Riverton, WY 82501 info@brunton.com www.brunton.com
BSA Guns Ltd., Armoury Rd. Small Heath, Birmingham B11 2PP, ENGLAND 011-021-772-8543; FAX: 011-021-773-0845 sales@bsagun.com www.bsagun.com
BSA Optics, 3911 SW 47th Ave., Ste. 914, Ft. Lauderdale, FL 33314 954-581-2144; FAX: 954-581-3165 info@bsaoptics.com www.bsaoptics.com
B-Square Company, Inc., 8909 Forum Way, Ft. Worth, TX 76140 / 800-433-2909; FAX: 817-926-7012 bsquare@b-square.com www.b-square.com
Buckhorn Gun Works, 8109 Woodland Dr., Black Hawk, SD 57718 / 605-787-6472
Buckskin Bullet Co., P.O. Box 1893, Cedar City, UT 84721 / 435-586-3286
Buehler Custom Sporting Arms, P.O. Box 4096, Medford, OR 97501 / 541-664-9109 rbrifle@earthlink.net
Buffalo Arms Co., 660 Vermeer Ct., Ponderay, ID 83852 / 208-263-6953; FAX: 208-265-2096 www.buffaloarms.com
Buffalo Bullet Co., Inc., 12637 Los Nietos Rd., Unit A, Santa Fe Springs, CA 90670 / 800-423-8069; FAX: 562-944-5054 rdanlitz@verizon.net
Buffalo Gun Center, 3385 Harlem Rd., Buffalo, NY 14225 / 716-833-2581; FAX: 716-833-2265 www.buffaloguncenter.com
Buffalo Rock Shooters Supply, R.R. 1, Ottawa, IL 61350 / 815-433-2471
Burris Co., Inc., P.O. Box 1747, 331 E. 8th St., Greeley, CO 80631 / 970-356-1670; FAX: 970-356-8702
Bushmaster Firearms, Inc., 999 Roosevelt Trail, Windham, ME 04062 / 800-998-7928; FAX: 207-892-8068 info@bushmaster.com www.bushmaster.com
Bushnell Outdoor Products, 9200 Cody, Overland Park, KS 66214 / 913-752-3400 or 800-423-3537; FAX: 913-752-3550
Butler Creek Corp., 9200 Cody St., Overland Park, KS 66214 / 800-845-2444 or 406-388-1356; FAX: 406-388-7204

C

C. Sharps Arms Co. Inc./Montana Armory, 100 Centennial Dr., P.O. Box 885, Big Timber, MT 59011 / 406-932-4353; FAX: 406-932-4443 www.csharpsarms.com
Cabela's, One Cabela Drive, Sidney, NE 69160 / 308-254-5505; FAX: 308-254-8420
Caesar Guerini USA, Inc., 700 Lake St., Cambridge, MD 21613 / 410-901-1131; FAX: 410-901-1137 info@gueriniusa.com www.gueriniusa.com
Cannon Safe, Inc., 216 S. 2nd Ave. #BLD-932, San Bernardino, CA 92400 800-242-1055; FAX: 909-382-0707 info@cannonsafe.com www.cannonsafe.com
Carl Walther GmbH, B.P. 4325, D-89033, Ulm, GERMANY
Carl Zeiss Inc., 13005 N. Kingston Ave., Chester, VA 23836 / 800-441-3005; FAX: 804-530-8481
Carolina Precision Rifles, 1200 Old Jackson Hwy., Jackson, SC 29831 803-827-2069

Carry-Lite, Inc., P.O. Box 1587, Fort Smith, AR 72902 / 479-782-8971;
FAX: 479-783-0234

Carter's Gun Shop, 225 G St., Penrose, CO 81240 / 719-372-6240
rlewiscarter@msn.com

Caspian Arms, Ltd., 14 North Main St., Hardwick, VT 05843 / 802-472-6454;
FAX: 802-472-6709

Cast Performance Bullet Company, P.O. Box 1466, Rainier, OR 97048 /
503-556-3006; FAX: 503-556-8037 info@bornhunter.com www.bornhunter.com

Casull Arms Corp., P.O. Box 1629, Afton, WY 83110 / 307-886-0200

Caywood Gunmakers, 18 Kings Hill Estates, Berryville, AR 72616 / 870-423-4741
www.caywoodguns.com

CCI/Speer Div of ATK, P.O. Box 856, 2299 Snake River Ave., Lewiston, ID 83501 /
800-627-3640 or 208-746-2351

Century International Arms, Inc., 430 S. Congress Ave. Ste. 1, Delray Beach, FL
33445-4701 / 800-527-1252; FAX: 561-265-4520 support@centuryarms.com
www.centuryarms.com

Champion Shooters' Supply, P.O. Box 303, New Albany, OH 43054 / 614-855-1603;
FAX: 614-855-1209

Champion Target Co., 232 Industrial Parkway, Richmond, IN 47374 / 800-441-4971

Champion's Choice, Inc., 201 International Blvd., LaVergne, TN 37086 / 615-793-
4066; FAX: 615-793-4070 champ.choice@earthlink.net www.champchoice.com

Champlin Firearms, Inc., P.O. Box 3191, Woodring Airport, Enid, OK 73701 / 580-
237-7388; FAX: 580-242-6922 info@champlinarms.com www.champlinarms.com

Chapman Academy of Practical Shooting, 4350 Academy Rd., Hallsville, MO
65255 / 573-696-5544; FAX: 573-696-2266 hq@chapmanacademy.com
chapmanacademy.com

Christensen Arms, 192 East 100 North, Fayette, UT 84630 / 435-528-7999;
FAX: 435-528-7494 www.christensenarms.com

Chuck's Gun Shop, P.O. Box 597, Waldo, FL 32694 / 904-468-2264

Clark Custom Guns, Inc., 336 Shootout Lane, Princeton, LA 71067 / 318-949-9884;
FAX: 318-949-9829

Classic Arms Company, Rt 1 Box 120F, Burnet, TX 78611 / 512-756-4001

Classic Arms Corp., P.O. Box 106, Dunsmuir, CA 96025-0106 / 530-235-2000

Classic Old West Styles, 1060 Doniphan Park Circle C, El Paso, TX 79936
915-587-0684

Clean Shot Technologies, 21218 St. Andrews Blvd. Ste 504, Boca Raton, FL 33433
888-866-2532

Colonial Arms, Inc., P.O. Box 636, Selma, AL 36702-0636 / 334-872-9455; FAX:
334-872-9540 colonialarms@mindspring.com www.colonialarms.com

Colt Blackpowder Arms Co., 110 8th Street, Brooklyn, NY 11215 / 718-499-4678;
FAX: 718-768-8056

Colt's Mfg. Co., Inc., P.O. Box 1868, Hartford, CT 06144-1868 / 800-962-COLT or
860-236-6311; FAX: 860-244-1449

Connecticut Shotgun Mfg. Co., P.O. Box 1692, 35 Woodland St., New Britain, CT
06051 / 860-225-6581; FAX: 860-832-8707

Cooper Arms, P.O. Box 114, Stevensville, MT 59870 / 406-777-0373;
FAX: 406-777-5228

Cor-Bon Inc./Glaser LLC, P.O. Box 173, 1311 Industry Rd., Sturgis, SD 57785 /
605-347-4544 or 800-221-3489; FAX: 605-347-5055 email@corbon.com www.
corbon.com

Crimson Trace Lasers, 8090 S.W. Cirrus Dr., Beverton, OR 97008 / 800-442-2406;
FAX: 503-627-0166 travis@crimsontrace.com www.crimsontrace.com

Crosman Airguns, Rts. 5 and 20, E. Bloomfield, NY 14443 / 716-657-6161;
FAX: 716-657-5405

CRR, Inc./Marble's Inc., 420 Industrial Park, P.O. Box 111, Gladstone, MI 49837 /
906-428-3710; FAX: 906-428-3711

CVA, 5988 Peachtree Corners East, Norcross, GA 30071 / 770-449-4687;
FAX: 770-242-8546 info@cva.com www.cva.com

CZ USA, P.O. Box 171073, Kansas City, KS 66117 / 913-321-1811;
FAX: 913-321-4901

D

Dakota Arms, Inc., 130 Industry Road, Sturgis, SD 57785 / 605-347-4686;
FAX: 605-347-4459 info@dakotaarms.com www.dakotaarms.com

Daly, Charles/KBI, P.O. Box 6625, Harrisburg, PA 17112 / 866-DALY GUN
damascususa@inteliport.com, 149 Deans Farm Rd., Tyner, NC 27980 /
252-221-2010 damascususa@inteliport.com www.damascususa.com

Dan Wesson Firearms, 5169 Rt. 12 South, Norwich, NY 13815 / 607-336-1174;
FAX: 607-336-2730 dwservice@cz-usa.com dz-usa.com

Dangler's Custom Flint Rifles, Homer L. Dangler, 2870 Lee Marie Dr., Adrian, MI
49221 / 517-266-1997 homerdangler@yahoo.com

Davide Pedersoli and Co., Via Artigiani 57, Gardone VT, Brescia 25063, ITALY /
030-8915000; FAX: 030-8911019 info@davidepedersoli.com
www.davide_pedersoli.com

Delta Arms Ltd., P.O. Box 1000, Delta, VT 84624-1000

Delta Enterprises, 284 Hagemann Drive, Livermore, CA 94550

Dillon Precision Products, Inc., 8009 East Dillon's Way, Scottsdale, AZ 85260 /
480-948-8009 or 800-762-3845; FAX: 480-998-2786 sales@dillonprecision.com
www.dillonprecision.com

Dina Arms Corporation, P.O. Box 46, Royersford, PA 19468 / 610-287-0266;
FAX: 610-287-0266 dinaarms@erols.com www.users.erds.com/dinarms

Dixie Gun Works, P.O. Box 130, Union City, TN 38281 / 731-885-0700;
FAX: 731-885-0440 info@dixiegunworks.com www.dixiegunworks.com

Dixon Muzzleloading Shop, Inc., 9952 Kunkels Mill Rd., Kempton, PA 19529 /
610-756-6271 dixonmuzzleloading.com

E

E.A.A. Corp., P.O. Box 1299, Sharpes, FL 32959 / 407-639-4842 or 800-536-4442;
FAX: 407-639-7006

Eagle Arms, Inc. (See ArmaLite, Inc.)

E-A-R, Inc., Div. of Cabot Safety Corp., 5457 W. 79th St., Indianapolis, IN 46268 /
800-327-3431; FAX: 800-488-8007

Ed Brown Products, Inc., P.O. Box 492, Perry, MO 63462 / 573-565-3261;
FAX: 573-565-2791 edbrown@edbrown.com www.edbrown.com

Ed Brown Products, Inc., 43825 Muldrow Trl., P.O. Box 492, Perry, MO 63462 /
573-565-3261; FAX: 573-565-2791 edbrown@edbrown.com www.edbrown.com

Electronic Shooters Protection, Inc., 15290 Gadsden Ct., Brighton, CO 80603 /
800-797-7791; FAX: 303-659-8668 esp@usa.net espamerica.com

Eley Ltd., Selco Way Minworth Industrial Estate, Minworth Sutton Coldfield, West
Midlands, B76 1BA ENGLAND / 44 0 121-313-4567; FAX: 44 0 121-313-4568
www.eleyammunition.com

Ellett Bros., 267 Columbia Ave., P.O. Box 128, Chapin, SC 29036 / 803-345-3751 or
800-845-3711; FAX: 803-345-1820 www.ellettbrothers.com

European American Armory Corp. (See E.A.A. Corp.)

Eversull Co., Inc., 1 Tracemont, Boyce, LA 71409 / 318-793-8728;
FAX: 318-793-5483 bestguns@aol.com

Evolution Gun Works, Inc., 48 Belmont Ave., Quakertown, PA 18951-1347
www.egw-guns.com

Excalibur Electro Optics, Inc., P.O. Box 400, Fogelsville, PA 18051-0400 /
610-391-9105; FAX: 610-391-9220

Excalibur Publications, P.O. Box 89667, Tucson, AZ 85752 / 520-575-9057
excalibureditor@earthlink.net

F

F+W Publications, Inc., 700 E. State St., Iola, WI 54990 / 715-445-2214;
FAX: 715-445-4087

Fabarm S.p.A., Via Averolda 31, 25039 Travagliato, Brescia, ITALY / 030-6863629;
FAX: 030-6863684 info@fabarm.com www.fabarm.com

Federal Cartridge Co., 900 Ehlen Dr., Anoka, MN 55303 / 612-323-2300;
FAX: 612-323-2506

Federal Champion Target Co., 232 Industrial Pkwy., Richmond, IN 47374 /
800-441-4971; FAX: 317-966-7747

FEG, Budapest, Soroksariut 158, H-1095, HUNGARY

Feinwerkbau Westinger & Altenburger, Neckarstrasse 43, 78727, Oberndorf a. N.,
GERMANY / 07423-814-0; FAX: 07423-814-200 info@feinwerkbau.de
www.feinwerkbau.de

Fieldsport Ltd., Bryan Bilinski, 3313 W. South Airport Rd., Traverse City, MI 49684
616-933-0767

Fiocchi Munizioni S.A. (See U.S. Importer-Fiocch

Fiocchi of America, Inc., 5030 Fremont Rd., Ozark, MO 65721 / 417-725-4118 or
800-721-2666; FAX: 417-725-1039

Flambeau, Inc., 15981 Valplast Rd., Middlefield, OH 44062 / 216-632-1631;
FAX: 216-632-1581 www.flambeau.com

Flayderman & Co., Inc., P.O. Box 2446, Fort Lauderdale, FL 33303 / 954-761-8855
www.flayderman.com

FN Manufacturing, P.O. Box 24257, Columbia, SC 29224 / 803-736-0522

Freedom Arms, Inc., P.O. Box 150, Freedom, WY 83120 / 307-883-2468; FAX: 307-
883-2005

Fujinon, Inc., 10 High Point Dr., Wayne, NJ 07470 / 201-633-5600; FAX: 201-633-
5216

G

Galati International, P.O. Box 10, 616 Burley Ridge Rd., Wesco, MO 65586 / 636-
584-0785; FAX: 573-775-4308 support@galatiinternational.com
www.galatiinternational.com

Galaxy Imports Ltd., Inc., P.O. Box 3361, Victoria, TX 77903 / 361-573-4867
galaxy06@suddenlink.net

GALCO International Ltd., 2019 W. Quail Ave., Phoenix, AZ 85027 / 623-474-7070; FAX: 623-582-6854 customerservice@usgalco.com www.usgalco.com

Galena Industries AMT, 5463 Diaz St., Irwindale, CA 91706 / 626-856-8883; FAX: 626-856-8878

Gamo USA, Inc., 3911 SW 47th Ave., Suite 914, Fort Lauderdale, FL 33314 / 954-581-5822; FAX: 954-581-3165 gamousa@gate.net www.gamo.com

Gander Mountain, Inc., 12400 Fox River Rd., Wilmont, WI 53192 / 414-862-6848

Gary Reeder Custom Guns, 2601 7th Ave. E., Flagstaff, AZ 86004 / 928-526-3313; FAX: 928-527-0840 gary@reedercustomguns.com www.reedercustomguns.com

Gator Guns & Repair, 7952 Kenai Spur Hwy., Kenai, AK 99611-8311

GDL Enterprises, 409 Le Gardeur, Slidell, LA 70460 / 504-649-0693

Gehmann, Walter (See Huntington Die Specialties)

Genco, P.O. Box 5704, Asheville, NC 28803

Genecco Gun Works, 10512 Lower Sacramento Rd., Stockton, CA 95210 209-951-0706; FAX: 209-931-3872

Gene's Custom Guns, P.O. Box 10534, White Bear Lake, MN 55110 / 651-429-5105; FAX: 651-429-7365

Glaser LLC, P.O. Box 173, Sturgis, SD 57785 / 605-347-4544 or 800-221-3489; FAX: 605-347-5055 email@corbon.com www.safetyslug.com

Glaser Safety Slug, Inc. (see CorBon/Glaser safetyslug.com)

Glock GmbH, P.O. Box 50, A-2232, Deutsch, Wagram, AUSTRIA

Glock, Inc., P.O. Box 369, Smyrna, GA 30081 / 770-432-1202; FAX: 770-433-8719

GOEX, Inc., P.O. Box 659, Doyline, LA 71023-0659 / 318-382-9300; FAX: 318-382-9303 mfahringer@goexpowder.com www.goexpowder.com

Green Mountain Rifle Barrel Co., Inc., P.O. Box 2670, 153 W. Main St., Conway, NH 03818 / 603-447-1095; FAX: 603-447-1099 info@gmriflebarrel.com www.gmriflebarrel.com

Gun Digest (See F+W Publications), 700 E. State St., Iola, WI 54990 715-445-2214; FAX: 715-445-4087 www.gundigestmagazine.com

Gun Vault, 7339 E. Acoma Dr., Ste. 7, Scottsdale, AZ 85260 / 602-951-6855

Gun Works, The, 247 S. 2nd St., Springfield, OR 97477 / 541-741-4118; FAX: 541-988-1097 info@thegunworks.com www.thegunworks.com

Gun-Alert, 1010 N. Maclay Ave., San Fernando, CA 91340 / 818-365-0864; FAX: 818-365-1308

GUNS Magazine, 12345 World Trade Dr., San Diego, CA 92128-3743 619-297-5350; FAX: 619-297-5353

Gunsight, The, 5292 Kentwater Pl., Yorba Linda, CA 92886

Gunsite Training Center, P.O. Box 700, Paulden, AZ 86334 / 520-636-4565; FAX: 520-636-1236

H

H&R 1871, LLC, 60 Industrial Rowe, Gardner, MA 01440 / 508-632-9393; FAX: 508-632-2300 hr1871@hr1871.com www.hr1871.com

H. Krieghoff Gun Co., Boschstrasse 22, D-89079, Ulm, GERMANY / 731-401820; FAX: 731-4018270

H.K.S. Products, 7841 Founion Dr., Florence, KY 41042 / 606-342-7841 or 800-354-9814; FAX: 606-342-5865

Hagn Rifles & Actions, P.O. Box 444, Cranbrook, BC V1C 4H9 Canada / 250-489-4861

Hammerli AG, Industrieplaz, a/Rheinpall, CH-8212 Neuhausen, SWITZERLAND info@hammerli.com www.haemmerliich.com

Hammerli Service-Precision Mac, Rudolf Marent, 9711 Tiltree St., Houston, TX 77075 / 713-946-7028 rmarent@webtv.net

Hammerli USA, 19296 Oak Grove Circle, Groveland, CA 95321 FAX: 209-962-5311

Harrington & Richardson (See H&R 1871, Inc.)

Harris Engineering Inc., Dept. GD54, 999 Broadway, Barlow, KY 42024 / 270-334-3633; FAX: 270-334-3000

Harris Enterprises, P.O. Box 105, Bly, OR 97622 / 503-353-2625

Hastings, P.O. Box 135, Clay Center, KS 67432 / 785-632-3169; FAX: 785-632-6554

Heckler & Koch GmbH, P.O. Box 1329, 78722 Oberndorf, Neckar, GERMANY 49-7423179-0; FAX: 49-7423179-2406

Heckler & Koch, Inc., 21480 Pacific Blvd., Sterling, VA 20166-8900 / 703-450-1900; FAX: 703-450-8160 www.hecklerkoch-usa.com

Heinie Specialty Products, 301 Oak St., Quincy, IL 62301-2500 / 217-228-9500; FAX: 217-228-9502 rheinie@heinie.com www.heinie.com

Henry Repeating Arms Co., 110 8th St., Brooklyn, NY 11215 / 718-499-5600; FAX: 718-768-8056 info@henryrepeating.com www.henryrepeating.com

Heritage Firearms (See Heritage Mfg., Inc.)

Heritage Manufacturing, Inc., 4600 NW 135th St., Opa Locka, FL 33054 305-685-5966; FAX: 305-687-6721 infohmi@heritagemfg.com www.heritagemfg.com

High Precision, Bud Welsh, 80 New Road, E. Amherst, NY 14051 / 716-688-6344; FAX: 716-688-0425 welsh5168@aol.com www.high-precision.com

High Standard Mfg. Co./F.I., Inc., 5200 Mitchelldale St., Ste. E17, Houston, TX 77092-7222 / 713-462-4200 or 800-272-7816; FAX: 713-681-5665 info@highstandard.com

Hi-Point Firearms/MKS Supply, 8611-A North Dixie Dr., Dayton, OH 45414 877-425-4867; FAX: 937-454-0503 www.hi-pointfirearms.com

Hodgdon Powder Co., 6231 Robinson, Shawnee Mission, KS 66202 913-362-9455; FAX: 913-362-1307

Hogue Grips, P.O. Box 1138, Paso Robles, CA 93447 / 800-438-4747 or 805-239-1440; FAX: 805-239-2553

Holland & Holland Ltd., 33 Bruton St., London, ENGLAND / 44-171-499-4411; FAX: 44-171-408-7962

Homak, 350 N. La Salle Dr. Ste. 1100, Chicago, IL 60610-4731 / 312-523-3100; FAX: 312-523-9455

Hoppe's Div. Penguin Industries, Inc., 9200 Cody St., Overland Park, KS 66214 / 800-845-2444

Hornady Mfg. Co., P.O. Box 1848, Grand Island, NE 68802 / 800-338-3220 or 308-382-1390; FAX: 308-382-5761

Howa Machinery, Ltd., 1900-1 Sukaguchi Kiyosu, Aichi 452-8601, JAPAN / 81-52-408-1231; FAX: 81-52-401-4999 howa@howa.co.jp http://www.howa.cojpl

H-S Precision, Inc., 1301 Turbine Dr., Rapid City, SD 57701 / 605-341-3006; FAX: 605-342-8964

Hunter's Specialties Inc., 6000 Huntington Ct. NE, Cedar Rapids, IA 52402-1268 / 319-395-0321; FAX: 319-395-0326

Hydrosorbent Dehumidifiers, P.O. Box 437, Ashley Falls, MA 01222 / 800-448-7903; FAX: 413-229-8743 orders@dehumidify.com www.dehumidify.com

I

Impact Case & Container, Inc., P.O. Box 1129, Rathdrum, ID 83858 / 877-687-2452; FAX: 208-687-0632 bradk@icc-case.com www.icc-case.com

INTEC International, Inc., P.O. Box 5708, Scottsdale, AZ 85261 / 602-483-1708

Inter Ordnance of America LP, 3305 Westwood Industrial Dr., Monroe, NC 28110-5204 / 704-821-8337; FAX: 704-821-8523

InterMedia Outdoors, Inc., 6420 Wilshire Blvd., Los Angeles, CA 90048 / 213-782-2000; FAX: 213-782-2867

Israel Arms Inc., 5625 Star Ln. #B, Houston, TX 77057 / 713-789-0745; FAX: 713-914-9515 www.israelarms.com

Ithaca Classic Doubles, Stephen Lamboy, No. 5 Railroad St., Victor, NY 14564 / 716-924-2710; FAX: 716-924-2737 ithacadoubles.com

Ithaca Guns, LLC, 420 N. Walpole St., Upper Sandusky, OH 43351 / 419-294-4113; FAX: 419-294-9433 service@ithacaguns.com www.ithacaguns-usa.com

J

J.G. Anschutz GmbH & Co. KG, Daimlerstr. 12, D-89079 Ulm, Ulm, GERMANY 49 731 40120; FAX: 49 731 4012700 JGA-info@anschuetz-sport.com www.anschuetz-sport.com

Jarrett Rifles, Inc., 383 Brown Rd., Jackson, SC 29831 / 803-471-3616 www.jarrettrifles.com

Jewell Triggers, Inc., 3620 Hwy. 123, San Marcos, TX 78666 / 512-353-2999; FAX: 512-392-0543

JG Airguns, LLC, John Groenewold, P.O. Box 830, Mundelein, IL 60060 847-566-2365; FAX: 847-566-4065 john@jgairguns.biz www.jgairguns.biz

K

Kahles A. Swarovski Company, 2 Slater Rd., Cranston, RI 02920 / 401-946-2220; FAX: 401-946-2587

Kahr Arms, P.O. Box 220, 630 Route 303, Blauvelt, NY 10913 / 845-353-7770; FAX: 845-353-7833 www.kahr.com

Kalispel Case Line, P.O. Box 267, Cusick, WA 99119 / 509-445-1121

Kel-Tec CNC Industries, Inc., P.O. Box 236009, Cocoa, FL 32923 / 321-631-0068; FAX: 321-631-1169 www.kel-tec.com

Kent Cartridge America, Inc., P.O. Box 849, 1000 Zigor Rd., Kearneysville, WV 25430

Kickeez, I.N.C., Inc., 13715 NE 384th St., La Center, WA 98629 / 877-542-5339; FAX: 954-656-4527 info@kickeezproducts www.kickeez.products.com

Kimber of America, Inc., 1 Lawton St., Yonkers, NY 10705 / 800-880-2418; FAX: 914-964-9340

Kleen-Bore, Inc., 8909 Forum Way, Ft. Worth, TX 76140 / 413-527-0300; FAX: 817-926-7012 info@kleen-bore.com www.kleen-bore.com

Knight Rifles, 21852 Hwy. J46, P.O. Box 130, Centerville, IA 52544 / 515-856-2626; FAX: 515-856-2628 www.knightrifles.com

Kolpin Outdoors, Inc., P.O. Box 107, 205 Depot St., Fox Lake, WI 53933 414-928-3118; FAX: 414-928-3687 cdutton@kolpin.com www.kolpin.com

KP Books Division of F+W Publications, 700 E. State St., Iola, WI 54990-0001 / 715-445-2214

Krieger Barrels, Inc., 2024 Mayfield Rd, Richfield, WI 53076 / 262-628-8558; FAX: 262-628-8748

Krieghoff Gun Co., H., Boschstrasse 22, D-89079 Elm, GERMANY / 731-4018270

Krieghoff International, Inc., 7528 Easton Rd., Ottsville, PA 18942 / 610-847-5173; FAX: 610-847-8691 info@krieghoff.com www.krieghoff.com

Kwik-Site Co., 5555 Treadwell St., Wayne, MI 48184 / 734-326-1500; FAX: 734-326-4120 kwiksitecorp@aol.com www.kwiksiteco@aol.com

L

Laser Devices, Inc., 2 Harris Ct. A-4, Monterey, CA 93940 / 831-373-0701; FAX: 831-373-0903 sales@laserdevices.com www.laserdevices.com

Laseraim Technologies, Inc., P.O. Box 3548, Little Rock, AR 72203 / 501-375-2227

Laserlyte, 2201 Amapola Ct., Torrance, CA 90501

LaserMax, 3495 Winton Place, Rochester, NY 14623-2807 / 800-527-3703; FAX: 585-272-5427 customerservice@lasermax-inc.com www.lasermax.com

Lazzeroni Arms Co., P.O. Box 26696, Tucson, AZ 85726 / 888-492-7247; FAX: 520-624-4250

Lee Precision, Inc., 4275 Hwy. U, Hartford, WI 53027 / 262-673-3075; FAX: 262-673-9273 info@leeprecision.com www.leeprecision.com

Leica Sport Optics, 1 Pearl Ct., Ste. A, Allendale, NJ 07401 / 201-995-1686 www.leica-camera.com/usa

Les Baer Custom, Inc., 29601 34th Ave., Hillsdale, IL 61257 / 309-658-2716; FAX: 309-658-2610 www.lesbaer.com

LesMerises, Felix. See: ROCKY MOUNTAIN ARMOURY

Lethal Force Institute (See Police Bookshelf), P.O. Box 122, Concord, NH 03301 / 603-224-6814; FAX: 603-226-3554 ayoob@attglobal.net www.ayoob.com

Leupold & Stevens, Inc., 14400 NW Greenbrier Pky., Beaverton, OR 97006 503-646-9171; FAX: 503-526-1455

Liberty Mfg., Inc., 2233 East 16th St., Los Angeles, CA 90021 / 323-581-9171; FAX: 323-581-9351 libertymfginc@aol.com

Liberty Safe, 999 W. Utah Ave., Payson, UT 84651-1744 / 800-247-5625; FAX: 801-489-6409

Lilja Precision Rifle Barrels, P.O. Box 372, Plains, MT 59859 / 406-826-3084; FAX: 406-826-3083 lilja@riflebarrels.com www.riflebarrels.com

Lyman Instant Targets, Inc. (See Lyman Products Corp.)

Lyman Products Corp., 475 Smith St., Middletown, CT 06457-1541 / 800-423-9704; FAX: 860-632-1699 lymansales@cshore.com www.lymanproducts.com

M

Mag-Na-Port International, Inc., 41302 Executive Dr., Harrison Twp., MI 48045-1306 / 586-469-6727; FAX: 586-469-0425 email@magnaport.com www.magnaport.com

Magnum Research, Inc., 7110 University Ave. NE, Minneapolis, MN 55432 / 800-772-6168 or 763-574-1868; FAX: 763-574-0109 info@magnumresearch.com

Magtech Ammunition Co. Inc., 248 Apollo Dr. Ste. 180, Linolakes, MN 55014 / 800-466-7191; FAX: 763-235-4004 www.magtechammunition.com

Marble Arms (See CRR, Inc./Marble's Inc.)

Marksman Products, 5482 Argosy Dr., Huntington Beach, CA 92649 714-898-7535 or 800-822-8005; FAX: 714-891-0782

Marlin Firearms Co., 100 Kenna Dr., North Haven, CT 06473 / 203-239-5621; FAX: 203-234-7991 www.marlinfirearms.com

Martini & Hagn, Ltd., 1264 Jimsmith Lake Rd., Cranbrook, BC V1C 6V6 CANADA / 250-417-2926; FAX: 250-417-2928 martini-hagn@shaw.ca www.martiniandhagngunmakers.com

Master Lock Co., 2600 N. 32nd St., Milwaukee, WI 53245 / 414-444-2800

Mauser Werke Oberndorf Waffensysteme GmbH, Postfach 1349, 78722, Oberndorf/ N., GERMANY

McMillan Fiberglass Stocks, Inc., 1638 W. Knudsen Dr. #101, Phoenix, AZ 85027 / 623-582-9635; FAX: 623-581-3825 mfsinc@mcmfamily.com www.mcmfamily.com

McMillan Optical Gunsight Co., 28638 N. 42nd St., Cave Creek, AZ 85331 602-585-7868; FAX: 602-585-7872

McMillan Rifle Barrels, 10456 State Highway 6 S, College Sta, TX 77845 979-690-3456

MEC, Inc., 715 South St., Mayville, WI 53050 reloaders@mayvl.com www.mecreloaders.com

MEC-Gar S.R.L., Via Madonnina 64, Gardone V.T. Brescia, ITALY / 39-030-3733668; FAX: 39-030-3733687 info@mec-gar.it www.mec-gar.it

MEC-Gar U.S.A., Inc., Hurley Farms Industr. Park, 905 Middle St., Middletown, CT 06457 / 203-262-1525; FAX: 203-262-1719 mecgar@aol.com www.mec-gar.com

Meopta USA, LLC, 50 Davids Dr., Hauppauge, NY 11788 / 631-436-5900 ussales@meopta.com www.meopta.com

Midway Arms, Inc., 5875 W. Van Horn Tavern Rd., Columbia, MO 65203 800-243-3220; FAX: 800-992-8312 www.midwayusa.com

Midwest Gun Sport, 1108 Herbert Dr., Zebulon, NC 27597 / 919-269-5570

Midwest Shooting School, The, Pat LaBoone, 2550 Hwy. 23, Wrenshall, MN 55797 218-384-3670 shootingschool@starband.net

Midwest Sport Distributors, Box 129, Fayette, MO 65248

Millett Sights, 16131 Gothard St., Huntington Beach, CA 92647 / 714-842-5575 or 800-645-5388; FAX: 714-843-5707 sales@millettsights.com www.millettsights.com

Mitchell's Mauser, P.O. Box 9295, Fountain Valley, CA 92728 / 714-979-7663; FAX: 714-899-3660

N

Naval Ordnance Works, 467 Knott Rd., Sheperdstown, WV 25443 / 304-876-0998; FAX: 304-876-0998 nvordfdy@earthlink.net

Navy Arms Company, 219 Lawn St., Martinsburg, WV 25405 / 304-262-9870; FAX: 304-262-1658 info@navyarms.com www.navyarms.com

New England Arms Co., Box 278, Lawrence Lane, Kittery Point, ME 03905 207-439-0593; FAX: 207-439-0525 info@newenglandarms.com www.newenglandarms.com

New England Custom Gun Service, 438 Willow Brook Rd., Plainfield, NH 03781 / 603-469-3450; FAX: 603-469-3471 bestguns@comcast.net www.newenglandcustom.com

Nighthawk Custom, 1306 W. Trimble, Berryville, AR 72616 / 877-268-GUNS; (4867) or 870-423-GUNS; FAX: 870-423-4230 www.nighthawkcustom.com

Nikon, Inc., 1300 Walt Whitman Rd., Melville, NY 11747 / 516-547-8623; FAX: 516-547-0309

Norma Precision AB (See U.S. Importers-Dynamit)

North American Arms, Inc., 2150 South 950 East, Provo, UT 84606-6285 800-821-5783 or 801-374-9990; FAX: 801-374-9998

Nosler, Inc., P.O. Box 671, Bend, OR 97709 / 800-285-3701 or 541-382-3921; FAX: 541-388-4667 www.nosler.com

O

O.F. Mossberg & Sons, Inc., 7 Grasso Ave., North Haven, CT 06473 / 203-230-5300; FAX: 203-230-5420

Obermeyer Rifled Barrels, 23122 60th St., Bristol, WI 53104 / 262-843-3537; FAX: 262-843-2129 www.obermeyerbarrels.com

October Country Muzzleloading, P.O. Box 969, Dept. GD, Hayden, ID 83835 / 208-772-2068; FAX: 208-772-9230 dawn@octobercountry.com www.octobercountry.com

Oklahoma Ammunition Co., 3701A S. Harvard Ave., No. 367, Tulsa, OK 74135-2265 918-396-3187; FAX: 918-396-4270

Old West Reproductions, Inc. R.M. Bachman, 446 Florence S. Loop, Florence, MT 59833 / 406-273-2615; FAX: 406-273-2615 rick@oldwestreproductions.com www.oldwestreproductions.com

Olympic Arms Inc., 620-626 Old Pacific Hwy. SE, Olympia, WA 98513 / 360-456-3471; FAX: 360-491-3447 info@olyarms.com www.olyarms.com

Olympic Optical Co., 5801 Safety Dr. NE, Belmont, MI 49306-0032 901-794-3890 or 800-238-7120; FAX: 901-794-0676

Op-Tec, P.O. Box L632, Langhorn, PA 19047 / 215-757-5037; FAX: 215-757-7097

Oregon Trail Bullet Company, P.O. Box 529, Dept. P, Baker City, OR 97814 800-811-0548; FAX: 514-523-1803

Otis Technology, Inc., RR 1 Box 84, Boonville, NY 13309 / 315-942-3320

Outers Laboratories Div. of ATK, Route 2, P.O. Box 39, Onalaska, WI 54650 608-781-5800; FAX: 608-781-0368

P

Pachmayr Div. Lyman Products, 475 Smith St., Middletown, CT 06457 860-632-2020 or 800-225-9626; FAX: 860-632-1699 lymansales@cshore.com www.pachmayr.com

Para-Ordnance Mfg., Inc., 980 Tapscott Rd., Scarborough, ON M1X 1E7 CANADA / 416-297-7855; FAX: 416-297-1289

Para-Ordnance, Inc., 1919 NE 45th St., Ste 215, Ft. Lauderdale, FL 33308 416-297-7855; FAX: 416-297-1289 info@paraord.com www.paraord.com

Pardini Armi Srl, Via Italica 154, 55043, Lido Di Camaiore Lu, ITALY / 584-90121; FAX: 584-90122

Pentax U.S.A., Inc., 600 12th St. Ste. 300, Golden, CO 80401 / 303-799-8000; FAX: 303-460-1628 www.pentaxlightseeker.com

Perazzi U.S.A. Inc., 1010 West Tenth, Azusa, CA 91702 / 626-334-1234; FAX: 626-334-0344 perazziusa@aol.com

PMC Ammunition, P.O. Box 940878, Houston, TX 77094-7878 / 281-759-9020; FAX: 281-759-0784 kbauer@pmcammo.com www.pmcammo.com

Powell & Son (Gunmakers) Ltd., William, 35-37 Carrs Lane, Birmingham, B4 7SX ENGLAND / 121-643-0689; FAX: 121-631-3504 sales@william-powell.co.uk www.william-powell.co.uk

Precision Cast Bullets, 101 Mud Creek Lane, Ronan, MT 59864 / 406-676-5135

Precision Shooting, Inc., 222 McKee St., Manchester, CT 06040 / 860-645-8776; FAX: 860-643-8215 www.precisionshooting.com

Precision Small Arms Inc., 9272 Jeronimo Rd., Ste. 121, Irvine, CA 92618 800-554-5515 or 949-768-3530; FAX: 949-768-4808 www.tcbebe.com

Q

Quality Arms, Inc., Box 19477, Dept. GD, Houston, TX 77224 / 281-870-8377 arrieta2@excite.com www.arrieta.com

Quality Cartridge, P.O. Box 445, Hollywood, MD 20636 / 301-373-3719 www.qual-cart.com

R

Ram-Line ATK, P.O. Box 39, Onalaska, WI 54650

Raytech Div. of Lyman Products Corp., 475 Smith Street, Middletown, CT 06457-1541 / 860-632-2020 or 800-225-9626; FAX: 860-632-1699 raysales@cshore.com www.raytech-

RCBS Operations/ATK, 605 Oro Dam Blvd., Oroville, CA 95965 / 800-533-5000; FAX: 530-533-1647 www.rcbs.com

Reardon Products, P.O. Box 126, Morrison, IL 61270 / 815-772-3155

Redfield Media Resource Center, 4607 N.E. Cedar Creek Rd., Woodland, WA 98674 / 360-225-5000; FAX: 360-225-7616

Remington Arms Co., Inc., 870 Remington Drive, P.O. Box 700, Madison, NC 27025-0700 / 800-243-9700; FAX: 336-548-8700 info@remington.com www.remington.com

Riley Ledbetter Airguns, 1804 E. Sprague St., Winston Salem, NC 27107-3521 / 919-784-0676

Rock River Arms, 101 Noble St., Cleveland, IL 61241

Rossi Firearms, Gary Mchalik, 16175 NW 49th Ave., Miami, FL 33014-6314 / 305-474-0401; FAX: 305-623-7506

Ruger (See Sturm Ruger & Co., Inc.)

RWS (See U.S. Importer-Umarex-USA), 6007 S. 29th St., Fort Smith, AR 72908

S

Sabatti SPA, Via A Volta 90, 25063 Gandome V.T.(BS), Brescia, ITALY / 030-8912207-831312; FAX: 030-8912059 info@sabatti.it www.sabatti.com

SAFE, P.O. Box 864, Post Falls, ID 83877 / 208-773-3624; FAX: 208-773-6819 staysafe@safe-llc.com www.safe-llc.com

Sako Ltd. (See U.S. Importer-Stoeger Industries)

Savage Arms (Canada), Inc., 248 Water St., P.O. Box 1240, Lakefield, ON K0L 2H0 CANADA / 705-652-8000; FAX: 705-652-8431 www.savagearms.com

Savage Arms, Inc., 100 Springdale Rd., Westfield, MA 01085 / 413-568-7001; FAX: 413-562-7764

Savage Range Systems, Inc., 100 Springdale Rd., Westfield, MA 01085 / 413-568-7001; FAX: 413-562-1152 snailtraps@savagearms.com www.snailtraps.com

Schmidt & Bender, Inc., P.O. Box 134, Meriden, NH 03770 / 603-469-3565; FAX: 603-469-3471 info@schmidtbender.com www.schmidtbender.com

Second Chance Body Armor, P.O. Box 578, Central Lake, MI 49622 / 616-544-5721; FAX: 616-544-9824

Sharps Arms Co., Inc., C., 100 Centennial, Box 885, Big Timber, MT 59011 406-932-4353

Shiloh Rifle Mfg., P.O. Box 279, Big Timber, MT 59011

Shooter's Choice Gun Care, 15050 Berkshire Ind. Pkwy., Middlefield, OH 44062 / 440-834-8888; FAX: 440-834-3388 www.shooterschoice.com

Shooter's Edge Inc., 3313 Creekstone Dr., Fort Collins, CO 80525

Shooters Supply, 153 Childs Rd., Trout Creek, MT 59874 / 509-452-1181

Shootin' Shack, 357 Cypress Drive, No. 10, Tequesta, FL 33469 / 561-746-2731; FAX: 772-545-4861 ckeays@comcast.net

Shoot-N-C Targets (See Birchwood Casey)

Sierra Bullets, 1400 W. Henry St., Sedalia, MO 65301 / 816-827-6300; FAX: 816-827-6300 www.sierrabullets.com

Sig Sauer, Inc., 18 Industrial Dr., Exeter, NH 03833 / 603-772-2302; FAX: 603-772-9082 siginfo@sigsauer.com www.sigsauer.com

Sightron, Inc., 1672B Hwy. 96, Franklinton, NC 27525 / 919-528-8783; FAX: 919-528-0995 info@sightron.com www.sightron.com

SIG-Sauer (See U.S. Importer-Sigarms, Inc.)

SKB Shotguns, 4441 S. 134th St., Omaha, NE 68137 / 800-752-2767; FAX: 402-330-8040 skb@skbshotguns.com www.skbshotguns.com

Smith & Wesson, 2100 Roosevelt Ave., Springfield, MA 01104 / 413-781-8300; FAX: 413-731-8980 qa@smith-wesson.com www.smith-wesson.com

Specialty Shooters Supply, Inc., 3325 Griffin Rd., Suite 9mm, Fort Lauderdale, FL 33317

Speer Bullets, P.O. Box 856, Lewiston, ID 83501 / 208-746-2351 www.speer-bullets.com

Sportsman Safe Mfg. Co., 6309-6311 Paramount Blvd., Long Beach, CA 90805 800-266-7150; or 310-984-5445

Springfield Armory, 420 W. Main St., Geneseo, IL 61254 / 309-944-5631; FAX: 309-944-3676 sales@springfield-armory.com www.springfieldarmory.com

Steyr Arms, P.O. Box 2609, Cumming, GA 30028 / 770-888-4201 www.steyrarms.com

Steyr Mannlicher GmbH & Co. KG, Ramingtal 46, A-4442 Kleinraming, Steyr, AUSTRIA / 0043-7252-896-0; FAX: 0043-7252-78620 office@steyr-mannlicher.com www.steyr-mannlicher.com

Stoeger Industries, 17603 Indian Head Hwy., Suite 200, Accokeek, MD 20607-2501 / 301-283-6300; FAX: 301-283-6986 www.stoegerindustries.com

Stoney Point Products, Inc., 9200 Cody St., Overland Park, KS 66214 800-845-2444; FAX: 507-354-7236 stoney@newulmtel.net www.stoneypoint.com

Sturm Ruger & Co. Inc., 200 Ruger Rd., Prescott, AZ 86301 / 928-541-8820; FAX: 520-541-8850 www.ruger.com

Swarovski Optik North America Ltd., 2 Slater Rd., Cranston, RI 02920 401-946-2220 or 800-426-3089; FAX: 401-946-2587

Swift Bullet Co., P.O. Box 27, 201 Main St., Quinter, KS 67752 / 913-754-3959; FAX: 913-754-2359

T

Tactical Defense Institute, 2174 Bethany Ridges, West Union, OH 45693 937-544-7228; FAX: 937-544-2887 tdiohio@dragonbbs.com www.tdiohio.com

Talley, Dave, P.O. Box 369, Santee, SC 29142 / 803-854-5700 or 307-436-9315; FAX: 803-854-9315 talley@diretway www.talleyrings.com

Tasco Sales, Inc., 2889 Commerce Pkwy., Miramar, FL 33025

Taurus Firearms, Inc., 16175 NW 49th Ave., Miami, FL 33014 / 305-624-1115; FAX: 305-623-7506

Taurus International Firearms (See U.S. Importer Taurus Firearms, Inc.)

Taurus S.A. Forjas, Avenida Do Forte 511, Porto Alegre, RS BRAZIL 91360 55-51-347-4050; FAX: 55-51-347-3065

The Midwest Shooting School, 2550 Hwy. 23, Wrenshall, MN 55797 218-384-3670 patrick@midwestshootingschool.com www.midwestshootingschool.com

Thompson/Center Arms, P.O. Box 5002, Rochester, NH 03866 / 603-332-2394; FAX: 603-332-5133 tech@tcarms.com www.tcarms.com

Thunder Ranch, 96747 Hwy. 140 East, Lakeview, OR 97630 / 541-947-4104; FAX: 541-947-4105 troregon@centurytel.net www.thunderranchinc.com

Tikka (See U.S. Importer-Stoeger Industries)

Tippman Sports, LLC, 2955 Adams Center Rd., Fort Wayne, IN 46803 260-749-6022; FAX: 260-441-8504 www.tippmann.com

Traditions Performance Firearms, P.O. Box 776, 1375 Boston Post Rd., Old Saybrook, CT 06475 / 860-388-4656; FAX: 860-388-4657 info@traditionsfirearms.com www.traditionsfirearms.com

Trigger Lock Division / Central Specialties Ltd., 220-D Exchange Dr., Crystal Lake, IL 60014 / 847-639-3900; FAX: 847-639-3972

Trijicon, Inc., 49385 Shafer Ave., P.O. Box 930059, Wixom, MI 48393-0059 248-960-7700; or 800-338-0563; FAX: 248-960-7725 info@trijicon.com www.trijicon.com

Tristar Sporting Arms, Ltd., 1816 Linn St. #16, N. Kansas City, MO 64116-3627
  816-421-1400; FAX: 816-421-4182 tristarsporting@sbcglobal.net
  www.tristarsportingarms
Truglo, Inc., P.O. Box 1612, McKinna, TX 75070 / 972-774-0300;
  FAX: 972-774-0323 www.truglosights.com

U

U.S. Optics, A Division of Zeitz Optics U.S.A., 5900 Dale St., Buena Park, CA 90621 /
  714-994-4901; FAX: 714-994-4904 www.usoptics.com
U.S. Repeating Arms Co., Inc., 275 Winchester Ave., Morgan, UT 84050-9333 /
  801-876-3440; FAX: 801-876-3737 www.winchester-guns.com
Uncle Mike's (See Michaels of Oregon, Co.)
Unertl Ordance Co., Inc., 2900 S. Highland Dr., Bldg. 19, Unit B, Las Vegas, NV
  89109 / 702-369-4092; FAX: 702-369-4571 info@unertloptics.com
  www.unertloptics.com

V

Volquartsen Custom Ltd., 24276 240th Street, P.O. Box 397, Carroll, IA 51401 /
  712-792-4238; FAX: 712-792-2542 info@volquartsen.com www.volquartsen.com

W

Walther America, P.O. Box 22, Springfield, MA 01102 / 413-747-3443
  www.walther-usa.com
Walther GmbH, Carl, B.P. 4325, D-89033 Ulm, GERMANY
Weatherby, Inc., 1605 Commerce Way, Paso Robles, CA 93446 / 805-227-2600;
  FAX: 805-237-0427 www.weatherby.com
Weaver Products ATK, P.O. Box 39, Onalaska, WI 54650 / 800-648-9624 or
  608-781-5800; FAX: 608-781-0368
Weaver Scope Repair Service, 1121 Larry Mahan Dr., Suite B, El Paso, TX 79925 /
  915-593-1005 frank@weaver-scope-repair.com www.weaver-scope-repair.com
Webley Limited, Universe House Planetary Rd., Key Industrial Park, Willenhall,
  WV13 3YA ENGLAND / 011-01902-722144; FAX: 011-1902-722880
  sales@webley.co.uk
Williams Gun Sight Co., 7389 Lapeer Rd., Box 329, Davison, MI 48423
  810-653-2131 or 800-530-9028; FAX: 810-658-2140 williamsgunsight.com
Williams Mfg. of Oregon, 110 East B St., Drain, OR 97435 / 503-836-7461;
  FAX: 503-836-7245
Wilson Combat, 2234 CR 719, Berryville, AR 72616-4573 / 800-955-4856;
  FAX: 870-545-3310 info@wilsoncombat.com www.wilsoncombat.com
Wilson Case, Inc., P.O. Box 1106, Hastings, NE 68902-1106 / 800-322-5493;
  FAX: 402-463-5276 sales@wilsoncase.com www.wilsoncase.com
Winchester Div. Olin Corp., 427 N. Shamrock, E. Alton, IL 62024 / 618-258-3566;
  FAX: 618-258-3599
Wolf Performance Ammunition, 2201 E. Winston Rd., Ste. K, Anaheim, CA
  92806-5537 / 702-837-8506; FAX: 702-837-9250

X

XS Sight Systems, 2401 Ludelle St., Fort Worth, TX 76105 / 888-744-4880;
  FAX: 800-734-7939

Y

Yavapai Firearms Academy Ltd., P.O. Box 27290, Prescott Valley, AZ 86312
  928-772-8262; FAX: 928-772-0062 info@yfainc.com www.yfainc.com

Z

Zabala Hermanos S.A., P.O. Box 97, Elbar Lasao, 6, Elgueta, Guipuzcoa, 20600
  SPAIN / 34-943-768076; FAX: 34-943-768201 imanol@zabalahermanos.com
  www.zabalabermanos.com

Web Directory

The whole world might not be online, but sometimes it seems like it. If you're one of the fifty percent of Americans who has an Internet connection in their home, this directory will be of particular use to you. If you don't have an Internet connection at home odds are you have access to one. In either event you'll find this directory to be one of the fastest and easiest ways to find out everything you want to know about the various models of guns and gun-related products.

AMMUNITION AND COMPONENTS

A-Square Co.:: www.asquarecompany.com
3-D Ammunition:: www.3dammo.com
Accurate Arms Co. Inc:: www.accuratepowder.com
ADCO/Nobel Sport Powder: www.adcosales.com
Aguila Ammunition: www.aguilaammo.com
Alexander Arms: www.alexanderarms.com
Alliant Powder: www.alliantpowder.com
American Ammunition: www.a-merc.com
American Derringer Co.: www.amderringer.com
American Pioneer Powder: www.americanpioneerpowder.com
Ammo Depot: www.ammodepot.com
Arizona Ammunition, Inc.: www.arizonaammunition.com
Ballistic Products,Inc.: www.ballisticproducts.com
Barnaul Cartridge Plant: www.ab.ru/~stanok
Barnes Bullets: www.barnesbullets.com
Baschieri & Pellagri: www.baschieri-pellagri.com
Beartooth Bullets: www.beartoothbullets.com
Bell Brass: www.bellbrass.com
Berger Bullets, Ltd.: www.bergerbullets.com
Berry's Mfg., Inc.: www.berrysmfg.com
Big Bore Bullets of Alaska: www.awloo.com/bbb/index.htm
Big Bore Express: www.powerbeltbullets.com
Bismuth Cartridge Co.: www.bismuth-notox.com
Black Dawge Cartridge: www.blackdawgecartridge.com
Black Hills Ammunition, Inc.: www.black-hills.com
Brenneke of America Ltd.: www.brennekeusa.com
Buffalo Arms: www.buffaloarms.com
Calhoon, James, Bullets: www.jamescalhoon.com
Cartuchos Saga: www.saga.es
Cast Performance Bullet: www.castperformance.com
CCI: www.cci-ammunition.com
Centurion Ordnance: www.aguilaammo.com
Century International Arms: www.centuryarms.com
Cheaper Than Dirt: www.cheaperthandirt.com
Cheddite France: www.cheddite.com
Claybuster Wads: www.claybusterwads.com
Clean Shot Powder: www.cleanshot.com
Cole Distributing: www.cole-distributing.com
Combined Tactical Systems: www.less-lethal.com
Cor-Bon/Glaser : www.cor-bon.com
Cowboy Bullets: www.cowboybullets.com
Defense Technology Corp.: www.defense-technology.com
Denver Bullet Co. denbullets@aol.com
Dillon Precision: www.dillonprecision.com
Dionisi Cartridge: www.dionisi.com
DKT, Inc.: www.dktinc.com
Down Range Mfg.: www.downrangemfg.com
Dynamit Nobel RWS Inc.: www.dnrws.com
Elephant/Swiss Black Powder:
   www.elephantblackpowder.com
Eley Ammunition: www.eleyusa.com
Eley Hawk Ltd.: www.eleyhawk.com
Environ-Metal: www.hevishot.com
Estate Cartridge: www.estatecartridge.com
Extreme Shock Munitions: www.extremeshockusa.net
Federal Cartridge Co.: www.federalpremium.com
Fiocchi of America: www.fiocchiusa.com
Fowler Bullets: www.benchrest.com/fowler
Gamebore Cartridge: www.gamebore.com
Garrett Cartridges: www.garrettcartridges.com
Gentner Bullets: www.benchrest.com/gentner/
Glaser Safety Slug, Inc.: www.corbon.com
GOEX Inc.: www.goexpowder.com
GPA: www.cartouchegpa.com
Graf & Sons: www.grafs.com
Hastings: www.hastingsammunition.com
Hawk Bullets: www.hawkbullets.com

Hevi.Shot: www.hevishot.com
Hi-Tech Ammunition: www.iidbs.com/hitech
Hodgdon Powder: www.hodgdon.com
Hornady: www.hornady.com
Hull Cartridge: www.hullcartridge.com
Huntington Reloading Products: www.huntingtons.com
Impact Bullets: www.impactbullets.com
IMR Smokeless Powders: www.imrpowder.com
International Cartridge Corp: www.iccammo.com
Israel Military Industries: www.imisammo.co.il
ITD Enterprise: www.itdenterpriseinc.com
Kent Cartridge America: www.kentgamebore.com
Knight Bullets: www.benchrest.com/knight/
Kynoch Ammunition: www.kynochammunition.com
Lapua: www.lapua.com
Lawrence Brand Shot: www.metalico.com
Lazzeroni Arms Co.: www.lazzeroni.com
Leadheads Bullets: www.proshootpro.com
Lightfield Ammunition Corp: www.lightfieldslugs.com
Lomont Precision Bullets: www.klomont.com/kent
Lost River Ballistic Technologies,Inc.:
    www.lostriverballistic.com
Lyman : www.lymanproducts.com
Magkor Industries.: www.magkor.com
Magnum Muzzleloading Products: www.mmpsabots.com
Magnus Bullets: www.magnusbullets.com
MagSafe Ammunition: www.realpages.com/magsafeammo
Magtech: www.magtechammunition.com
Masterclass Bullet Co.: www.mastercast.com
Meister Bullets: www.meisterbullets.com
Midway USA: www.midwayusa.com
Miltex,Inc.: www.miltexusa.com
Mitchell Mfg. Co.: www.mitchellsales.com
MK Ballistic Systems: www.mkballistics.com
Mullins Ammunition: www.mullinsammunition.com
National Bullet Co.: www.nationalbullet.com
Navy Arms: www.navyarms.com
Nobel Sport: www.nobelsportammo.com
Norma: www.norma.cc
North Fork Technologies: www.northforkbullets.com
Nosler Bullets,Inc.: www.nosler.com
Old Western Scrounger: www.ows-ammunition.com
Oregon Trail/Trueshot Bullets: www.trueshotbullets.com
Pattern Control: www.patterncontrol.com
PMC: www.pmcammo.com
Polywad: www.polywad.com
PowerBelt Bullets: www.powerbeltbullets.com
PR Bullets: www.prbullet.com
Precision Ammunition: www.precisionammo.com
Precision Reloading: www.precisionreloading.com
Pro Load Ammunition: www.proload.com
Quality Cartridge: www.qual-cart.com
Rainier Ballistics: www.rainierballistics.com
Ram Shot Powder: www.ramshot.com
Reloading Specialties Inc.: www.reloadingspecialties.com
Remington: www.remington.com
Rio Ammo: www.rioammo.com
Rocky Mountain Cartridge: www.rockymountaincartridge.com
RUAG Ammotec: www.ruag.com
Samco Global Arms: www.samcoglobal.com
Schuetzen Powder: www.schuetzenpowder.com
Sellier & Bellot USA inc.: www.sb-usa.com
Shilen: www.shilen.com
Sierra: www.sierrabullets.com
Simunition.: www.simunition.com
SinterFire, Inc.: www.sinterfire.com
Speer Bullets: www.speer-bullets.com
Sporting Supplies Int'l Inc.: www.ssiintl.com
Starline: www.starlinebrass.com

Swift Bullets Co.: **www.swiftbullet.com**
Ten-X Ammunition: **www.tenxammo.com**
Top Brass: **www.top-brass.com**
Triton Cartridge: **www.a-merc.com**
Trueshot Bullets: **www.trueshotbullets.com**
Tru-Tracer: **www.trutracer.com**
Ultramax Ammunition: **www.ultramaxammunition.com**
Vihtavuori Lapua: **www.vihtavuori-lapua.com**
Weatherby: **www.weatherby.com**
West Coast Bullets: **www.westcoastbullet.com**
Western Powders Inc.: **www.westernpowders.com**
Widener's Reloading & Shooters Supply: **www.wideners.com**
Winchester Ammunition: **www.winchester.com**
Windjammer Tournament Wads.: **www.windjammer-wads.com**
Wolf Ammunition: **www.wolfammo.com**
Woodleigh Bullets: **www.woodleighbullets.com.au**
Zanders Sporting Goods: **www.gzanders.com**

CASES, SAFES, GUN LOCKS, AND CABINETS

Ace Case Co.: **www.acecase.com**
AG English Sales Co.: **www.agenglish.com**
All Americas' Outdoors: **www.innernet.net/gunsafe**
Alpine Cases: **www.alpinecases.com**
Aluma Sport by Dee Zee: **www.deezee.com**
American Security Products: **www.amsecusa.com**
Americase: **www.americase.com**
Avery Outdoors, Inc.: **www.averyoutdoors.com**
Bear Track Cases: **www.beartrackcases.com**
Boyt Harness Co.: **www.boytharness.com**
Bulldog Gun Safe Co.: **www.gardall.com**
Cannon Safe Co.: **www.cannonsafe.com**
CCL Security Products: **www.cclsecurity.com**
Concept Development Corp.: **www.saf-t-blok.com**
Doskocil Mfg. Co.: **www.doskocilmfg.com**
Fort Knox Safes: **www.ftknox.com**
Franzen Security Products: **www.securecase.com**
Frontier Safe Co.: **www.frontiersafe.com**
Granite Security Products: **www.granitesafe.com**
Gunlocker Phoenix USA Inc.: **www.gunlocker.com**
GunVault: **www.gunvault.com**
Hakuba USA Inc.: **www.hakubausa.com**
Heritage Safe Co.: **www.heritagesafecompany.com**
Hide-A-Gun: **www.hide-a-gun.com**
Homak Safes: **www.homak.com**
Hunter Company: **www.huntercompany.com**
Kalispel Case Line: **www.kalispelcaseline.com**
Knouff & Knouff, Inc.: **www.kkair.com**
Knoxx Industries: **www.knoxx,com**
Kolpin Mfg. Co.: **www.kolpin.com**
Liberty Safe & Security: **www.libertysafe.com**
New Innovative Products: **www.starlightcases**
Noble Security Systems Inc.: **www.noble.co.ll**
Phoenix USA Inc.: **www.gunlocker.com**
Plano Molding Co.: **www.planomolding.com**
Rhino Gun Cases: **www.rhinoguns.com**
Rhino Safe: **www.rhinosafe.com**
Safe Tech, Inc.: **www.safrgun.com**
Saf-T-Hammer: **www.saf-t-hammer.com**
Saf-T-Lok Corp.: **www.saf-t-lok.com**
San Angelo All-Aluminum Products Inc.:
 sasptuld@x.netcom.com
Securecase: **www.securecase.com**
Shot Lock Corp.: **www.shotlock.com**
Smart Lock Technology Inc.: **www.smartlock.com**
Sportsmans Steel Safe Co.: **www.sportsmansteelsafes.com**
Stack-On Products Co.: **www.stack-on.com**
Starlight Cases: **www.starlightcases.com**
Sun Welding: **www.sunwelding.com**
T.Z. Case Int'l : **www.tzcase.com**

Versatile Rack Co.: **www.versatilegunrack.com**
V-Line Industries: **www.vlineind.com**
Winchester Safes: **www.fireking.com**
Ziegel Engineering: **www.ziegeleng.com**
Zonetti Armor: **www.zonettiarmor.com**

CHOKE DEVICES, RECOIL REDUCERS, SUPPRESSORS AND ACCURACY DEVICES

Advanced Armament Corp.: **www.advanced-armament.com**
100 Straight Products: **www.100straight.com**
Answer Products Co.: **www.answerrifles.com**
Briley Mfg: **www.briley.com**
Carlson's: **www.choketube.com**
Colonial Arms: **www.colonialarms.com**
Comp-N-Choke: **www.comp-n-choke.com**
Gemtech: **www.gem-tech.com**
Hastings: **www.hastingsbarrels.com**
Kick's Industries: **www.kicks-ind.com**
LimbSaver: **www.limbsaver.com**
Mag-Na-Port Int'l Inc.: **www.magnaport.com**
Metro Gun: **www.metrogun.com**
Patternmaster Chokes: **www.patternmaster.com**
Poly-Choke: **www.poly-choke.com**
Sims Vibration Laboratory: **www.limbsaver.com**
Teague Precision Chokes: **www.teague.ca**
Truglo: **www.truglo.com**

CHRONOGRAPHS AND BALLISTIC SOFTWARE

Barnes Ballistic Program: **www.barnesbullets.com**
Ballisticard Systems: **www.ballisticards.com**
Competition Electronics: **www.competitionelectronics.com**
Competitive Edge Dynamics: **www.cedhk.com**
Hodgdon Shotshell Program: **www.hodgdon.com**
Lee Shooter Program: **www.leeprecision.com**
Load From A Disk: **www.loadammo.com**
Oehler Research Inc.: **www.oehler-research.com**
PACT: **www.pact.com**
ProChrony: **www.competitionelectronics.com**
Quickload: **www.neconos.com**
RCBS Load: **www.rcbs.com**
Shooting Chrony Inc: **www.shootingchrony.com**
Sierra Infinity Ballistics Program: **www.sierrabullets.com**

CLEANING PRODUCTS

Accupro: **www.accupro.com**
Ballistol USA: **www.ballistol.com**
Battenfeld Technologies: **www.battenfeldtechnologies.com**
Birchwood Casey: **www.birchwoodcasey.com**
Blue Wonder: **www.bluewonder.com**
Bore Tech: **www.boretech.com**
Break-Free, Inc.: **www.break-free.com**
Bruno Shooters Supply: **www.brunoshooters.com**
Butch's Bore Shine: **www.lymanproducts.com**
C.J. Weapons Accessories: **www.cjweapons,com**
Clenzoil: **www.clenzoil.com**
Corrosion Technologies: **www.corrosionx.com**
Dewey Mfg.: **www.deweyrods.com**
Eezox Inc.: **www.xmission.com**
G 96: **www.g96.com**
Gunslick Gun Care: **www.gunslick.com**
Gunzilla: **www.topduckproducts.com**
Hollands Shooters Supply: **www.hollandgun.com**
Hoppes: **www.hoppes.com**
Hydrosorbent Products: **www.dehumidify.com**
Inhibitor VCI Products: **www.theinhibitor.com**
Iosso Products: **www.iosso.com**
KG Industries: **www.kgcoatings.com**

Kleen-Bore Inc.: **www.kleen-bore.com**
L&R Mfg.: **www.lrultrasonics.com**
Lyman: **www.lymanproducts.com**
Mil-Comm Products: **www.mil-comm.com**
Militec-1: **www.militec-1.com**
Mpro7 Gun Care: **www.mp7.com**
Otis Technology, Inc.: **www.otisgun.com**
Outers: **www.outers-guncare.com**
Ox-Yoke Originals Inc.: **www.oxyoke.com**
Parker-Hale Ltd.: **www.parker-hale.com**
Prolix Lubricant: **www.prolixlubricant.com**
ProShot Products: **www.proshotproducts.com**
ProTec Lubricants: **www.proteclubricants.com**
Rusteprufe Labs: **www.rusteprufe.com**
Sagebrush Products: **www.sagebrushproducts.com**
Sentry Solutions Ltd.: **www.sentrysolutions.com**
Shooters Choice Gun Care: **www.shooters-choice.com**
Silencio: **www.silencio.com**
Slip 2000: **www.slip2000.com**
Stony Point Products: **www.uncle-mikes.com**
Tetra Gun: **www.tetraproducts.com**
The TM Solution thetmsolution@comsast.net
Top Duck Products: **www.topduckproducts.com**
Ultra Bore Coat: **www.ultracoatingsinc.com**
World's Fastest Gun Bore Cleaner: **www.michaels-oregon.com**

FIREARM MANUFACTURERS AND IMPORTERS

AAR, Inc.: **www.iar-arms.com**
A-Square: **www.asquarecompany.com**
Accuracy Int'l North America: **www.accuracyinternational.org**
Accuracy Rifle Systems: **www.mini-14.net**
Ace Custom 45's: **www.acecustom45.com**
Advanced Weapons Technology: **www.AWT-Zastava.com**
AIM: **www.aimsurplus.com**
AirForce Airguns: **www.airforceairguns.com**
Air Gun, Inc.: **www.airrifle-china.com**
Airguns of Arizona: **www.airgunsofarizona.com**
Airgun Express: **www.airgunexpress.com**
Alchemy Arms: **www.alchemyltd.com**
Alexander Arms: **www.alexanderarms.com**
American Derringer Corp.: **www.amderringer.com**
American Spirit Arms Corp.: **www.gunkits.com**
American Western Arms: **www.awaguns.com**
Anics Corp.: **www.anics.com**
Anschutz: **www.anschutz-sporters.com**
Answer Products Co.: **www.answerrifles.com**
AR-7 Industries,LLC: **www.ar-7.com**
Ares Defense Systems: **www.aresdefense.com**
Armalite: **www.armalite.com**
Armi Sport: **www.armisport.com**
Armory USA: **www.globaltraders.com**
Armsco: **www.armsco.net**
Armscorp USA Inc.: **www.armscorpusa.com**
Arnold Arms: **www.arnoldarms.com**
Arsenal Inc.: **www.arsenalinc.com**
Arthur Brown Co.: **www.eabco.com**
Atlanta Cutlery Corp.: **www.atlantacutlery.com**
Auction Arms: **www.auctionarms.com**
Autauga Arms,Inc.: **www.autaugaarms.com**
Auto-Ordnance Corp.: **www.tommygun.com**
AWA Int'l: **www.awaguns.com**
Axtell Rifle Co.: **www.riflesmith.com**
Aya: **www.aya-fineguns.com**
Baikal: **www.baikalinc.ru/eng/**
Ballard Rifles,LLC: **www.ballardrifles.com**
Barrett Firearms Mfg.: **www.barrettrifles.com**
Beeman Precision Airguns: **www.beeman.com**
Benelli USA Corp.: **www.benelliusa.com**
Benjamin Sheridan: **www.crosman.com**

Beretta U.S.A. Corp.: **www.berettausa.com**
Bernardelli: **www.bernardelli.com**
Bersa: **www.bersa-llama.com**
Bill Hanus Birdguns: **www.billhanusbirdguns.com**
Blaser Jagdwaffen Gmbh: **www.blaser.de**
Bleiker: **www.bleiker.ch**
Bluegrass Armory: **www.bluegrassarmory.com**
Bond Arms: **www.bondarms.com**
Borden's Rifles, Inc.: **www.bordensrifles.com**
Boss & Co.: **www.bossguns.co.uk**
Bowen Classic Arms: **www.bowenclassicarms.com**
Briley Mfg: **www.briley.com**
BRNO Arms: **www.zbrojovka.com**
Brown, David McKay: **www.mckaybrown.com**
Brown, Ed Products: **www.brownprecision.com**
Browning: **www.browning.com**
BSA Guns: **www.bsaguns.com**
BUL Ltd.: **www.bultransmark.com**
Bushmaster Firearms/Quality Parts: **www.bushmaster.com**
BWE Firearms: **www.bwefirearms.com**
Caesar Guerini USA: **www.gueriniusa.com**
Cape Outfitters: **www.doublegun.com**
Carbon 15: **www.professional-ordnance.com**
Caspian Arms, Ltd.: **www.caspianarmsltd.8m.com**
Casull Arms Corp.: **www.casullarms.com**
Calvary Arms: **www.calvaryarms.com**
CDNN Investments, Inc.: **www.cdnninvestments.com**
Century Arms: **www.centuryarms.com**
Chadick's Ltd.: **www.chadicks-ltd.com**
Champlin Firearms: **www.champlinarms.com**
Chapuis Arms: **www.doubleguns.com/chapuis.htm**
Charles Daly: **www.charlesdaly.com**
Charter Arms: **www.charterfirearms.com**
CheyTac USA: **www.cheytac.com**
Christensen Arms: **www.christensenarms.com**
Cimarron Firearms Co.: **www.cimarron-firearms.com**
Clark Custom Guns: **www.clarkcustomguns.com**
Cobra Enterprises: **www.cobrapistols.com**
Cogswell & Harrison: **www.cogswell.co.uk/home.htm**
Colt's Mfg Co.: **www.colt.com**
Compasseco, Inc.: **www.compasseco.com**
Connecticut Valley Arms: **www.cva.com**
Cooper Firearms: **www.cooperfirearms.com**
Corner Shot: **www.cornershot.com**
Crosman: **www.crosman.com**
Crossfire, L.L.C.: **www.crossfirelle.com**
C.Sharp Arms Co.: **www.csharparms.com**
CVA: **www.cva.com**
CZ USA: **www.cz-usa.com**
Daisy Mfg Co.: **www.daisy.com**
Dakota Arms Inc.: **www.dakotaarms.com**
Dan Wesson Firearms: **www.danwessonfirearms.com**
Davis Industries: **www.davisindguns.com**
Detonics USA: **www.detonicsusa.com**
Diana: **www.diana-airguns.de**
Dixie Gun Works: **www.dixiegunworks.com**
Dlask Arms Corp.: **www.dlask.com**
D.P.M.S., Inc.: **www.dpmsinc.com**
D.S.A, Inc.: **www.dsarms.com**
Dumoulin: **www.dumoulin-herstal.com**
Dynamit Noble: **www.dnrws.com**
Eagle Imports,Inc.: **www.bersa-llama.com**
Ed Brown Products: **www.edbrown.com**
EDM Arms: **www.edmarms.com**
E.M.F. Co.: **www.emf-company.com**
Enterprise Arms: **www.enterprise.com**
E R Shaw: **www.ershawbarrels.com**
European American Armory Corp.: **www.eaacorp.com**
Evans, William: **www.williamevans.com**

Excel Arms: www.excelarms.com
Fabarm: www.fabarm.com
FAC-Guns-N-Stuff: www.gunsnstuff.com
Falcon Pneumatic Systems: www.falcon-airguns.com
Fausti Stefano: www.faustistefanoarms.com
Firestorm: www.firestorm-sgs.com
Flodman Guns: www.flodman.com
FN Herstal: www.fnherstal.com
FNH USA: www.fnhusa.com
Franchi: www.franchiusa.com
Freedom Arms: www.freedomarms.com
Galazan: www.connecticutshotgun.com
Gambo Renato: www.renatogamba.it
Gamo: www.gamo.com
Gary Reeder Custom Guns: www.reeder-customguns.com
Gazelle Arms: www.gazellearms.com
German Sport Guns: www.germansportguns.com
Gibbs Rifle Company: www.gibbsrifle.com
Glock: www.glock.com
Griffin & Howe: www.griffinhowe.com
Grizzly Big Boar Rifle: www.largrizzly.com
GSI Inc.: www.gsifirearms.com
Guerini: www.gueriniusa.com
Gunbroker.Com: www.gunbroker.com
Hammerli: www.carl-walther.com
Hatfield Gun Co.: www.hatfield-usa.com
Hatsan Arms Co.: www.hatsan.com.tr
Heckler and Koch: www.hk-usa.com
Henry Repeating Arms Co.: www.henryrepeating.com
Heritage Mfg.: www.heritagemfg.com
Heym: www.heym-waffenfabrik.de
High Standard Mfg.: www.highstandard.com
Hi-Point Firearms: www.hi-pointfirearms.com
Holland & Holland: www.hollandandholland.com
H&R 1871 Firearms: www.hr1871.com
H-S Precision: www.hsprecision.com
Hunters Lodge Corp.: www.hunterslodge.com
IAR Inc.: www.iar-arms.com
Imperial Miniature Armory: www.1800miniature.com
Interarms: www.interarms.com
International Military Antiques, Inc.: www.ima-usa.com
Inter Ordnance: www.interordnance.com
Intrac Arms International LLC: www.hsarms.com
Israel Arms: www.israelarms.com
Iver Johnson Arms: www.iverjohnsonarms.com
Izhevsky Mekhanichesky Zavod: www.baikalinc.ru
Jarrett Rifles,Inc.: www.jarrettrifles.com
J&G Sales, Ltd.: www.jgsales.com
Johannsen Express Rifle: www.johannsen-jagd.de
Jonathan Arthur Ciener: www.22lrconversions.com
JP Enterprises, Inc.: www.jprifles.com
Kahr Arms/Auto-Ordnance: www.kahr.com
K.B.I.: www.kbi-inc.com
Kel-Tec CNC Ind., Inc.: www.kel-tec.com
Kifaru: www.kifaru.net
Kimber: www.kimberamerica.com
Knight's Mfg. Co.: www.knightsarmco.com
Knight Rifles: www.knightrifles.com
Korth: www.korthwaffen.de
Krieghoff GmbH: www.krieghoff.de
KY Imports, Inc.: www.kyimports.com
Krieghoff Int'l: www.krieghoff.com
L.A.R Mfg: www.largrizzly.com
Lazzeroni Arms Co.: www.lazzeroni.com
Legacy Sports International: www.legacysports.com
Les Baer Custom, Inc.: www.lesbaer.com
Lewis Machine & Tool Co.: www.lewismachine.net
Linebaugh Custom Sixguns: www.sixgunner.com/linebaugh
Ljutic: www.ljuticgun.com

Llama: www.bersa-llama.com
Lone Star Rifle Co.: www.lonestarrifle.com
Magnum Research: www.magnumresearch.com
Majestic Arms: www.majesticarms.com
Markesbery Muzzleloaders: www.markesbery.com
Marksman Products: www.marksman.com
Marlin: www.marlinfirearms.com
Mauser: www.mauser.com
McMillan Bros Rifle Co.: www.mcfamily.com
MDM: www.mdm-muzzleloaders.com
Meacham Rifles: www.meachamrifles.com
Merkel: www.hk-usa.com
Miller Arms: www.millerarms.com
Miltech: www.miltecharms.com
Miltex, Inc.: www.miltexusa.com
Mitchell's Mausers: www.mitchellsales.com
MK Ballistic Systems: www.mkballistics.com
M-Mag: www.mmag.com
Montana Rifle Co.: www.montanarifleman.com
Mossberg: www.mossberg.com
Navy Arms: www.navyarms.com
Nesika: www.nesika.com
New England Arms Corp.: www.newenglandarms.com
New England Custom Gun Svc, Ltd.:
    www.newenglandcustomgun.com
New England Firearms: www.hr1871.com
New Ultra Light Arms: www.newultralight.com
North American Arms: www.northamericanarms.com
Nosler Bullets,Inc.: www.nosler.com
Nowlin Mfg. Inc.: www.nowlinguns.com
O.F. Mossberg & Sons: www.mossberg.com
Ohio Ordnance Works: www.ohioordnanceworks.com
Olympic Arms: www.olyarms.com
Panther Arms: www.dpmsinc.com
Para-Ordnance: www.paraord.com
Pedersoli Davide & Co.: www.davide-pedersoli.com
Perazzi: www.perazzi.com
Pietta: www.pietta.it
PKP Knife-Pistol: www.sanjuanenterprise.com
Power Custom: www.powercustom.com
Professional Arms: www.professional-arms.com
PTR 91,Inc.: www.ptr91.com
Purdey & Sons: www.purdey.com
Remington: www.remington.com
Republic Arms Inc.: www.republicarmsinc.com
Rhineland Arms, Inc.: www.rhinelandarms.com
Rigby: www.johnrigbyandco.com
Rizzini USA: www.rizziniusa.com
Robar Companies, Inc.: www.robarguns.com
Robinson Armament Co.: www.robarm.com
Rock River Arms, Inc.: www.rockriverarms.com
Rogue Rifle Co. Inc.: www.chipmunkrifle.com
Rohrbaugh Firearms: www.rohrbaughfirearms.com
Rossi Arms: www.rossiusa.com
RPM: www.rpmxlpistols.com
Russian American Armory: www.raacfirearms.com
RUAG Ammotec: www.ruag.com
Sabatti SPA: www.sabatti.com
Sabre Defense Industries: www.sabredefense.com
Saco Defense: www.sacoinc.com
Safari Arms: www.olyarms.com
Sako: www.berettausa.com
Samco Global Arms Inc.: www.samcoglobal.com
Sarco Inc.: www.sarcoinc.com
Savage Arms Inc.: www.savagearms.com
Scattergun Technologies Inc.: www.wilsoncombat.com
Searcy Enterprises: www.searcyent.com
Shiloh Rifle Mfg.: www.shilohrifle.com
SIGARMS,Inc.: www.sigarms.com

Simpson Ltd.: www.simpsonltd.com
SKB Shotguns: www.skbshotguns.com
Smith & Wesson: www.smith-wesson.com
SOG International, Inc.: soginc@go-concepts.com
Sphinx System: www.sphinxarms.com
Springfield Armory: www.springfield-armory.com
SSK Industries: www.sskindustries.com
Stag Arms: www.stagarms.com
Steyr Arms, Inc. : www.steyrarms.com
Stoeger Industries: www.stoegerindustries.com
Strayer-Voigt Inc.: www.sviguns.com
Sturm,Ruger & Company: www.ruger-firearms.com
Tactical Solutions: www.tacticalsol.com
Tar-Hunt Slug Guns, Inc.: www.tar-hunt.com
Taser Int'l: www.taser.com
Taurus: www.taurususa.com
Taylor's & Co., Inc.: www.taylorsfirearms.com
Tennessee Guns: www.tennesseeguns.com
The 1877 Sharps Co.: www.1877sharps.com
Thompson Center Arms: www.tcarms.com
Tikka: www.berettausa.com
TNW, Inc. tncorp@aol.com
Traditions: www.traditionsfirearms.com
Tristar Sporting Arms: www.tristarsportingarms.com
Uberti: www.ubertireplicas.com
Ultra Light Arms: www.newultralight.com
Umarex: www.umarex.com
U.S. Firearms Mfg. Co.: www.usfirearms.com
Valkyrie Arms: www.valkyriearms.com
Vektor Arms: www.vektorarms.com
Verney-Carron: www.verney-carron.com
Volquartsen Custom Ltd.: www.volquartsen.com
Vulcan Armament: www.vulcanarmament.com
Walther USA: www.waltheramerica.com
Weatherby: www.weatherby.com
Webley and Scott Ltd.: www.webley.co.uk
Westley Richards: www.westleyrichards.com
Widley: www.widleyguns.com
Wild West Guns: www.wildwestguns.com
William Larkin Moore & Co.: www.doublegun.com
Wilson Combat: www.wilsoncombat.com
Winchester Rifles and Shotguns: www.winchesterguns.com

GUN PARTS, BARRELS, AFTER-MARKET ACCESSORIES

300 Below: www.300below.com
Accuracy International of North America:
    www.accuracyinternational.org
Accuracy Speaks, Inc.: www.accuracyspeaks.com
Advanced Barrel Systems: www.carbonbarrels.com
Advantage Arms: www.advantagearms.com
Aim Surplus: www.aimsurplus.com
AK-USA: www.ak-103.com
American Spirit Arms Corp.: www.gunkits.com
AMT Gun Parts: www.amt-gunparts.com
Armatac Industries: www.armatac.com
Badger Barrels, Inc.: www.badgerbarrels.com
Bar-Sto Precision Machine: www.barsto.com
Battenfeld Technologies: www.battenfeldtechnologies.com
Bellm TC's: www.bellmtcs.com
Belt Mountain Enterprises: www.beltmountain.com
Bergara Barrels: www.bergarabarrels.com
Briley: www.briley.com
Brownells: www.brownells.com
B-Square: www.b-square.com
Buffer Technologies: www.buffertech.com
Bullberry Barrel Works: www.bullberry.com
Bulldog Barrels: www.bulldogbarrels.com

Bushmaster Firearms/Quality Parts: www.bushmaster.com
Butler Creek Corp: www.butler-creek.com
Cape Outfitters Inc.: www.capeoutfitters.com
Caspian Arms Ltd.: www.caspianarms.com
Cheaper Than Dirt: www.cheaperthandirt.com
Chesnut Ridge: www.chestnutridge.com/
Chip McCormick Corp: www.chipmccormickcorp.com
Choate Machine & Tool Co.: www.riflestock.com
Cierner, Jonathan Arthur: www.22lrconversions.com
CJ Weapons Accessories: www.cjweapons.com
Colonial Arms: www.colonialarms.com
Comp-N-Choke: www.comp-n-choke.com
Cylinder & Slide Shop: www.cylinder-slide.com
Dave Manson Precision Reamers.: www.mansonreamers.com
Digi-Twist: www.fmtcorp.com
Dixie Gun Works: www.dixiegun.com
Douglas Barrels: www.benchrest.com/douglas/
DPMS: www.dpmsinc.com
D.S.Arms,Inc.: www.dsarms.com
eBay: www.ebay.com
Ed Brown Products: www.edbrown.com
EFK Marketing/Fire Dragon Pistol Accessories:
    www.flmfire.com
E.R. Shaw: www.ershawbarrels.com
Forrest Inc.: www.gunmags.com
Fulton Armory: www.fulton-armory.com
Galazan: www.connecticutshotgun.com
Gemtech: www.gem-tech.com
Gentry, David: www.gentrycustom.com
GG&G: www.gggaz.com
Green Mountain Rifle Barrels: www.gmriflebarrel.com
Gun Parts Corp.: www.e-gunparts.com
Harris Engineering: www.harrisbipods.com
Hart Rifle Barrels: www.hartbarrels.com
Hastings Barrels: www.hastingsbarrels.com
Heinie Specialty Products: www.heinie.com
Holland Shooters Supply: www.hollandgun.com
H-S Precision: www.hsprecision.com
100 Straight Products: www.100straight.com
I.M.A.: www.ima-usa.com
Jack First Gun Shop: www.jackfirstgun.com
Jarvis, Inc.: www.jarvis-custom.com
J&T Distributing: www.jtdistributing.com
John's Guns: www.johnsguns.com
John Masen Co.: www.johnmasen.com
Jonathan Arthur Ciener, Inc.: www.22lrconversions.com
JP Enterprises: www.jpar15.com
Keng's Firearms Specialities: www.versapod.com
KG Industries: www.kgcoatings.com
Kick Eez: www.kickeez.com
Kidd Triggers: www.coolguyguns.com
King's Gunworks: www.kingsgunworks.com
Knoxx Industries: www.knoxx.com
Krieger Barrels: www.kriegerbarrels.com
K-VAR Corp.: www.k-var.com
Les Baer Custom, Inc.: www.lesbaer.com
Lilja Barrels: www.riflebarrels.com
Lone Star Rifle Co.: www.lonestarrifles.com
Lone Wolf Dist.: www.lonewolfdist.com
Lothar Walther Precision Tools Inc.: www.lothar-walther.de
M&A Parts, Inc.: www.m-aparts.com
MAB Barrels: www.mab.com.au
Majestic Arms: www.majesticarms.com
Marvel Products, Inc.: www.marvelprod.com
MEC-GAR SrL: www.mec-gar.it
Mesa Tactical: www.mesatactical.com
Michaels of Oregon Co.: www.michaels-oregon.com
North Mfg. Co.: www.rifle-barrels.com
Numrich Gun Parts Corp.: www.e-gunparts.com

Pachmayr: **www.pachmayr.com**
Pac-Nor Barrels: **www.pac-nor.com**
Para Ordinance Pro Shop: **www.ltms.com**
Point Tech Inc.: **pointec@ibm.net**
Promag Industries: **www.promagindustries.com**
Power Custom, Inc.: **www.powercustom.com**
Red Star Arms: **www.redstararms.com**
Rocky Mountain Arms: **www.rockymountainarms.com**
Royal Arms Int'l: **www.royalarms.com**
R.W. Hart: **www.rwhart.com**
Sarco Inc.: **www.sarcoinc.com**
Scattergun Technologies Inc.: **www.wilsoncombat.com**
Schuemann Barrels: **www.schuemann.com**
Seminole Gunworks Chamber Mates:
  www.chambermates.com
Shilen: **www.shilen.com**
Sims Vibration Laboratory: **www.limbsaver.com**
Smith & Alexander Inc.: **www.smithandalexander.com**
Speed Shooters Int'l: **www.shooternet.com/ssi**
Sprinco USA Inc.: **sprinco@primenet.com**
STI Int'l: **www.stiguns.com**
S&S Firearms: **www.ssfirearms.com**
SSK Industries: **www.sskindustries.com**
Sunny Hill Enterprises: **www.sunny-hill.com**
Tactical Innovations: **www.tacticalinc.com**
Tapco: **www.tapco.com**
Trapdoors Galore: **www.trapdoors.com**
Triple K Manufacturing Co. Inc.: **www.triplek.com**
U.S.A. Magazines Inc.: **www.usa-magazines.com**
Verney-Carron SA: **www.verney-carron.com**
Volquartsen Custom Ltd.: **www.volquartsen.com**
W.C. Wolff Co.: **www.gunsprings.com**
Waller & Son: **www.wallerandson.com**
Weigand Combat Handguns: **www.weigandcombat.com**
Western Gun Parts: **www.westerngunparts.com**
Wilson Arms: **www.wilsonarms.com**
Wilson Combat: **www.wilsoncombat.com**
Wisner's Inc.: **www.wisnerinc.com**
Z-M Weapons: **www.zmweapons.com/home.htm**

GUNSMITHING SUPPLIES AND INSTRUCTION

American Gunsmithing Institute: **www.americangunsmith.com**
Battenfeld Technologies: **www.battenfeldtechnologies.com**
Bellm TC's: **www.bellmtcs.com**
Brownells, Inc.: **www.brownells.com**
B-Square Co.: **www.b-square.com**
Clymer Mfg. Co.: **www.clymertool.com**
Craftguard Metal Finishing: **crftgrd@aol.com**
Dem-Bart: **www.dembartco.com**
Doug Turnbull Restoration: **www.turnbullrestoration,com**
Du-Lite Corp.: **www.dulite.com**
Dvorak Instruments: **www.dvorakinstruments.com**
Gradiant Lens Corp.: **www.gradientlens.com**
Grizzly Industrial: **www.grizzly.com**
Gunline Tools: **www.gunline.com**
Harbor Freight: **www.harborfreight.com**
JGS Precision Tool Mfg. LLC: **www.jgstools.com**
Mag-Na-Port International: **www.magnaport.com**
Manson Precision Reamers: **www.mansonreamers.com**
Midway: **www.midwayusa.com**
Murray State College: **www.mscok.edu**
Olympus America Inc.: **www.olympus.com**
Pacific Tool & Gauge: **www.pacifictoolandgauge.com**
Trinidad State Junior College: **www.trinidadstate.edu**

HANDGUN GRIPS

Ajax Custom Grips, Inc.: **www.ajaxgrips.com**
Altamont Co.: **www.altamontco.com**

Aluma Grips: **www.alumagrips.com**
Badger Grips: **www.pistolgrips.com**
Barami Corp.: **www.hipgrip.com**
Blu Magnum Grips: **www.blumagnum.com**
Buffalo Brothers: **www.buffalobrothers.com**
Crimson Trace Corp.: **www.crimsontrace.com**
Eagle Grips: **www.eaglegrips.com**
Falcon Industries: **www.ergogrips.net**
Herrett's Stocks: **www.herrettstocks.com**
Hogue Grips: **www.getgrip.com**
Kirk Ratajesak: **www.kgratajesak.com**
Lett Custom Grips: **www.lettgrips.com**
N.C. Ordnance: **www.gungrip.com**
Nill-Grips USA: **www.nill-grips.com**
Pachmayr: **www.pachmayr.com**
Pearce Grips: **www.pearcegrip.com**
Trausch Grips Int.Co.: **www.trausch.com**
Tyler-T Grips: **www.t-grips.com**
Uncle Mike's:: **www.uncle-mikes.com**

HOLSTERS AND LEATHER PRODUCTS

Akah: **www.akah.de**
Aker Leather Products: **www.akerleather.com**
Alessi Distributor R&F Inc.: **www.alessiholsters.com**
Alfonso's of Hollywood: **www.alfonsogunleather.com**
Armor Holdings: **www.holsters.com**
Bagmaster: **www.bagmaster.com**
Bianchi International: **www.bianchi-intl.com**
Blackhills Leather: **www.blackhillsleather.com**
BodyHugger Holsters: **www.nikolais.com**
Boyt Harness Co.: **www.boytharness.com**
Brigade Gun Leather: **www.brigadegunleather.com**
Chimere: **www.chimere.com**
Classic Old West Styles: **www.cows.com**
Conceal It: **www.conceal-it.com**
Concealment Shop Inc.: **www.theconcealmentshop.com**
Coronado Leather Co.: **www.coronadoleather.com**
Covert Carry: **www.covertcarry.com**
Creedmoor Sports, Inc.: **www.creedmoorsports.com**
Custom Leather Wear: **www.customleatherwear.com**
Defense Security Products: **www.thunderwear.com**
Dennis Yoder: **www.yodercustomleather.com**
DeSantis Holster: **www.desantisholster.com**
Dillon Precision: **www.dillonprecision.com**
Don Hume Leathergoods, Inc.: **www.donhume.com**
Ernie Hill International: **www.erniehill.com**
Fist: **www.fist-inc.com**
Fobus USA: **www.fobusholster.com**
Front Line Ltd. **frontlin@internet-zahav.net**
Galco: **www.usgalco.com**
Gilmore's Sports Concepts: **www.gilmoresports.com**
Gould & Goodrich: **www.gouldusa.com**
Gunmate Products: **www.gun-mate.com**
Hellweg Ltd.: **www.hellwegltd.com**
Hide-A-Gun: **www.hide-a-gun.com**
Holsters.Com: **www.holsters.com**
Horseshoe Leather Products: **www.horseshoe.co.uk**
Hunter Co.: **www.huntercompany.com**
Kirkpatrick Leather Company: **www.kirkpatrickleather.com**
KNJ: **www.knjmfg.com**
Kramer Leather: **www.kramerleather.com**
Law Concealment Systems: **www.handgunconcealment.com**
Levy's Leathers Ltd.: **www.levysleathers.com**
Michaels of Oregon Co.: **www.michaels-oregon.com**
Milt Sparks Leather: **www.miltsparks.com**
Mitch Rosen Extraordinary Gunleather: **www.mitchrosen.com**
Old World Leather: **www.gun-mate.com**
Pacific Canvas & Leather Co.:
  paccanadleather@directway.com

Pager Pal: www.pagerpal.com
Phalanx Corp.: www.smartholster.com
PWL: www.pwlusa.com
Rumanya Inc.: www.rumanya.com
S.A. Gunleather: www.elpasoleather.com
Safariland Ltd. Inc.: www.safariland.com
Shooting Systems Group Inc.: www.shootingsystems.com
Strictly Anything Inc.: www.strictlyanything.com
Strong Holster Co.: www.strong-holster.com
The Belt Co.: www.conceal-it.com
The Leather Factory Inc.: lflandry@flash.net
The Outdoor Connection: www.outdoorconnection.com
Top-Line USA inc.: www.toplineusa.com
Triple K Manufacturing Co.: www.triplek.com
Wilson Combat: www.wilsoncombat.com

MISCELLANEOUS SHOOTING PRODUCTS

10X Products Group: www.10Xwear.com
Aero Peltor: www.aearo.com
American Body Armor: www.americanbodyarmor.com
Armor Holdings Products: www.armorholdings.com
Battenfeld Technologies: www.battenfeldtechnologies.com
Beamhit: www.beamhit.com
Beartooth: www.beartoothproducts.com
Bodyguard by S&W: www.yourbodyguard.com
Burnham Brothers: www.burnhambrothers.com
Collectors Armory: www.collectorsarmory.com
Dalloz Safety: www.cdalloz.com
Deben Group Industries Inc.: www.deben.com
Decot Hy-Wyd Sport Glasses: www.sportyglasses.com
E.A.R., Inc.: www.earinc.com
First Choice Armor: www.firstchoicearmor.com
Gunstands: www.gunstands.com
Howard Leight Hearing Protectors: www.howardleight.com
Hunters Specialities: www.hunterspec.com
Johnny Stewart Wildlife Calls: www.hunterspec.com
Merit Corporation: www.meritcorporation.com
Michaels of Oregon: www.michaels-oregon.com
MPI Outdoors: www.mpioutdoors.com
MTM Case-Gard: www.mtmcase-gard.com
North Safety Products: www.northsafety-brea.com
Plano Molding: www.planomolding.com
Pro-Ears: www.pro-ears.com
Second Chance Body Armor Inc.: www.secondchance.com
Silencio: www.silencio.com
Smart Lock Technologies: www.smartlock.com
Surefire: www.surefire.com
Taser Int'l: www.taser.com
Walker's Game Ear Inc.: www.walkersgameear.com

MUZZLELOADING FIREARMS AND PRODUCTS

American Pioneer Powder: www.americanpioneerpowder.com
Armi Sport: www.armisport.com
Barnes Bullets: www.barnesbullets,com
Black Powder Products: www.bpiguns.com
Buckeye Barrels: www.buckeyebarrels.com
CVA: www.cva.com
Davide Perdsoli & co.: www.davide-pedersoli.com
Dixie Gun Works, Inc.: www.dixiegun.com
Elephant/Swiss Black Powder:
   www.elephantblackpowder.com
Goex Black Powder: www.goexpowder.com
Green Mountain Rifle Barrel Co.: www.gmriflebarrel.com
Harvester Bullets: www.harvesterbullets.com
Hornady: www.hornady.com
Jedediah Starr Trading Co.: www.jedediah-starr.com
Jim Chambers Flintlocks: www.flintlocks.com
Kahnke Gunworks: www.powderandbow.com/kahnke/

Knight Rifles: www.knightrifles.com
L&R Lock Co.: www.lr-rpl.com
Log Cabin Shop: www.logcabinshop.com
Lyman: www.lymanproducts.com
Magkor Industries : www.magkor.com
MDM Muzzleloaders: www.mdm-muzzleloaders.com
Millennium Designed Muzzleloaders:
   www.mdm-muzzleloaders.com
MSM, Inc.: www.msmfg.com
Muzzleload Magnum Products: www.mmpsabots.com
Muzzleloading Technologies, Inc.: www.mtimuzzleloading.com
Navy Arms: www.navyarms.com
Northwest Trade Guns: www.northstarwest.com
Nosler, Inc.: www.nosler.com
October Country Muzzleloading: www.oct-country.com
Ox-Yoke Originals Inc.: www.oxyoke.com
Pacific Rifle Co.: pacificrifle@aol.com
Palmetto Arms: www.palmetto.it
Pietta: www.pietta.it
Powerbelt Bullets: www.powerbeltbullets.com
PR Bullets: www.prbullets.com
Precision Rifle Dead Center Bullets: www.prbullet.com
R.E. Davis CVo.: www.redaviscompany.com
Remington: www.remington.com
Rightnour Mfg. Co. Inc.: www.rmcsports.com
The Rifle Shop trshoppe@aol.com
Savage Arms, Inc.: www.savagearms.com
Schuetzen Powder: www.schuetzenpowder.com
TDC: www.tdcmfg.com
Thompson Center Arms: www.tcarms.com
Traditions Performance Muzzleloading:
   www.traditionsfirearms.com

PUBLICATIONS, VIDEOS, AND CD'S

A&J Arms Booksellers: www.ajarmsbooksellers.com
Airgun Letter: www.airgunletter.com
American Cop: www.americancopmagazine.com
American Firearms Industry: www.amfire.com
American Handgunner: www.americanhandgunner.com
American Hunter: www.nrapublications.org
American Rifleman: www.nrapublications.org
American Shooting Magazine: www.americanshooting.com
Blacksmith: sales@blacksmithcorp.com
Black Powder Cartridge News: www.blackpowderspg.com
Black Powder Guns & Hunting: www.bpghmag.com
Black Powder Journal: www.blackpowderjournal.com
Blue Book Publications: www.bluebookinc.com
Combat Handguns: www.combathandguns.com
Concealed Carry: www.uscca.us
Cornell Publications: www.cornellpubs.com
Countrywide Press: www.countrysport.com
DBI Books/Krause Publications: www.krause.com
Delta Force: www.infogo.com/delta
Gun List: www.gunlist.com
Gun Video: www.gunvideo.com
GUNS Magazine: www.gunsmagazine.com
Guns & Ammo: www.gunsandammomag.com
Gunweb Magazine: www Links: www.imags.com
Gun Week: www.gunweek.com
Gun World: www.gunworld.com
Harris Publications: www.harrispublications.com
Heritage Gun Books: www.gunbooks.com
Krause Publications: www.krause.com
Law and Order: www.hendonpub.com
Moose Lake Publishing: MooselakeP@aol.com
Munden Enterprises Inc.: www.bob-munden.com
Outdoor Videos: www.outdoorvideos.com
Precision Shooting: www.precisionshooting.com
Predator Extreme: www.predatorextreme.com

Predator & Prey: **www.predatorandpreymag.com**
Ray Riling Arms Books: **www.rayrilingarmsbooks.com**
Rifle and Handloader Magazines: **www.riflemagazine.com**
Safari Press Inc.: **www.safaripress.com**
Shoot! Magazine: **www.shootmagazine.com**
Shooters News: **www.shootersnews.com**
Shooting Illustrated: **www.nrapublications.org**
Shooting Industry: **www.shootingindustry.com**
Shooting Sports Retailer: **www.shootingsportsretailer.com**
Shooting Sports USA: **www.nrapublications.org**
Shotgun News: **www.shotgunnews.com**
Shotgun Report: **www.shotgunreport.com**
Shotgun Sports Magazine: **www.shotgun-sports.com**
Small Arms Review: **www.smallarmsreview.com**
Small Caliber News: **www.smallcaliber.com**
Sporting Clays Web Edition: **www.sportingclays.net**
Sports Afield: **www.sportsafield.com**
Sports Trend: **www.sportstrend.com**
Sportsmen on Film: **www.sportsmenonfilm.com**
SWAT Magazine: **www.swatmag.com**
The Gun Journal: **www.shooters.com**
The Shootin Iron: **www.off-road.com/4x4web/si/si.html**
The Single Shot Exchange Magazine:
   singleshot@earthlink.net
The Sixgunner: **www.sskindustries.com**
Voyageur Press: **www.voyageurpress.com**
VSP Publications: **www.gunbooks.com**
Vulcan Outdoors Inc.: **www.vulcanpub.com**

RELOADING TOOLS

Ballisti-Cast Mfg.: **www.ballisti-cast.com**
Battenfeld Technologies: **www.battenfeldtechnologies.com**
Bruno Shooters Supply: **www.brunoshooters.com**
Camdex, Inc.: **www.camdexloader.com**
CH/4D Custom Die: **www.ch4d.com**
Colorado Shooters Supply: **www.hochmoulds.com**
Corbin Mfg & Supply Co.: **www.corbins.com**
Dillon Precision: **www.dillonprecision.com**
Forster Precision Products: **www.forsterproducts.com**
GSI International, Inc.: **www.gsiinternational.com**
Hanned Line: **www.hanned.com**
Harrell's Precision: **www.harrellsprec.com**
Holland's Shooting Supplies: **www.hollandgun.com**
Hornady: **www.hornady.com**
Huntington Reloading Products: **www.huntingtons.com**
J & J Products Co.: **www.jandjproducts.com**
Lead Bullet Technology: **LBTisaccuracy@lmbris.net**
Lee Precision,Inc.: **www.leeprecision.com**
Littleton Shotmaker: **www.leadshotmaker.com**
Load Data: **www.loaddata.com**
Lyman: **www.lymanproducts.com**
Magma Engineering: **www.magmaengr.com**
Mayville Engineering Co. (MEC): **www.mecreloaders.com**
Midway: **www.midwayusa.com**
Moly-Bore: **www.molybore.com**
MTM Case-Guard: **www.mtmcase-guard.com**
NECO: **www.neconos.com**
NEI : **www.neihandtools.com**
Neil Jones Custom Products: **www.neiljones.com**
Ponsness/Warren: **www.reloaders.com**
Ranger Products:
   www.pages.prodigy.com/rangerproducts.home.htm
Rapine Bullet Mold Mfg Co.: **www.bulletmoulds.com**
RCBS: **www.rcbs.com**
Redding Reloading Equipment: **www.redding-reloading.com**
Russ Haydon's Shooting Supplies: **www.shooters-supply.com**
Sinclair Int'l Inc.: **www.sinclairintl.com**
Stoney Point Products Inc: **www.stoneypoint.com**
Thompson Bullet Lube Co.: **www.thompsonbulletlube.com**

Vickerman Seating Die: **www.castingstuff.com**
Wilson(L.E. Wilson): **www.lewilson.com**

RESTS— BENCH, PORTABLE, ATTACHABLE

Battenfeld Technolgies: **www.battenfeldtechnologies.com**
Bench Master: **www.bench-master.com**
B-Square: **www.b-square.com**
Bullshooter: **www.bullshooterssightingin.com**
Desert Mountain Mfg.: **www.benchmasterusa.com**
Harris Engineering Inc.: **www.harrisbipods**
Kramer Designs: **www.snipepod.com**
L Thomas Rifle Support: **www.ltsupport.com**
Level-Lok: **www.levellok.com**
Midway: **www.midwayusa.com**
Predator Sniper Styx: **www.predatorsniperstyx.com**
Ransom International: **www.ransom-intl.com**
R.W. Hart: **www.rwhart.com**
Sinclair Intl, Inc.: **www.sinclairintl.com**
Stoney Point Products: **www.uncle-mikes.com**
Target Shooting: **www.targetshooting.com**
Varmint Masters: **www.varmintmasters.com**
Versa-Pod: **www.versa-pod.com**

SCOPES, SIGHTS, MOUNTS AND ACCESSORIES

Accumount: **www.accumounts.com**
Accusight: **www.accusight.com**
ADCO: **www.shooters.com/adco/index/htm**
Adirondack Opitcs: **www.adkoptics.com**
Advantage Tactical Sight: **www.advantagetactical.com**
Aimpoint: **www.aimpoint.com**
Aim Shot, Inc.: **www.miniosprey.com**
Aimtech Mount Systems: **www.aimtech-mounts.com**
Alpec Team, Inc.: **www.alpec.com**
Alpen Outdoor Corp.: **www.alpenoutdoor.com**
American Technologies Network, Corp.: **www.atncorp.com**
AmeriGlo, LLC: **www.ameriglo.net**
AO Sight Systems Inc.: **www.aosights.com**
Ashley Outdoors, Inc.: **www.ashleyoutdoors.com**
ATN: **www.atncorp.com**
Badger Ordnance: **www.badgerordnance.com**
Beamshot-Quarton: **www.beamshot.com**
BSA Optics: **www.bsaoptics.com**
B-Square Company, Inc.: **www.b-square.com**
Burris: **www.burrisoptics.com**
Bushnell Performance Optics: **www.bushnell.com**
Carl Zeiss Optical Inc.: **www.zeiss.com**
Carson Optical: **www.carson-optical.com**
CenterPoint Precision Optics: **www.centerpointoptics.com**
C-More Systems: **www.cmore.com**
Conetrol Scope Mounts: **www.conetrol.com**
Crimson Trace Corp.: **www.crimsontrace.com**
Crossfire L.L.C.: **www.amfire.com/hesco/html**
DCG Supply Inc.: **www.dcgsupply.com**
D&L Sports: **www.dlsports.com**
DuraSight Scope Mounting Systems: **www.durasight.com**
EasyHit, Inc.: **www.easyhit.com**
EAW: **www.eaw.de**
Elcan Optical Technologies: **www.armament.com,:**
   www.elcan.com
Electro-Optics Technologies: **www.eotechmdc.com/holosight**
Europtik Ltd.: **www.europtik.com**
Fujinon, Inc.: **www.fujinon.com**
Gilmore Sports: **www.gilmoresports.com**
Gradient Lens Corp.: **www.gradientlens.com**
Hakko Co. Ltd.: **www.hakko-japan.co.jp**
Hesco: **www.hescosights.com**
Hi-Lux Optics: **www.hi-luxoptics.com**

Hitek Industries: **www.nightsight.com**
HIVIZ: **www.hivizsights.com**
Hollands Shooters Supply: **www.hollandguns.com**
Horus Vision: **www.horusvision.com**
Hunter Co.: **www.huntercompany.com**
Innovative Weaponry,Inc.: **www.ptnightsights.com**
Ironsighter Co.: **www.ironsighter.com**
ITT Night Vision: **www.ittnightvision.com**
Kahles: **www.kahlesoptik.com**
Kowa Optimed Inc.: **www.kowascope.com**
Kwik-Site Co.: **www.kwiksitecorp.com**
L-3 Communications-Eotech: **www.l-3com.com**
Laser Bore Sight: **www.laserboresight.com**
Laser Devices Inc.: **www.laserdevices.com**
Lasergrips: **www.crimsontrace.com**
LaserLyte: **www.laserlytesights.com**
LaserMax Inc.: **www.lasermax.com**
Laser Products: **www.surefire.com**
Leapers, Inc.: **www.leapers.com**
Leatherwood: **www.hi-luxoptics.com**
Leica Camera Inc.: **www.leica-camera.com/usa**
Leupold: **www.leupold.com**
LightForce/NightForce USA: **www.nightforcescopes.com**
Lyman: **www.lymanproducts.com**
Lynx: **www.b-square.com**
Marble's Outdoors: **www.marblesoutdoors.com**
MDS,Inc.: **www.mdsincorporated.com**
Meopta: **www.meopta.com**
Meprolight: **www.kimberamerica.com**
Micro Sight Co.: **www.microsight.com**
Millett : **www.millettsights.com**
Miniature Machine Corp.: **www.mmcsight.com**
Montana Vintage Arms: **www.montanavintagearms.com**
Mounting Solutions Plus: **www.mountsplus.com**
NAIT: **www.nait.com**
Newcon International Ltd.: **newconsales@newcon-optik.com**
Night Force Optics: **www.nightforcescopes.com**
Night Optics USA, Inc.: **www.nightoptics.com**
Night Owl Optics: **www.nightowloptics.com**
Night Vision Systems: **www.nightvisionsystems.com**
Nikon Inc.: **www.nikonusa.com**
North American Integrated Technologies: **www.nait.com**
O.K. Weber, Inc.: **www.okweber.com**
Optolyth-Optic: **www.optolyth.de**
Pentax Corp.: **www.pentaxlightseeker.com**
Premier Reticles: **www.premierreticles.com**
Redfield: **www.redfieldoptics.com**
Rifle Electronics: **www.theriflecam.com**
R&R Int'l Trade: **www.nightoptic.com**
Schmidt & Bender: **www.schmidt-bender.com**
Scopecoat: **www.scopecoat.com**
Scopelevel: **www.scopelevel.com**
Segway Industries: **www.segway-industries.com**
Shepherd Scope Ltd.: **www.shepherdscopes.com**
Sightron: **www.sightron.com**
Simmons: **www.simmonsoptics.com**
S&K: **www.scopemounts.com**
Springfield Armory: **www.springfield-armory.com**
Sure-Fire: **www.surefire.com**
Swarovski/Kahles: **www.swarovskioptik.com**
Swift Optics: **www.swiftoptics.com**
Talley Mfg. Co.: **www.talleyrings.com**
Tasco: **www.tascosales.com**
Trijicon Inc.: **www.trijicon.com**
Truglo Inc.: **www.truglo.com**
UltraDot: **www.ultradotusa.com**
Unertl Optical Co.: **www.unertloptics.com**
US Night Vision: **www.usnightvision.com**
U.S. Optics Technologies Inc.: **www.usoptics.com**

Valdada-IOR Optics: **www.valdada.com**
Warne: **www.warnescopemounts.com**
Weaver Mounts: **www.weaver-mounts.com**
Weaver Scopes: **www.weaveroptics.com**
Wilcox Industries Corp.: **www.wilcoxind.com**
Williams Gun Sight Co.: **www.williamsgunsight.com**
XS Sight Systems: **www.xssights.com**
Zeiss: **www.zeiss.com**

SHOOTING ORGANIZATIONS, SCHOOLS AND RANGES

Amateur Trapshooting Assoc.: **www.shootata.com**
American Custom Gunmakers Guild: **www.acgg.org**
American Gunsmithing Institute: **www.americangunsmith.com**
American Pistolsmiths Guild: **www.americanpistol.com**
American Shooting Sports Council: **www.assc.com**
American Single Shot Rifle Assoc.: **www.assra.com**
Antique Shooting Tool Collector's Assoc.:
   www.oldshootingtools.org
Assoc. of Firearm & Tool Mark Examiners: **www.afte.org**
BATF: **www.atf.ustreas.gov**
Blackwater Lodge and Training Center:
   www.blackwaterlodge.com
Boone and Crockett Club: **www.boone-crockett.org**
Buckmasters, Ltd.: **www.buckmasters.com**
Cast Bullet Assoc.: **www.castbulletassoc.org**
Citizens Committee for the Right to Keep & Bear Arms:
   www.ccrkba.org
Civilian Marksmanship Program: **www.odcmp.com**
Colorado School of Trades: **www.gunsmith-school.com**
Ducks Unlimited: **www.ducks.org**
4-H Shooting Sports Program: **www.4-hshootingsports.org**
Fifty Caliber Institute: **www.fiftycal.org**
Fifty Caliber Shooters Assoc.: **www.fcsa.org**
Firearms Coalition: **www.nealknox.com**
Front Sight Firearms Training Institute: **www.frontsight.com**
German Gun Collectors Assoc.: **www.germanguns.com**
Gun Clubs: **www.associatedgunclubs.org**
Gun Owners' Action League: **www.goal.org**
Gun Owners of America: **www.gunowners.org**
Gun Trade Asssoc. Ltd.: **www.brucepub.com/gta**
Gunsite Training Center,Inc.: **www.gunsite.com**
Handgun Hunters International: **www.sskindustries.com**
Hunting and Shooting Sports Heritage Fund:
   www.huntandshoot.org
International Defense Pistol Assoc.: **www.idpa.com**
International Handgun Metallic Silhouette Assoc.:
   www.ihmsa.org
International Hunter Education Assoc.: **www.ihea.com**
International Single Shot Assoc.: **www.issa-schuetzen.org**
Jews for the Preservation of Firearms Ownership: **www.jpfo.org**
Mule Deer Foundation: **www.muledeer.org**
Muzzle Loaders Assoc. of Great Britain: **www.mlagb.com**
National 4-H Shooting Sports: **www.4-hshootingsports.org**
National Association of Sporting Goods Wholesalers:
   www.nasgw.org
National Benchrest Shooters Assoc.: **www.benchrest.com**
National Muzzle Loading Rifle Assoc.: **www.nmlra.org**
National Reloading Manufacturers Assoc:
   www.reload-nrma.com
National Rifle Assoc.: **www.nra.org**
National Rifle Assoc. ILA: **www.nraila.org**
National Shooting Sports Foundation: **www.nssf.org**
National Skeet Shooters Association: **www.nssa-nsca.com**
National Sporting Clays Assoc.: **www.nssa-nsca.com**
National Wild Turkey Federation: **www.nwtf.com**
NICS/FBI: **www.fbi.gov**
North American Hunting Club: **www.huntingclub.com**

Order of Edwardian Gunners (Vintagers): **www.vintagers.org**
Outdoor Industry Foundation:
    www.outdoorindustryfoundation.org
Pennsylvania Gunsmith School: **www.pagunsmith.com**
Quail Unlimited: **www.qu.org**
Right To Keep and Bear Arms: **www.rkba.org**
Rocky Mountain Elk Foundation: **www.rmef.org**
SAAMI: **www.saami.org**
Safari Club International: **www.scifirstforhunters.org**
Scholastic Clay Target Program: **www.nssf.org/sctp**
Second Amendment Foundation: **www.saf.org**
Second Amendment Sisters: **www.2asisters.org**
Shooting Ranges Int'l: **www.shootingranges.com**
Single Action Shooting Society: **www.sassnet.com**
Students for Second Amendment: **www.sf2a.org**
S&W Academy and Nat'l Firearms Trng. Center:
    www.sw-academy.com
Tactical Defense Institute: **www.tdiohio.com**
Ted Nugent United Sportsmen of America: **www.tnugent.com**
Thunder Ranch: **www.thunderranchinc.com**
Trapshooters Homepage: **www.trapshooters.com**
Trinidad State Junior College: **www.trinidadstate.edu**
U.S. Concealed Carry Association: **www.uscca.us**
U.S. Int'l Clay Target Assoc.: **www.usicta.com**
United States Fish and Wildlife Service: **www.fws.gov**
U.S. Practical Shooting Assoc.: **www.uspsa.org**
USA Shooting: **www.usashooting.com**
Varmint Hunters Assoc.: **www.varminthunter.org**
U.S. Sportsmen's Alliance: **www.ussportsmen.org**
Women Hunters: **www.womanhunters.com**
Women's Shooting Sports Foundation: **www.wssf.org**

STOCKS

Advanced Technology: **www.atigunstocks.com**
Battenfeld Technologies: **www.battenfeldtechnologies.com**
Bell & Carlson, Inc.: **www.bellandcarlson.com**
Boyd's Gunstock Industries, Inc.: **www.boydgunstocks.com**
Butler Creek Corp: **www.butler-creek.com**
Calico Hardwoods, Inc.: **www.calicohardwoods.com**
Choate Machine: **www.riflestock.com**
Elk Ridge Stocks: **www.reamerrentals.com/elk_ridge.htm**
Fajen: **www.battenfeldtechnologies.com**
Great American Gunstocks: **www.gunstocks.com**
Herrett's Stocks: **www.herrettstocks.com**
High Tech Specialties: **www.bansnersrifle.com/hightech**
Holland's Shooting Supplies: **www.hollandgun.com**
Knoxx Industries: **www.blackhawk.com**
Lone Wolf: **www.lonewolfriflestocks.com**
McMillan Fiberglass Stocks: **www.mcmfamily.com**
MPI Stocks: **www.mpistocks.com**
Precision Gun Works: **www.precisiongunstocks.com**
Ram-Line: **www.outers-guncare.com**
Rimrock Rifle Stock: **www.rimrockstocks.com**
Royal Arms Gunstocks: **www.imt.net/~royalarms**
S&K Industries: **www.sandkgunstocks.com**
Speedfeed, Inc.: **www.speedfeedinc.com**
Tiger-Hunt Curly Maple Gunstocks: **www.gunstockwood.com**
Wenig Custom Gunstocks Inc.: **www.wenig.com**

TARGETS AND RANGE EQUIPMENT

Action Target Co.: **www.actiontarget.com**
Advanced Interactive Systems: **www.ais-sim.com**
Birchwood Casey: **www.birchwoodcasey.com**
Bullet Proof Electronics: **www.thesnipertarget.com**
Caswell Meggitt Defense Systems: **www.mds-caswell.com**
Champion Traps & Targets: **www.championtarget.com**
Handloader/Victory Targets: **www.targetshandloader.com**
Just Shoot Me Products: **www.ballistictec.com**

Laser Shot: **www.lasershot.com**
Mountain Plains Industries: **www.targetshandloader.com**
MTM Products: **www.mtmcase-gard.com**
Natiional Target Co.: **www.nationaltarget.com**
Newbold Target Systems: **www.newboldtargets.com**
Porta Target,Inc.: **www.portatarget.com**
Range Management Services Inc.: **www.casewellintl.com**
Range Systems: **www.shootingrangeproducts.com**
Reactive Target Systems Inc.: **chrts@primenet.com**
ShatterBlast Targets: **www.daisy.com**
Super Trap Bullet Containment Systems: **www.supertrap.com**
Thompson Target Technology: **www.thompsontarget.com**
Tombstone Tactical Targets: **www.tttargets.com**
Visible Impact Targets: **www.crosman.com**
White Flyer: **www.whiteflyer.com**

TRAP AND SKEET SHOOTING EQUIPMENT AND ACCESSORIES

Auto-Sporter Industries: **www.auto-sporter.com**
10X Products Group: **www.10Xwear.com**
Claymaster Traps: **www.claymaster.com**
Do-All Traps, Inc.: **www.doalloutdoors.com**
Laporte USA: **www.laporte-shooting.com**
Outers: **www.blount.com**
Trius Products Inc.: **www.triustraps.com**
White Flyer: **www.whiteflyer.com**

TRIGGERS

Brownells: **www.brownells.com**
Chip McCormick Corp.: **www.chipmccormickcorp.com**
Huber Concepts: **www.huberconcepts.com**
Kidd Triggers.: **www.coolguyguns.com**
Shilen: **www.shilen.com**
Timney Triggers: **www.timneytrigger.com**

MAJOR SHOOTING WEB SITES AND LINKS

24 Hour Campfire: **www.24hourcampfire.com**
Alphabetic Index of Links: **www.gunsgunsguns.com**
Ammo Guide: **www.ammoguide.com**
Auction Arms: **www.auctionarms.com**
Benchrest Central: **www.benchrest.com**
Big Game Hunt: **www.biggamehunt.net**
Bullseye Pistol: **www.bullseyepistol.com**
Firearms History: **www.researchpress.co.uk/firearms**
Gun Broker Auctions: **www.gunbroker.com**
Gun Index: **www.gunindex.com**
Gun Industry: **www.gunindustry.com**
Gun Blast: **www.gunblast.com**
Gun Boards: **www.gunboards.com**
GunsAmerica.com: **www.gunsamerica.com**
Guns Unified Nationally Endorsing Dignity: **www.guned.com**
Gun Shop Finder: **www.gunshopfinder.com**
Hunt and Shoot (NSSF): **www.huntandshoot.org**
Keep and Bear Arms: **www.keepandbeararms.com**
Leverguns: **www.leverguns.com**
Load Swap: **www.loadswap.com**
Outdoor Press Room: **www.outdoorpressroom.com**
Outdoor Yellow Pages: **www.outdoorsyp.com**
Real Guns: **www.realguns.com**
Shooters Forum: **www.shootersforum.com**
Shooter's Online Services: **www.shooters.com**
Shotgun Sports Resource Guide: **www.shotgunsports.com**
Sixgunner: **www.sixgunner.com**
Sniper's Hide: **www.snipershide.com**
Sportsman's Web: **www.sportsmansweb.com**
Surplus Rifles: **www.surplusrifle.com**
Wing Shooting USA: **www.wingshootingusa.org**

About the Author
(and his photographer)

James Morgan Ayres got his first gun, a .22 rifle, at age seven and has been shooting ever since. During military service he served with the 82nd Airborne Division and the Seventh Special Forces Group (ABN), qualified for Sniper's School and fired Expert or Distinguished Expert on every weapon the Army provided from the Government Model 1911 .45 ACP to the 106 Recoilless Rifle.

His work as a consultant for various government agencies and private companies has taken him to over thirty countries. He has hunted big and small game and been involved in armed conflicts on four continents. In addition to his work as a consultant he has founded four companies, three of them internationally-based; produced and directed video productions in Asia and Europe; and, authored numerous White Papers for government agencies. In addition, Ayres has written three children's books, two books of nonfiction, and over a hundred articles for publications including *The South China Morning Post, The Los Angeles Times, Backpacker, Blade*, and *France*. His first novel, *The Jaguar's Heart* is scheduled for publication in 2009.

He is currently on extended sabbatical from Nomadic Productions International.

M.L. Ayres has been shooting since she learned to hunt jackrabbits in the West Texas desert at the age of ten. She first learned the craft of photography with film cameras while apprenticed to a photojournalist. After some years of shooting fashion for publications including *GQ, Playboy, Women's Wear Daily,* and *Daily News Report* she moved into production management, and has managed video productions on location from Hong Kong and Shenzhen China to Barcelona and Prague. In addition to her film work, she has managed operations for an import/export company based in Hong Kong, handled technical support for a systems company, and is a Fixer-of-All-Things.

While on sabbatical from Nomadic Productions International, M.L. returned to her first vocation—photography. Her current professional work, both editorial and commercial, has appeared in national and international publications and in videos distributed in over twenty countries. (She no longer hunts jackrabbits, but she can shoot the pips out of a playing card with her pocket pistol.)

More About Arms Identifying and Handling

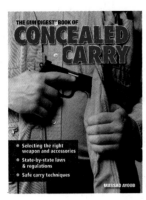

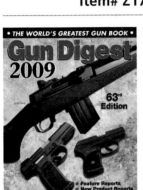

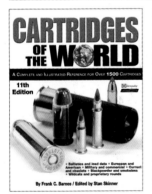